BLIGHTY

BLIGHTY

Steve Lowe
&
Alan McArthur

sphere

SPHERE

First published in Great Britain in 2008 by Sphere

A CIP catalogue record for this book
is available from the British Library.

ISBN 978-1-84744-179-9

Design and motifs by D.R.ink

Typeset in Sabon by M Rules
Printed and bound in Great Britain by
Clays Ltd, St Ives plc

Papers used by Sphere are natural, renewable and recyclable
products made from wood grown in sustainable forests and certified
in accordance with the rules of the Forest Stewardship Council.

Mixed Sources
Product group from well-managed
forests and other controlled sources
www.fsc.org   Cert no. SGS-COC-004081
© 1996 Forest Stewardship Council
FSC

Sphere
An imprint of
Little, Brown Book Group
100 Victoria Embankment
London EC4Y 0DY

An Hachette Livre UK Company
www.hachettelivre.co.uk

www.littlebrown.co.uk

CONTENTS

AUTUMN

WINTER

LISTS

ACKNOWLEDGEMENTS

Firstly, we would like to thank our venerable publisher Antonia Hodgson and our esteemed agent Karolina Sutton. We would also like to thank Sean Garrehy, Tamsyn Berryman, Kirsteen Astor, Catherine Duncan, Diane Spivey, Andy Hine, Marie Hrynczak, Nathalie Morse, Andrew Edwards, Linda Silverman and everyone else at Little, Brown, Sian Rance at D.R.ink and Laura Sampson at Curtis Brown/ICM.

Thanks to everyone who helped us along the way, including Stan Crooke, Ian Tucker for the portrait of Prince William, Karl Rhys, our friends in the north who put us up in Beeston, Patrick Murphy, our friend who was kind enough to sort out the polo for us, Chris Harvie and Neil McEvoy for giving generously of their time, and everybody else we met along the way.

Finally, to the greatly missed Kate Jones.

INTRODUCTION

WE'D BEEN SCEPTICAL. A council-run British Citizenship Ceremony sounds like very much the worst sort of party. Would there even be a bar? (There wasn't.)

We watched intently. Before us, inside the curvy wood-panelled Hackney Town Hall council chamber, sat 20 British-citizens-in-waiting. At this moment, they were Algerian, Australian, Iraqi, Israeli, Sierra Leonian, Turkish, Latvian, Cameroonian . . . But within the hour, they would turn British and henceforward would remain British. They were going to be touched with the British vibe stick. (That's a metaphor; nobody actually touches them with a stick.) We were here to witness the Spirit of Britain enter these expectant people. We wanted to see what it looked like. For the examination of Britishness is what we were about. In all its facets. This was our quest. And we were putting the hours in.

The proto-Britishers had all passed the fiendish Citizenship Test and, having paid the requisite £625, had now each been issued a special citizenship folder with pictures on the front, representing Britain: Stonehenge; a castle; the Forth Railway Bridge (British!); a family jumping up and down in a field . . . This – this! – is Britain. An ancient land where jumping is entirely permissible. Welcome!

An hour later, it was all over. Armed with their complimentary Hackney Council recycling mugs, with the kind and stirring words of Councillor Faizullah Khan reverberating in their ears, and having pledged undying allegiance to the Crown in the sight of Almighty God (as you do), and then all joining in a rousing rendition of 'God Save the Queen', these new Brits emerged into the light: presumably to get pissed, hail Nelson and dance around a maypole. 'You've got to watch the Boche,' one of them might say. It would seem only fitting.

But Britishness is not just for people from Abroad. These days, even British people are being encouraged to be British. To have Britishness days. To fly flags in their gardens (British flags). To swear oaths. But what does any of it mean? In a post-Empire, devolved, globalised Britain, what does it mean to be British? Obviously it means *something*. But what does it mean? Anything?

Many people are newly concerned with questions of identity. Genealogy is all the rage. The television schedules are full of programmes about national culture and landscape: *How We Built Britain*, *Britain from Above*, *Britain's Got Talent* . . . With the current jiggling and jostling between England, Scotland and Wales and the potential collapse of Britain altogether, we realised it was vitally important – of national importance, in fact – for someone to answer the question of Britishness, to metaphorically explore the idea of Britain by literally exploring some key sites and events of Britishness. And deep down, we knew that this someone was us.

So we set out, in the year of the 300th anniversary of the Union that created Britain, to clear a few matters up once and for all: is Britain a nation, or just a state? Was Robin Hood real? Did Churchill exist? Magna Carta, or did she go of her own accord?

As it turns out, there are masses of things going on all over Britain that somehow shine a light on the British dilemma. British people are, alarmingly often, doing British things. We set ourselves the task of looking at them, starting on the first day of spring – with druids on Tower Hill, in London – and, following the year round, finishing exactly one year later, on the north Norfolk coast.

So we begin at the start of British history and end at the end (well, the present – is that the end?), passing along the way, in roughly chronological order, Romans, pagans, Normans, Tudorbethans, industrialists, imperialists, Islamists and *Sun* columnists. And including five extended mini-odysseys (odysseys within odysseys) into Scotland, Wales, southern

England, northern England and, of course, the Empire (which *still* exists – don't listen to the doubters).

You can read chronologically, or dip in and out like you've got some crazy voodoo time machine or something. Up to you.

But, whatever you do, be warned: things are about to get very British.

SPRING

ONE

WITH FOUR THOUSAND GODS ON OUR SIDE

BARBAROUS RITES
THE ONENESS
COMMUNAL SNACKING

SPRING. A TIME of new beginnings. A time that symbolises the rebirth of nature and the renewal of hope. What better time to begin our quest, to cultivate ourselves anew, to traverse this sceptred isle and satisfy, once and for all, the age-old question: what's it all about? The weather tends to pick up around then, too, which is always a bonus if you're going to spend a lot of time outdoors.

And thus we found ourselves on Tower Hill Terrace, by the Tower of London, in the shadow of the City on a morning of bright sun and high, fast clouds and polite showers. It was 21 March, the spring equinox – one of the two times in the sun's cycle when the day and night are equal in length. We were here to see druids, and druids like that sort of thing.

To the south lay the river Thames, which is a sacred river (at least that is the main contention of Peter Ackroyd's book *Thames: Sacred River*). Every vernal equinox, the Druid Order meets here on a stone enclosure sandwiched between the Tower ticket office and a church, All Hallows-by-the-Tower, to give thanks and praise to the earth, the sun, the moon; everything natural, all gushing with newness like a tap that flows nature. We were to begin our quest with them. For history begins – that is, proper written accounts – with the arrival of the Romans, who found druids here. Before the druids, the priest-caste of the Celts, there were hunter-gatherers walking in from Europe, traders from the Med, primitive farmers . . . We could have squinted at little artefacts in museums and burial mounds dotted across the countryside, but really: mud and bits of broken pot? Balls to it. No one really knows much about all that stuff anyway, and here were druids – up close and personal. Druid flesh – made flesh. Come on!

In truth, we weren't sure what to expect. We were hoping for some sooth. But would the druids just hand out sooth to people who tip up on the day, or do you have to get more involved first – you know, like with *Which?* or *Reader's Digest?* The ancient druids may well have come to this ancient holy place to eat the flesh of a dog, or maybe toss the decapitated heads of their enemies into the river as an offering. They thought that eating the dog would enable them to divine secrets of the future, which may seem far-fetched to modern readers. But what would the new-style druids do? We weren't expecting them to eat a dog. That was probably quite unlikely. (The whole event had been advertised in *Time Out*, after all.)

But if there is any collective memory in these isles, any ahistorical group-think, any 'ness', then the descendants of the remembrancers must surely be tuned right into it.

Just before midday, around 30 figures in freshly ironed brilliant white smocks and headdresses emerged slowly from the church meeting hall on the other side of a wall. The smocks really were *very* white. The druids would make a very effective, if freaky, advert for washing powder. Silently they processed down the path to the main road, Byward Street, led by a middle-aged man in spectacles holding a huge sheathed sword. One brandished a crook, another a six-foot-long horn. A queen figure in a Celtic torc held aloft a basket of daffodils and white tulips. Seeds on a plate. Another horn. Banners, one showing the sun over a Stonehenge-style trilothon, another with scales above a pyramid. These symbols were, presumably, highly symbolic.

THE DRUID ORDER: VERY CLEAN DRUIDS.

The entourage processed beside the grizzling midday traffic before turning through the terrace gateway – an open-top Big Bus Sightseeing Tour bus stopping between them and the lunchtime drinkers outside Foxtrot Oscar, the passengers gawping at the neo-ancients. Then, slowly, oh so slowly, really very slowly indeed, they came among us, forming a circle with a fluency that suggested they'd been practising.

Poking from under their white smocks, all wore identical footwear; footwear that matched the hue of their garb and that also suited the druid's active lifestyle. That is to say, they all wore white trainers. ('White trainers,' we both independently wrote in our new British Odyssey notebooks.)

Only one of the circle dared break away from this uniform with a renegade pair of scuffed brown loafers. ('Brown shoes,' we scribbled.) Perhaps this act of rebellion indicated his difficulty with some tenet of the group's principles; a footwear-based expression of essential doubt. Perhaps it was a statement warning how all religious orders – all tribes – have the potential to stifle individuality. Perhaps he didn't have any white trainers.

At noon, the man with the straight horn, taller than himself, took the centre and held his instrument up to the sky, letting out a tight, vulnerable parp towards each corner in turn. Then the chief druid began his eulogy to the supreme force governing the sun and the earth and the crops. This was clearly going to be the main event; no dog-eating would be going down today.

We were here to begin at the beginning. British history officially starts in 55 BC. Before that, barely anything had been written about the inhabitants of Britain/Britannia/Albion/whatever, but that year, Julius Caesar – keen to impress the Roman populace – decided to come, see and conquer this island off the edge of civilisation. In fact, he came and saw the Kent coast before leaving hurriedly when his ships were wrecked in a storm. Next year, he came again, saw again and got bogged down around Brentford (this would have been before the M4 came), finally leaving with some token prisoners. The locals were left wondering: why all the hype about Caesar?

The land he found was populated by Celts, separate, warring tribes of farmers who liked a fight, which they often did in the nuddy ('Those people want to kill us . . . quick, let's take all our clothes off!'). The Druids were their practical and spiritual leaders, wise men and women hanging around in oak groves bedecked with mistletoe saying sooths about when to plant the crops and how best to appease their fantastic array of possibly up to 4,000 gods and goddesses.

OLD MEN

The oldest complete skeleton found in Britain is called the Cheddar Man (he was found in the Cheddar Gorge, he's not made of cheese – you're thinking of the moon). He dates from around 7150 BC: about 4,500 years before the first stones at Stonehenge were erected (really, really, really a long time ago). Older *parts* of humans have been found but the Cheddar Man, who now resides in the Natural History Museum, is the oldest complete true Brit.

Mr Cheddar has butchery marks on his bones, as if he's been professionally sliced up in some way. Naturally, this being prehistory, this is contested: he may for example just have over-enthusiastically scratched an itch. (If you're turned off history because it's a bit argumentative, don't even go there with pre-history. The prehistory guys are animals.) Turn away if you're of a nervous disposition, but basically: he was probably eaten.

The Lindow Man, meanwhile, is the naturally preserved body of an Iron Age man discovered in a peat bog at Lindow Moss, Cheshire. He lives in the British Museum and looks like a deflated football. (Complete set of bones, complete set of skin: come on, they must have been at least *tempted* to put them together.) An eyeball and bits of the Lindow Man's brain had been preserved by the bog. (They even found some of his bum.)

The Lindow Man dates from sometime between 2 BC and AD 119, the time of the Celts and the druids, and the good news is that he wasn't eaten.

On the down side, he was probably a human sacrifice.

THE CHEDDAR MAN: A BIT BEARDY.
Suzanne Hubbard/Rex Features

Of course, all the sources saying the druids/Celts sacrificed humans are Roman, and therefore possibly fabricated, as they were unlikely to give good reviews to a population they were ruthlessly subduing. The Roman writer Tacitus wrote of 'religious groves dedicated to superstition and barbarous rites'; Lucian of 'trees ... sprinkled with human blood'. But the archaeological evidence indicates that they did like a touch of the human sacrificing, probably usually criminals or slaves, possibly burnt alive in huge baskets or effigies made from wicker.

Human butchery in these isles. It's a shocker. That's your roots for you, though. You watch programmes like Bruce Parry's *Tribe* and you see a world where everyone is close to nature and to each other and no one is ever ignored for long and it all seems quite inspiring. Then some elder wise man figure starts beating the kiddies with sticks to ward off evil spirits or something, and you think: balls to that for a game of soldiers, and move to Swindon.

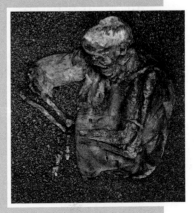

We actually popped in to see the Cheddar Man one day on our way somewhere else, and guess what: he was out. That is to say, he wasn't on display. Now, the books all say he's in the Natural History Museum. He's on the museum website. Who would feel the need to check? He's the oldest complete skeleton found

LINDOW MAN HANGS AROUND THE BOGS.
Peter Brooker/Rex Features

in Britain – *of course* he's going to be on display in the country's foremost natural history repository. And what would you do anyway: ring the Natural History Museum and ask: 'Is the Cheddar Man in?'

It's all dinosaurs now, of course. Old Cheddar Man is upstairs in a cupboard somewhere. We're sure he will be put out again one day. Well, if they haven't chucked him in a skip or something.

No one knows very much about them. They never wrote anything down, passing on their deep knowledge orally. From this we can deduce that they were always busy (which you would be with 4,000 gods to attend to). Druidism was common to the entire Celtic world (Gaul, Ireland, etc.), but budding druids often came here for their training. Britain, then: a true centre of excellence. For druids.

Back on the terrace, as the presider started eulogising in a broad West Country accent the 'super-essential light of light', one of the circle sheepishly edged his way out and off back towards the hall where the druids had left their everyday stuff. Maybe he had a meeting. Or just nicked off for a jimmy. Maybe he had an unavoidable lunch appointment. He might have blown off the druid ceremony altogether, but clearly, as a druid, he had decided that some goddess-worship on the equinox was better than no goddess-worship and, dammit, he would just have to try and fit in both. His neighbours hesitantly shuffled along to fill the gap.

By now, it was hard to ignore the pungent smell wafting across the terrace. Chicken. More particularly, fried chicken. Directly beneath our feet – in an infernal underground mini-mall called the Tower Vaults – the Tower Hill Diner was frying buy-one-get-one-free chicken (we'd been handed a flier near the Tube station). Caesar claimed the ancient Brits didn't eat chickens – merely kept them as pets, along with hares and geese. But here today, in modern Britain, people were eating chickens. (Kept chickens as pets, ate dogs: arse about tit.)

Finally done with the appeasing, the druids processed back to the All Hallows vestry hall. Inside were refreshments; everyone seemed to have brought a contribution. The smocks came off to reveal people who could more easily pass themselves off as twenty-first-century Londoners. Laid out was a feast of Kettle Chips, stollen, Brie, and (for druids less keen on wheat than perhaps their beliefs dictate) Sainsbury's Free From chocolate brownies. 'Must have a drink of cider,' gasped a knackered druid to no one in particular as he headed for the drinks table.

We chatted with Jerome Whitney, an American, and herald for the ceremony. Druidry, he said, was about 'upholding common basic values, like stewardship of the land. We preach merit over inheritance, and a respect for nature.' (That would explain all the seeds, we thought.)

The old druids believed that the soul is eternal and, on death, migrates to another being. Maybe Jerome is actually an old druid incarnate, we wondered. Equally that pigeon might be a druid. Or us? We might be druids. Probably not, though. Just to be on the safe side, we decided to be very polite to our new friend.

Modern neo-druidism is of course a reimagining of what went before. The revival's chief architect was eighteenth-century vicar William Stukeley, an antiquarian who explored Britain's stone circles and earthworks – initially to get more country air for his gout, an ailment he blamed on lavish dinners 'where we drank nothing but French wine'. Wrongly

FOR SOME REASON, WILLIAM STUKELEY'S WICKER MAN DRAWING HAS A REAL HEAD.
Rex Features

believing that these stones were built by the druids, Stukeley became obsessed with druidism until he felt pretty sure he was one. So he started expounding druidic principles from the pulpit and calling himself Chyndonax, Druid of Mount Haemus. Since then, generations of Britons have believed that making stuff up about druids will bring them closer to The Source Of Everything. Maybe it does? William Blake was probably initiated as a druid. Winston Churchill definitely was.* Updating the ancient druidic interest in rejuvenation, it was a latter-day druid who invented Sanatogen.

Today, around 7,000 practising druids are split between a

* Standard historians tend to skirt over this fact (probably because it's not very important), but the future PM was initiated into the Albion Lodge of the Ancient Order of Druids in August 1908, in a ceremony held at Blenheim Palace. Pictures show the young Winston staring sternly at the camera, surrounded by druids in massive white false beards, positively daring the viewer to laugh at him. What, though, could possibly be more British than Winston Churchill at a druid ceremony? Maybe he'd been binge-drinking too.

wild profusion of sects: there's the British Druid Order, the Nomadic Order of Minstrels and Druids, the Ancient Order of Druids, the Insular Order of Druids (presumably for druids who prefer to keep themselves to themselves), the Secular Order of Druids . . . raising the question: how do you split if you're just celebrating seasons? You can't fall out over entering the euro, or Iraq. Maybe one of them forgot the seeds one year and it all kicked off: 'You're *always* doing this. That's it. That is it. If there's any pestilence this year, we know who to blame.'

We asked Jerome about the splits and the numerous druid organisations. He gnomically replied that the different groups have 'different purposes'. What might this mean, we wondered. Maybe some of them do building work on the side or something? Or rent themselves out as security – you know, like the Hell's Angels. 'Your name's not down – hail the sun!' That kind of thing.

We left the druids to their Bombay mix and fruit teas and wished our new friends well. It's all a bit like a *Star Trek* convention with people talking Klingon to each other, but really, what's the harm? Even if they did eat the occasional dog, would that really be so wrong? And maybe the druids are on to something: couldn't we all be paying a bit more attention to nature? Certainly nature appears to be increasingly clamouring for our attention.

At least the worst that could befall the neo-druids were accusations of rendering themselves daft; their fortunes had to be better than those of their forebears. Inevitably, as Spring follows Winter, the Romans returned – under Claudius, in AD 43 – to finish off the conquering. During the first years of the occupation, druids were crucial in keeping alive what the Roman historian Tacitus called the 'mutinous spirit of the Britons', sheltering rebels and calling for armed insurrection from their base on the island of Ynys Mon, or Mona – modern-day Anglesey.

But by AD 60 these renegades had run out of time. Gathered at the Menai Straits, 6,000 troops under Seutonius Paulinus were about to board their rafts to cross the treacherous waters, awash with strong tides and dotted with quicksands, when they looked across to the opposite shore. There before them were the Britons. According to Tacitus, a line of druids in white, hands aloft, was invoking the gods and 'pouring forth horrible imprecations'. Meanwhile, the women (some in black like the warriors, some naked) ran around in wild disorder, shouting, waving flaming torches above their heads, 'their whole appearance resembling the frantic rage of the Furies'. Faced with this vision, Tacitus reports the soldiers paralysed in 'stupid amazement', 'their limbs shaking in terror' – so dumbstruck that they momentarily dropped their defences and laid themselves open to counterattack. They couldn't take the madness!

Then they realised they could take the madness, what with being the greatest fighting force that had ever been assembled and got their unleashing-hell shit together. The Britons reportedly didn't aid their own cause: with all the imprecating and wailing, many of the torch-wielders accidentally set themselves on fire. And that was the last thing they needed.

When the soldiers arrived on the other bank, the druids, women and rebel warriors were massacred in a manic blood frenzy, many thrown alive into the burning funeral pyres. The sacred oaks were shown no mercy.

In time, smashing up the resistance of other, less organised peoples would become a key British skill. But for now, these tribes were on the losing end of civilisation. History had arrived. From now on, chicken was on the menu.

THE FIRST TOGA PARTY

A ROMANO-BRITON AT PLAY.
Universal/The Kobal Collection

Britain's first known chronicler was Pytheas, a Greek merchant based in Marseille, who visited the south coast and Thames estuary in about 322 BC. His journal *About the Ocean* has not survived, but he reported the south-east tribes as growing grain, noting 'the gradual disappearance of various kinds of grain as one advanced towards the north'. So that's the very first mention of Britain ever, and there's already a north–south divide.

Greek writer Strabo said the British were 'bandy-legged' and 'although well supplied with milk, make no cheese'. Instead, the Celtic diet mainly consisted of eating meat with your hands (presumably in a pitta with a choice of 'Garlic sauce? Chilli sauce?'), washed down with strong beer. And you thought strong beer was a new invention from the Continent.

After his visit in 55 BC, Caesar wrote: 'The most civilised of all these nations are they who inhabit Kent.' (Presumably he left before the weekend.) The Britons' sexual preferences also raised Caesar's eyebrows: 'Ten and even twelve have wives common to them, and particularly brothers among brothers, and parents among their children.' (The potential for a primetime sitcom on these guys is immense.)

So how were these proud weirdos subdued? After a patchy start (including much of Roman Britain being burned to the ground during Boudica's revolt), Agricola hit upon a cunning plan. He decided to seduce the tribal leaders with nice togas, plus 'assembly rooms, bathing establishments and smart dinner parties'. By praising those who quickly got involved with the 'pleasures' of Roman life, 'competition for public recognition took the place of compulsion . . . Little by little there was a slide towards the allurements of degeneracy.' Tacitus concluded: 'In their inexperience the Britons called it civilisation when it was really all part of their servitude.'

And so it came to pass that the Britons were suckered by The Man. The Ro-Man. 'I really think we just need to work with these people,' they said, eyeing up a nice villa in Islingtonia. 'More olives?'

TWO

HANKIES AT DAWN

DANCING THE MORRIS
HORNED MAN-BEAST
A TRIUMPH, OVER TITCHMARSH

WE WERE PLUNGING towards the merriest of months, the merry, merry month of May. May is the month the rest of the folk calendar dances around, merrily; with the very Mayest day of all being May Day, the first day of May, when May begins, and the may comes out. This was a time for pre-Puritan Britons to throw off their mental chains and celebrate themselves and the coming of May via the means of boozing, sexing and dancing. Kind of like Brits abroad, but without the abroad.

But how to see in the May? Clearly we'd have to do it at the start of May – that much was obvious – and we opted to get up before dawn to climb a Dorset hillside and behold the Wessex Morris Men dancing the morris as the rising sun aligned itself with the 30-foot-long erection of the Rude Man of Cerne Abbas. The Cerne Abbas giant is the largest chalk figure in Britain, cut into the side of a hill in the chalky uplands above the Dorset village of the same name. And who wouldn't want to get up at dawn to watch white-clad middle-aged men dance with hankies atop a huge chalky tumescence? Who? Let the revels commence!

We arrived at Cerne Abbas, snuggled in the rolling Dorset downs, in the balmy early evening. After checking into the village's sixteenth-century New Inn (room names: 'Lovebird', 'Duck', 'Swallow' . . .), we took a pre-May Day trek to find the giant. This seemed wise: before sun-up tomorrow we might struggle to find our own feet, let alone a footpath in the deepest countryside. We must apprise ourselves immediately, we decided, of the Rude Man's limestone lumbar area.

We followed the signs along a bramble-edged footpath out of the village, running past playing fields alongside a stream. It was a tortuous route, though we didn't really pay much attention to this at the time. Crossing a stone bridge in some woods and entering a field of rapeseed, we faced north towards the steep hillside looming over the village. And there he stood. Proud. Almost too proud. He's a big bugger, mind – generally, that is, not just down below.

Why he's there – and for how long – is a matter of conjecture. Is he prehistoric? Certainly he appears in 'prehistoric Britain' books beside neolithic landmarks like the Uffington Horse. Another theory claims he was made by Roman soldiers who hero-worshipped Hercules – very much the original hero to worship – but why then does he go unmentioned until 1694,

'YEAH? WHAT?'
ALAMY

totally absent from the welter of medieval documents surviving at Cerne Abbey?

Some claim this be no ancient lob-on, but merely a latter-day put-on, possibly pre-Reformation graffiti to wind up the monks of the abbey below: 'Hey, monks! Get a load of this big cock!' That sort of thing. One local legend has it that he's the outline of a real giant, tied down and killed by villagers during a post-murderous rampage kip. (Locals, eh? What are they like?)

More likely the giant may be a Civil War-era carving ordered by a local landowner to mock the Herculean ego of Oliver Cromwell. Even then, it's not written down: maybe he just thought carving a massive cock and balls into the hillside was statement enough? So the Giant remains an enigma. Well, as enigmatic as anything can be while also sporting a large erection.

We stood in the evening sunlight considering the giant's facial expression. He's a funny one all right. His eyebrows are raised in surprise. As though he's been discovered on the hill up to no good, and up they've gone. Maybe there were originally a series of scenes cut across the hillside, like cartoon boxes. In this one he's got his arms open and eyebrows up in a conciliatory gesture of surprise. In the next, he's saying: 'Now I know what you're thinking, but I can explain the club.' And the people motion to his down-below bits and he just gets really embarrassed and runs away.

Whatever his provenance, the giant became a symbol of virility and fertility for local people (possibly because of his big willy). Childless couples have reputedly sought an extra leg-up by fornicating on his slopes, the mucky so-and-so's. Ladies feeling themselves in need of a husband have slept on the giant's giant manhood for good luck (choosing to ignore the huge raised club and gaping mouth, which do not, let's face it, scream husband material). On this particular evening, no one was taking advantage of the Rude Man's powers. The hills were rolling, but no one was rolling on the hills. All was quiet. Peace was in the valley. Across the chalk downland, undulating greenly, the dusky sky imbued everything with a warm orange glow. We went for a pint.

As the evening progressed, we asked around at the village pubs for details of the following morning's events, hoping for some roisteringly told tales of vivid local colour; but at the first two pubs, the landlords in this unchanging idyll (oft featured in England's Finest Village polls) had all recently moved to the area and didn't know anything about it. After last orders in the Royal Oak, we were promised a lock-in at another establishment down the road. We poked our heads round the door, hoping to be heartily welcomed and regaled with fragrant tales of May Days of yore. And we would laugh and laugh, possibly banging our tankards (do people still have tankards?) on the table with gusto and also gay abandon. But it was closed.

Four forty a.m. Although dawn was supposedly nearing, no one had yet told the sky, which was doing a fine impression of still being properly night-time. The lanes were silent. No morris men were lurking. (They weren't even nearby: we'd have heard their bells.) We poked around between the cottages on the main street to find the alleyway leading to the footpath. This was a strange hour to be poking about the streets of an English village. It was very dark, and a bit nippy.

The journey up the bramble-edged footpath was now a fraught affair involving perilous ravines and treacherous mud pools. We found the bottom of the giant's hill, only to realise we had no idea how to penetrate the enclosure's barbed-wire fence. The wire was blocking the way. The way to morris!

It was now, huffing and puffing our way up a bloody great big hill in the dark, doing battle with puddles and our beer-heads, that we wondered if this whole Britishness quest might be a terrible mistake.

Digging deep, we found a well of inner strength from somewhere, at about the same time we found a crumpled blister-pack of paracetamol in a jacket pocket. Everything was going to be all right.

It was clear that someone, or something, had been testing

us – but who? The National Trust would have put the fence up, and you wouldn't put anything past those bastards. Well, tough titty, National Trust – we're going on!

We decided to climb over the barbed wire. Through sheer dumb luck we survived without injury to our lower body areas or even our trousers, and started climbing the precipitous slope beside the giant. All was silent. All was dark. Where was this alleged daybreak morris revelry? Where? The faintest wash of slightly lighter blue in the east indicated some progress on the daylight front.

Finally (we're talking some minutes here), we reached the summit. Amazingly, a huddle of figures came into view silhouetted against the yellowy rim where the hillside met the sky. Rising arrestingly above them was a horned man-beast about ten feet tall. Gathered around this strange, otherworldly creature were 12 or so morris men – all-weather coats over their dancing garb – and about 10 other bystanders. We'd made it. Everyone else had decided to enter through the open gate at the top of the hill, which was quite clever of them all in all. (We made a mental note to, in future, just kind of generally look out for gates on our trek.)

This flattened grass square on top of the hill, surrounded by a shallow ditch – actually a small earthwork called the Trendle (or Frying Pan) that might (or might not) date from the Iron Age – was the former site of the village's maypole. Dancing around a maypole has strong phallic overtones. As, clearly, does the Giant himself: nothing has more phallic overtones than a phallus. So villagers dancing round a phallic symbol above a 30-foot-long phallic symbol: that's no longer mere overtone. That's a full tone, that is. Just thinking about it could take your eye out.

At 5.15 it was still fairly murky, but the eastern horizon now shimmered with orange. The morris men discarded their coats and welcomed the spectators, the numbers now swelled to 30 or 40, as more people arrived. Through the gate. The two accordion players sparked up and locked in together, bells were shaken and the dancers got on the good foot. The morris was go!

Pulling our thin jackets tight, with the wind roaring across the tops of the hills and straight into our ears, we felt horribly underdressed. But the dancers, wearing only cotton shirts, gave not a hoot for the cold and instead, waving their handkerchiefs and skipping to and fro, seemed almost hypnotised by the strange cat's-cradle patterns they were weaving. It's not often you see grown men skipping before sunrise, or any time, and we marvelled at the intricacy of their inexplicable gyrations. They were really going at it, and we respected them for that.

The man-bull, a large leather-wood mask with a scary hinged jaw, sometimes stood at the back, just sort of looking on, weird and menacing, and sometimes acted as a kind of totem at the centre of the formations, a weird knobble on his forehead resembling an untended wart or third eye struggling to break out. A giant horned folk creature does add a real touch of freakiness to any gathering, we thought.

The bagman then held out his bag full of sticks. The dancers took one each before lining up and setting about a furious stick dance. They really cracked those sticks.

Looking out across the valley, stretching, rolling, for miles and miles, we shared a little out-of-body vision of our little huddle on this hillside in early-morning Britain, the sound of chinging bells and cracking sticks blowing into the void, looking very small, somewhat forlorn but slightly heroic. This whole thing was inexplicable, but with a certain charm: inexplicable, but why not?

THE WESSEX MORRIS MEN: IT'S NOT OFTEN YOU SEE MEN SKIPPING.

Next up was a dance to bring abundant crops. 'This dance is for the growing of beans,' said the leader. 'That's English beans,' he added. 'Not French beans. Or any other foreign beans. English beans!' Because it's never too early for some jovial leguminous xenophobia.

Morris dancing could hardly be more redolent of a beardy, real-ale variety of monocultural Merrie Olde England. As white and English as the white cliffs of Dover. English English English. White white white. Dover Dover Dover.

Or, you know, African . . . First mentioned in 1458, the word 'morris' is thought to derive from '*moresco*' meaning 'Moorish', with the fashion possibly being brought back by John of Gaunt's troops on a Spanish military jaunt. Then again, it might not be. No one really knows for sure. (The white cliffs of Dover are a bit greyish, too. Can you trust nothing in this world?)

The tradition would probably have died out altogether were it not for the efforts of Edwardian folk revivalist Cecil Sharp, who believed – despite the total (that's total) lack of evidence – that these dances were relics of England's pagan, racially pure, past: ancient rites performed by ancient whites.*

Back on the hill it was getting lighter but also, if anything, getting colder. It was a paradox. A big brain-freezing bastard of a paradox. We were by now swaying and nodding our heads in time to the music. The relentless tum-te-tum melodies and on-the-one repetitive beats were a welcome distraction from the early-morning elements, and before long the effect honestly became slightly incantatory. As the eastern half of the cloudless sky turned properly sky-blue, the thought arose: this is a rave. Maybe these folk tunes are the original banging tunes. This lot are tripping their tits off – on the morris! Come on, morris men! Take us into insanity! It's just the sun rising. We call it acieeed. Rhythm is. A dancer. Es are good.

At the climax of their last dance, the morris men raised their hankies triumphantly to the sky. At that exact moment, the sun finally pierced the horizon. 'It's a sign!' we almost exclaimed. Or a coincidence. Either way, this moment could not be topped, and the side (morris teams are called sides, like beef) finally rested. Each spectator got issued with a nice green-on-white sticker with a jolly bearded dancer on it plus the legend 'I've Seen Wessex Morris Men'. (We've still got ours and wear them with pride. Although, to be fair, they should do a separate set that read 'I've Seen Wessex Morris Men Having Climbed Up A Fucking Big Hill At Dawn – And You Haven't',

---

* Not all folk dancers use the dances as exercises in racial purity: some use the occasion as an excuse to black up. And how into black stuff is that? In the past, some blacked-up groups would even refer to morris dancing as 'nigger dancing' or 'going niggering'. (The term probably doesn't hold the same connotations of street-smart camaraderie as used by, say, Samuel L. Jackson's character in *Jackie Brown*.)

to distinguish dilettantes who have only ever seen them outside a village pub by accident from the real fans.)

We headed back down to the village following the crowd, taking the normal, much easier route past the abbey at the base of the hill. It's from the Benedictine abbey that the name 'Abbas' comes. There's a legend that St Augustine himself (the father of British Christianity) came here and founded an earlier abbey, and magicked up a well by touching the ground with his stick. He didn't, though. Hoping to attract pilgrims, the local monks in the eleventh century hired fibbing monk Goscelin to make the story up from his head. But that's local legends for you: like legends, only more bollocks. (They were always doing shit like that, the church of yore – making stuff up to attract pilgrims. Thank God that these days they just stick to the facts.)

CECIL SHARP. AND FRIENDS.
Topfoto

In the village shop, an elderly woman customer saw the procession pass and recalled the May Days of her childhood in the 1920s, with the whole school marching up to the Trendle to dance around the maypole. Great days. We didn't ask her about the phallic overtones. Well, you wouldn't really, would you?

After parading through the village with hawthorn twigs, the dancers convened at the New Inn for breakfast, taking over the pub's wood-beamed front room. Like proper musicians, they started boozing at 8 a.m. If we're keying into a time before the Puritans made people work all the hours God sent (and the Victorians started repressing people into not stumbling around before elevenses), maybe getting pissed at breakfast-time might, every now and then, help put things in perspective, we thought. Pissed perspective, obviously, but perspective nonetheless.

After the first pints had been swiftly consumed, the singing began: hearty songs of sorrow and joy. It was heartening. Our hearts were heartened. Then our hearts were sorrowed. Our hearts moved accordingly, while our mouths ate bacon. One morris man explained that the horned man-beast was the Dorset Ooser – a mythic local figure used to harry local wrong-doers like adulterers. This was a 1975 replica of an original from nearby village Melbury Osmond that went missing in the 1930s. 'It was rumoured to be used by a witches' coven, but that's just a rumour . . .' he said. 'It was there to keep the community in line. Sort of intended to scare children. A personification of the beast within.' Adding brightly: 'It's evil, basically.' Cool.

This year's dance was judged particularly fine. No one could remember such a clear sky; they have danced in deep fog and even snow. The morris men told us that Alan Titchmarsh had turned up the year before, and it had absolutely pissed down, the crew drying out the insides of cameras with hairdryers in the back bar of the New Inn. Ha! Wrong year, Titchmarsh. The elements were on *our* side. The spirit of Britain is with us, not you! Screw you, Titchmarsh! Screw you!

Maybe the early start was beginning to hit, but soon the songs rolling away in the corner started feeling slightly repetitive, even oppressive. Particularly when they took a turn for the bawdy. Sadly, this is often where observing folk tradition can lead: beery old guys singing jaunty songs about groping teenage girls. Let the revels stop commencing!

Leaving the village, we pulled into a layby on the A352 for a photograph of the giant. Again we pondered the giant's mystery, considering how the problem with folk memory is that, left to their own devices, folks often remember precisely naff all. Most people struggle to remember to buy more milk, never mind pass on stories from ages back in some sort of generational game of Chinese whispers.

Then we recalled another theory that the Rude Man's member was once a smaller member that somehow got conjoined with a belly button. Can this be true? Surely not. If you're taking the trouble to carve a giant's erection into the hillside, would you really keep it on the small side? Maybe standing back halfway through and going: 'Hmm, is it too much? We don't want to seem tasteless . . .'

BRITAIN'S TOP ENEMIES

DANES, THE: You wouldn't think it to look at them now, but they were once huge bastards.

FRENCH, THE: In the eighteenth century, Britishness was built on four mainstays, according to top Britishness academic Linda Colley: Protestantism, war, the pursuit of profit, and hating the French. Nelson prescribed: 'You must hate a Frenchman as you hate the devil.' (The devil has the best tunes. Not something you could say for the French.)

ROMANS, THE: Slaughtered Boudica and subjugated the noble, woad-spattered Britons. On the plus side, introduced underfloor heating, which cuts radiator clutter.

NORMANS, THE: Prototype French. Cunningly, also Danish.

SPANISH, THE: No gip for ages on this front, but at the opening of Parliament in 1656, Cromwell was moved to declare: 'Why, truly, your great enemy is the Spaniard. He is

YOUR ENEMY.
Rex Features

a natural enemy, he is naturally so.' You don't get speeches like that at the opening of Parliament any more. More's the pity.

ARGIES, THE: All smoothed over now, though. So it's okay to eat corned beef again. Except it's revolting. Here's an idea: let's have a war with whichever nation is responsible for luncheon meat.

IRAQ: Clearly posed a major threat – but, well, they won't be bothering *us* for a while.

DUTCH, THE: Attempted to rival Britain for naval supremacy, before giving up to become pot-sodden whore-masters.

GERMANS, THE: No. 1 All-Time Top Enemy. The wave of anti-German feeling during WWI even saw angry mobs attacking dachshunds. We have it on the strictest authority of our grans that 'the Boche' will 'rise again'. Achtung! Achtung!

YOUR ENEMY.
Jupiter Images

YANKS, THE: And after all we'd done for them. At the time of the War of Independence, it was feared defeat would mean the 'dismemberment of the Empire'. But the Empire went on to be the largest the world had ever seen. So who's laughing now, eh?

THREE

MILLIONAIRE'S SHORTBREAD

BRITAIN IN PERIL
MEL GIBSON
FREEDOM!

NO ONE IN BRITAIN takes nationalism as seriously as the Scots, Scotland, the Scottish and the Scots. They even elect nationalists. And how nationalist is that!?

We arrived in Scotland 300 years, almost to the day, since the birth of Great Britain – the moment that the 1707 Acts Of Union took effect to form a new Kingdom out of two very different, often fairly hostile, kingdoms. That's if spending the previous few centuries raiding and grabbing and invading and slaughtering and jeering while waving one's fist in a hostile manner can be called hostile. Which it probably can.

We were in Scotland to peel away the layers of the nationalist onion; to look under the stone of Scottish history; and to possibly witness Britain getting broken. Or at least the first little baby steps towards Britain getting broken. A cute baby that would grow up into a huge oil-powered nationalist titan smashing Britain to pieces wildly with a fucking great big claymore. That sort of baby.

Because now, after 300 years of submersion within a newer nation, the elections on May 3 looked set to see the Scottish National Party – very much the people who were too Scottish to also be British – taking over the Scottish Parliament. We arrived on May 2, the day before this day of reckoning. And this meant one thing: the day of reckoning was near.

We would be venturing to the heart of Scottish nationhood, the key mythic sites of an ancient independent Scotland, before the vile Union with the English ruined everything. In a word: swords. (In a few more words: swords, and also stones.) But first: Edinburgh. Which is also in Scotland.

Arriving in the city centre, we hit Princes Street, the main drag of the post-Union New Town (designed by the nephew of the bloke who wrote 'Rule Britannia'), looking up at the colonialist street signs. In 2005, to commemorate the 700th anniversary of the death of William Wallace, a group called the Irrepressible Wing of Scotland's Frank Zapatistas (yeah, those guys again) covered these signs with new ones reading 'William Wallace Street', so ridding the drag of its Hanoverian taint. 'The Princes of Princes Street,' they claimed, 'were drunken German oafs whose memory does not deserve to be commemorated in the capital of Scotland.'

These guys really hate drunken Germans. Do you ever see the Irrepressible Wing of Scotland's Frank Zapatistas down the

EDINBURGH. PICTURED HERE MERCIFULLY FREE OF COMEDIANS.
Art Gallery of New South Wales and Australia/The Bridgeman Art Library

Oktoberfest, quaffing Pils and hailing passing pissed-up Boche? You do not.

The city's lampposts were festooned with election placards – for the SNP, for Labour, for the madpants' 8% Growth Party (we didn't look into it too deeply, but basically they were in favour of 8% growth), for some crazy Christian party with a thistle-based logo we couldn't understand . . .

We checked into the Britannia Hotel on Princes Street. It stands on the edge of the tainted Georgian New Town, but facing towards the ancient Old Town: it's sort of a symbol. And a hotel.

On a fine evening, we went out searching for the Scottish Parliament building, potential new centre of an independent Scotland. When the Union was proposed in 1706, the Scottish people were still fairly negative about joining with England. That's if rioting in the streets of Edinburgh, pelting the Commissioner with stones on his way into Parliament and burning copies of the Articles can be taken as being fairly negative, which it probably can.

Okay, these two kingdoms did already share the same king; the unification process had begun a century earlier with the 1603 Union Of The Crowns, when England, stuck for a monarch following The Virgin Queen's virgin death, picked the frankly quite weird Scots King James VI, who promptly naffed off to London, possibly saying: 'I'd love to stay, but . . . well, er . . . oh, fuck it, no reason! *Byeee!*' (It might cheer Scottish readers to know that, upon arriving in London, James literally offered to show the crowds his arse.)

But the Union of parliaments was obviously of a different order and even pro-Union writer Daniel Defoe, spying for the English, reported the Scottish people to be 99-1 against. Even so, Scottish MPs voted to dissolve themselves by 110 to 67. How come? Sorry, but there is no easy way to put this: cash was involved. Yes, we know, it's scarcely believable.

In fact, after a disastrous coffers-emptying stab at imperialism called the Darien Scheme (two words: Panama, malaria), the Scottish gentry were tripping over themselves for a bit of English money-money-money. Even Defoe was shocked by what he witnessed of the Scottish elite's willingness to sell their nationfolk down the Forth: 'I never saw so much trick, sham, pride, jealousy and cutting of friends' throats as there is among the noblemen.'

Back in Edinburgh, we'd reached our quarry. Nestling in a dead zone at the bottom of the Royal Mile underneath Arthur's Seat (which is a mountain), this new Scottish Parliament building was, in its pointy-steel-and-glass-and-bits-of-wood way, undoubtedly an impressive building. An impressive building that cost £431m, ten times the original budget. That is one expensive building. Never let it be called a cheap building. Because it's not. To be fair, it's priceyness has been noted.

Hope no one breaks it. It cost a lot of money.

On the Parliament's walls were numerous quotations from noted Scots summing up their beloved, if submerged, nation, including Scots nationalist Hugh MacDiarmid's weepy ode, since taken up by the SNP: 'The rose of all the world is not for me/I want for my part/Only the little white rose of Scotland/That smells sharp and sweet – and breaks the heart.' A mixture of Celtic romance and borderline xenophobia that is indeed touching to behold.*

Would this clearly expensive building one day host a proper

---

* MacDiarmid has the interesting distinction of being the only person ever expelled by the Communist Party for being a Scotttish Nationalist and expelled by the Scots Nationalists for being a Communist. What a guy.

independent Parliament? It certainly could. It looks to be big enough for that. At the moment, though, SNP leader Alex Salmond was checking hot-headed demands for independence, firmly hoping to keep 'moderate opinion' on side: the SNP pledged to keep the pound, swear allegiance to the Queen and delay any referendum at least until 2010 (presumably believing a future Tory government would push even more not-really-nationalists into their arms).

From humble acorns mighty Scots pines may yet grow, but it did all seem a bit mealy-mouthed. Why not just come and say it like a man: 'Fuck you and fuck your Queen!'

People respect that kind of honesty.

For dinner, we hit the Royal Mile. Real Scotland. Old school. Having sampled the delights of Tourist Scotland – shops like The Really Scottish Shop and Thistle Do Nicely – we dived into a pub to get a taste of the real thing. That is, we had haggis, tatties and neeps. In a pub with a tartan carpet. While listening to folk songs played by a bloke wearing what looked like tartan pyjamas.

Folk songs about heather. Now *that*'s Scottish.

It's nice, we thought, and also time-efficient, to have all the national clichés so neatly wrapped up in one mealtime. How about a one-man military tattoo while we're at it?

Election day. Morning. Today. Was the day. In the next few hours, the Hand of History might be called into play. Would the Scots emulate their historic heroes and throw off centuries of cruel English oppression? Or not bother? That was the question.

Before checking out the totemic sites of Old Scotland, we were to Kirkcaldy (aka Broon's Backyard™) in search of a guru: Professor Chris Harvie, foremost academic of Scottish nationhood and also a fully paid-up SNP-er and prospective MSP for Kirkcaldy. Chris Harvie knows more about Scotland than we will ever know. That isn't to say we're not interested in Scotland – we are; or that we don't like Scotland – we do. But the eminent Mr Harvie loves Scotland like only a Scotsman can. A Scotsman who has read many, many books. About Scotland.

Kirkcaldy is called the Lang Toun. As we drove along Kirkcaldy's long – very long – seafront, we realised that this is because it is quite long. This was the town that gave the world Adam Smith and, of course, James Gordon 'Gordon Brown'

HAIL TO THE CHIEF

When Scotsmen proudly don their kilt for another wedding, they are expressing a rich tradition – a rich tradition that was invented way back in the msits of time: in 1822. But then, 1822 *was* quite a long time ago . . .

This was the year that Scots literary giant Sir Walter *'Ivanhoe'* Scott and military man David Stewart of Garth prepared a massive pageant for the fat, drunken monarch George IV (the first visit north of the border by a reigning monarch since Charles II). Basically wanting to show off a bit, the Lowland Scots suddenly stopped thinking of their moor-dwelling neighbours as dangerous lowlife and instead got well Highland: out came the kilts and the tartan, and the immortal pipes – all nearly as novel for the Lowlanders as for the fat King himself.

GEORGE IV. THE FOURTH, AND MOST USELESS, OF ALL THE GEORGES.
Wellington Museum, London/ The Bridgeman Art Library

George's visit – 'one and twenty daft days', according to one observer – included balls (oh, the balls), walkabouts (oh, the walkabouts) and general 'huzzas' from adoring crowds (this was quite a turn-up, because people usually thought he was a fucking arsehole). Now, finally, all of the Scots looked Scottish.

Ironically, this festival of kitsch Highlandism was just after the first and before the second load of Highland Clearances, which saw hired thugs brutally expunging the Highlands of your actual Highlanders. These Clearances were not really post-Culloden English revenge on rebel clans, more the northern lords developing a brutal eye for sheep-related profit . . . so *anyone* wearing a Scottish sweater is basically a bastard.

CHRIS HARVIE. PICTURED HERE
THINKING ABOUT SCOTLAND.

Brown, one of whom would often warn of the dangers of letting capitalists get away with murder, and one of whom is a Labour prime minister. Adam Smith was among the leading lights of the eighteenth-century Scottish Enlightenment, the forward-thinking (post-Union) intellectual flowering that inspired Voltaire to declare: 'We look to Scotland for all our ideas of civilisation.' Reason: that was the main deal with these guys. Thinking about stuff.

Climbing a steep hill away from the seafront, we reached a granite hotel, the Strathearn, where we sat out on the lawn in the morning sun to discuss Scottishness and Britishness.

As you do.

At Chris's behest, we all enjoyed a cold glass of Irn-Bru, the fizzy orange pop from Glasgow that has never really caught on in southern Britain. This seemed to amuse him greatly, and nationalists with a sense of humour are definitely the best sort of nationalists. (A couple of years ago, the drink's advertisers ran into trouble for employing a Glasgae hardman stereotype for their television ads – the Glasgae hardman in the ad was actually a Glasgae hard-cuckoo, but it still caused offence. You just can't generalise about Glasgow cuckoos. Some of them are really sensitive.) (Alan, for the record, quite likes Irn-Bru.)

Labour was now desperate. Party leaders were virtually claiming that anyone who dared vote SNP would have the sky fall in on their tins of shortbread. Some rumours even alleged scare tactics to ward off Muslim voters, claiming the SNP were the Scottish equivalent to the BNP (a political tactic just shy of posting leaflets through people's letterboxes reading: PLEASE PLEASE PLEASE VOTE FOR US, WE'RE ABSOLUTELY FUCKING DESPERATE HERE – SO COME ON).

Broon styled himself as Mr Economy. But as Kirkcaldy and Cowdenbeath MP he'd only managed to rustle up one major new employer: MTI, a call centre offering low-paid, part-time work. (Yes. Broon had opened a call centre in his backyard.) Anti-Labour feeling was everywhere, said Chris.

He recounted some 'almost renaissance turns of phrase' of constituents, one man saying to him: 'I wouldn't piss on Broon if he was on fire; but if you were on fire, I would piss on you.' (This seemed to sum up the SNP's position very well. Is it not the very definition of 'critical support'?)

A modern civic nationalist, Chris had no time for *Braveheart*, tub-thumping patriotism ('terrible rubbish . . . total bollocks'), but he couldn't help breaking out some harder stuff about deal-making and ingenuity being 'hard-wired' into the national psyche. He seemed to envisage a glorious future of canny Scots feverishly making deals all over the place, free from endlessly kowtowing to the English.

It's a lovely image. But one that sat oddly with the SNP's casual acceptance of support from Brian Souter, the Stagecoach millionaire evangelist, who had just that March given them half a million pounds. Souter, who made his money from privatised bus services, is a well-known union-basher renowned for trying to drive competitors out of business by offering parallel cheaper (or even free) services. He's also a world-famous homophobe, who spent up to a million pounds trying to drum up opposition to the abolition of Clause 28.

A month after Souter's donation, the SNP had coincidentally done him a gigantic favour by dropping its commitment to re-regulate the buses. So the SNP's stirring vision seemed to be an independent, free Scotland in hock to no one except the oil industry, multinational corporations and Brian Souter. Still, at least it's not 'the English', eh?

Maybe this is the fullest expression of the Scots' renown for deal-making: getting into bed with anyone. Not that we're suggesting that Brian Souter would literally get into bed with Alex Salmond, not with his reputation as a world-famous homophobe. (That's Souter, not Salmond.)

As we left Kirkcaldy, we stopped for snacks at a corner shop owned by a sombre, grey-haired Muslim man. On the magazine rack, the top shelf was filled with pornography. As was the middle shelf. And also the bottom shelf (a sizeable proportion of the road traffic north of the central belt are truckers).

Maybe this was what Adam Smith had in mind when he spoke of the importance of appealing to people's instinct for self-love?

Intellect only gets you so far in matters of nationalisticism: now for the *heart*. First up, Stirling: Gateway to the Highlands. There we would climb the National Wallace Monument, a nineteenth-century shrine to the medieval Scottish hero nestled on a craig above the scene of his greatest victory against the cruel invaders. Once up there, we might roar.

Scotland can claim to have been a nation for longer than England, being first unified in either 843 (when Kenneth McAlpin brought together the Scots and Picts) or 1035 (when Duncan I became the first king of Scotland). Roughly speaking, that is (many nobles up north never really united under anyone except themselves). But then, in 1296, England invaded, and this really gave the Scots something to unite against.

The nickname of English – or, if we're being pedantic: French-Plantagenet – King Edward I was 'Hammer of the Scots'. This gives a good idea of what he had in mind for Scotland, and it wasn't everyone having a big cuddle. 'Emotional Counsellor of the Scots'? That wasn't his nickname.

At this point, Scotland needed a hero. Or two. And so they came. Men with names that sound tough from even the most effeminate mouth. William Wallace. Robert the Bruce. Say names like that too often and you too will end up wanting to duff up an English. (Robert the Bruce sounds much harder than the original Robert de Bruis, which rather gives away his Norman-aristo ancestry.)

As we approached, the pointed tip of the grey-stone monument way up on the hill was shrouded in mist. Was this some sort of sign, we wondered. Or just some mist?

At the bottom of the hill, by the shop, was a statue of William Wallace. Or rather Mel Gibson. An inscription told us how this sandstone statue, called *The Spirit of Wallace*, helped Brechin sculptor Tom Church revive his spirits after being brought low by life-threatening heart problems. 'At this low point, Tom watched the film *Braveheart*. So inspired was he by Wallace's patriotism and determination that Tom resolved to produce a sculpture that would capture the spirit of one of Scotland's greatest heroes.'

It's the best way for any Scot to summon the strength needed when adversity strikes hard: imagine smashing up an English! With a ruddy great claymore!

Walking up the steep, winding slope to the wooded craig, it was a beautiful early summer's day. We were nearly run over by the minibus that shuttles old people up the hill from the car park. Was *that* a sign? It was definitely a sign that we shouldn't stand round in the road looking for signs, but was it more than that?

At the base of the monument, sitting on a bench, a middle-aged woman was reading the Scottish edition of the *Daily Mail* bearing a full-page picture of Alex Salmond and the headline: THIS

WILLIAM WALLACE/MEL GIBSON. PICTURED HERE CRYING FREEDOM.

MAN WANTS TO DESTROY GREAT BRITAIN. Was *this* a sign?

We climbed the monument's many, many steps, round and round up the tower. Emerging into the brilliant sunshine, we surveyed the lands before us. This was the crucible of Scottish history; the key to Scotland. Strategically, controlling the crossing of the river at Stirling meant controlling the gate between Highlands and Lowlands. Hence all the battles. The Battle of Stirling Bridge (William Wallace beating Edward I's army in 1297) beneath us. Bannockburn there (Bruce's momentous victory over Edward II). Falkirk off in the distance (something else). The river snaked about below, glinting in the sun like a twisty-turny, wet snaky thing.

At the Battle of Bannockburn in June 1314 Robert the Bruce decisively smashed a massive English force under Edward II. The English were routed with Edward himself taking flight in panic. No such mighty invasion force ever went north of the border again. Because Scotland was not – not – conquered by the English. So in a sense, we agreed, it's because of Bannockburn that Scotland now doesn't have tuition fees. You know, kind of. If you're entering into the spirit of things.

Back inside the tower were exhibits like the Wallace sword, a truly massive claymore with which he supposedly did some battering. Standing at over five feet (including handle), you certainly wouldn't want it up you. Sadly, though, some clever-dicks have claimed it is two centuries too young to be Braveheart's blade (historians like spoiling people's fun).

On another floor was the Hall of Heroes – a room dedicated to Scottish heroes. Scottish people mostly, people like Rabbie Burns, James Watt and Muriel Gray.

On the middle floor was a crazy animated thing – a robot top half of Wallace with his face projected on to it looking like a hologram, wobbling about weirdly, arguing with a film projected on to the adjoining wall. A legless robot declaiming to the English? Come on! 'For, as long as but a hundred of us remain alive, never will we on any conditions be brought under English rule,' the head wobbled about, shouting. Bet it puts the shits up kids, we agreed.

Heading back down the hill, it seemed incredible that Wallace's men 'swooped down' from this steep craggy hillside in full armour with battleaxes and swords to slaughter the invaders. Even without all those encumbrances, you'd surely want to tread very carefully down slopes like this. Even with the correctly supportive footwear.

But Wallace's men had no fear of twisted ankles. These were people who, when faced with a steep slope, really went for it, probably yelling: 'AAAAAAARRRRRRRGHHHHH!!!!'

And also: 'CAAAANN'T STOOOOOOPPPPPP!!'

We ploughed on. Like the Scottish people, we had a date with destiny. The Stone of Destiny.

We were on our way to Scone Palace, just outside Perth. Or Perth: Gateway to the Highlands. Another gateway. Not sure if we ever went through one of the gateways to the Highlands into the actual proper Highlands. But we were definitely getting higher. The cows were getting beefier. The views were getting wider. The dead animals lying by the roadside were getting heftier. Badgers are big animals. We half expected to see some donkeys or moose lying there. Where were we? Oh yes, the Highlands. We did see some hills: put it that way.

The sun was still shining. We couldn't help thinking mist might have been more appropriate, but you can't have everything. The stereotypical *Highlander* view of Scottish history is of endless blood-feuds lasting centuries: clan forever clashing with clan to avenge their dead clansmen, clan inviting clan round for dinner before murdering clan after pudding.

But the reality wasn't even remotely like *Highlander* (thus negating a full two hours of our research). As one Scottish history book states, it is 'easy to infer a state of almost perpetual warfare', but that was simply not the case. For a start, fighting was largely confined to the summer. 'Hey, kids, summer's here!' 'Can we go swimming, Daddy?' 'Yes, we can go swimming in the blood of the MacNabs!'

A field just outside Perth was the scene of possibly the weirdest clan battle of them all. In September 1396, Robert II organised a sponsored slayathon between two clan teams, each of 30 warriors armed with claymores, to finally settle their differences. An arena was set up for townsfolk to get a good view of the claymore-based action. As the gory death toll mounted, the King and spectators were, according to reports, seized with 'an inexpressible horror'. The thing is, though: what were they actually expecting?

Scone Palace is a largely nineteenth-century mansion built on the spot where ancient Scottish kings ruled, ancient parliaments sat and ancient monastic song was sung . . . It is home to the Stone of Destiny. Which might sound like a fantasy trilogy from the eighties, but is actually a stone containing Scotland's mystical power. It's the ancient lump of sandstone on which the ancient kings were crowned – the stone they touched (usually after they had killed the previous king) to show their devotion to the Scottish dream.

After buying our tickets, we were accosted by one of the guides standing at the house entrance. Resembling a Scottish Kenneth Williams, and the man for whom the term waspish was invented, he upbraided us for our unkempt attire and inability to stand up straight when being spoken to.

We told our new friend, Alisdair MacDonald, that we thought Scotland had been trying to tell us something all morning, so we were going to check out the Stone for Scotland Rising vibes. Bet you've had a few through today, we enquired. 'You're not the full shilling, you two, are you?' he pronounced cheerfully.

After defeating William Wallace's army in Falkirk, Edward sent men straight over to Scone to take the stone. This wasn't

HALF-REMEMBER CULLODEN!

On the local radio came news that up near Inverness a reconstruction of Culloden was being filmed for the new battlefield visitor centre. This 1746 vicious slaughter by British soldiers of 4,000 retreating Jacobite rebels led by exiled Stuart heir Bonnie Prince

CULLODEN RECREATION SKIMPS ON
PARTICIPANTS?
ALAMY

Charlie has always stirred Scottish blood: the last battle on British soil, it's the moment the English really took over, bayoneting the heart out of the Highland clans on a cold, rain-flecked moor (the weather conditions are always mentioned, like it somehow makes it *much* worse).

This new National Trust for Scotland centre – with its 'revisionist' take on the events of the 1745 rising – had stirred the blood too, with one *Scotsman* article provoking anger from Edinburgh to Australia: 'A puerile attempt to degrade Scottish history and make it a "better fit" with Unionist propaganda.' Also: 'The anti Scottish National Trust . . . are the equivalent of the Native Americans who fought for the white settlers.' Plus: 'And so the British conquistadors continue to rewrite Scottish history . . . Same as it ever was.'

So they weren't keen. The Trust's crime? Oh, you know, just going with the facts. No question: Culloden was grim stuff – the mass slaughter and mutilation of the injured ordered by the so-called Butcher Cumberland would these days land you in the Hague.

But 'The 45' was not another Bannockburn: they were invading England, not defending Scotland. Invading England in support of a spoilt brat to reinstall the divine right of kings, feudalism and all that (all with the hopeful assistance of a non-existent French invasion). The rebels reached Derby before hurriedly retreating.

And how Scottish was 'The 45'? There were always more Scottish people fighting on the British side than against, and it wasn't even just Lowlander versus Highlander – many Highland clans (notably the Campbells, who you should never trust) fought with the British too.

As one modern folk song, 'Ghosts of Culloden', moistly claims: 'They fought to save their land, and died for liberty.' This statement is absolutely correct. Except for all of it.

THE STONE OF DESTINY. INCLUDES DESTINY.

just any stone. This was the Stone of Destiny. Edward knew
about crushing the life out of a fledgling nation – he'd just
done it to Wales back in the eighties ('Ah yes, remember those
days: crushing the life out of the fledgling nation of Wales?' he
would reminisce) – and decided to take all great symbols of
Scottish nationhood back home to London. That's it: Scotland
over. And what a souvenir of a trip to Scotland: Scotland.

For seven centuries, the Stone of Destiny sat in Westminster,
a centrepiece of all future coronation ceremonies. Except for a
short period in 1950 when it was stolen by four Scots nationalist students who drove it back to Scotland in the boot of their
Austin, eventually touting it round Scotland's historic sites.
(The lord of this palace was offered it, but refused because he'd
just pledged allegiance to the new Queen . . . he was scared of
the Queen.)

That is, if it was even the real stone. Alisdair insisted we
come and meet another guide, Blair, a Scottish history PhD stu-
dent who would prove a mine of information. Blair had
thought about the Stone of Scone. A lot. He was a fully paid-
up subscriber to the Westminster Stone theory, holding that the
stolen stone was never actually The Stone: when Edward's men
raided Scone Abbey, the monks had enough time to substitute

the real stone, a grander basalt supposedly bearing ancient hieroglyphs (possibly Roman).

As it happens, that stone – the 'substutite' stone – isn't the one on display at Scone. That one (that is, the one snatched by Edward I) is in Edinburgh (Scone 'didn't have the security' for the stone on its 1996 return from Westminster). The stone actually at Scone is a replica: according to Blair, 'a fake of a fake'. This may seem confusing, but it really isn't (actually, that's a lie – it is confusing).

Blair believed the real, more spectacular stone was still buried in the palace grounds. We'd already decided on Scone because of its ancient totemic significance, and because that's where the Stone *should be*. But Blair's belief that the *real* stone was beneath our very feet enabled us to increase our already rising level of self-imposed delusion most satisfactorily. If we were ever going to be tuned in to the Scottish Frequency, this would be the time.

We went back outside. It was *still* sunny. (Although a video showing in the main house absolutely sodden with mist had helped conjure up the right mood.) The stone – the fake one – stands on a mound across a courtyard from the house. Our plan involved looking at it. It looked unavoidably like the *Spinal Tap* Stonehenge.

We knew – *knew* – the real stone was buried below our feet somewhere. But the fake was as close as we were going to get to the Stone of Destiny, so that's where the vibes would be. The question was: would it quiver?

We stood on the mound, looking at it intently. Was that a quiver? It was not.

We tried nonchalantly walking away from the stone, then turning back suddenly, in case it would only move if it thought no one was looking. We tried crouching down behind long grass, pretending to look at the peacocks that were wandering about all over the place.

Nothing. Not a quiver.

Don't know if you've ever tried nonchalantly watching a stone to see if it quivers, but it's harder work than you'd think.

This was the very mound on which Robert The Bruce was crowned in 1306. It was a heroic occasion in which the brave Scots hero heroically, and fairly hurriedly, usurped the Scottish crown, having just been excommunicated by the Pope after a meeting with rival claimant John Comyn inside Greyfriars Kirk in Dumfries went deeply awry: an argument led to the drawing of swords and Bruce stabbing Comyn to death. (Meetings that don't go that well, where you end up stabbing someone to death? They're the worst type of meetings.)

Then we wheeled round super-sharp to see if we could catch the stone at it . . . But no.

Perhaps in recognition of our efforts, Kenneth Williams came over again and gave us some pieces of cake for free left over from the now-closing cafeteria. Millionaire's shortbread: now, that *had to be* a sign.

A few hours later we were walking through Glasgow looking for somewhere to watch the election results. Glasgow has historically been seen as a fairly tough, downtrodden place. With some justification. But the city centre is also rather grand, with its swooping Georgian vistas being very much the physical embodiment of the high days of Britishness, the benefits of Union to Scotland's ruling elite, and the opportunities for booty that now came their way. In a word: fags

We strolled up Trongate – built as a private street for the Tobacco lords, where they could lord it up, on their own special lordy street, and any ordinary poor Scots, if found using the lords' street, could be soundly beaten. So the Union worked in part because Scots businessmen really loved using the slaves that England had transported to the New World. (Glaswegians still keep up their historic links with tobacco by smoking lots of fags.)

We checked out George Square, where tanks confronted the Red Clydesiders in 1919. Tens of thousands of workers had gathered in the square as part of a campaign for shorter working hours (56 hours was often the norm in the city's factories). Fearing a Bolshevik-style revolution, the Liberal government sent in the troops – the only time tanks have squared up to civilians on British soil. Were any English tanks secreted up side streets tonight? Not that we could see. But it could happen. So could an SNP clampdown on foreign dissidents. And we were ready to break for the border at any given moment.

We retired to a bar near our hotel. It turned out to be a rock bar. A bar that plays rock. Rock! On a big-screen telly they were showing results coming in. A rock bar with the election on. Now that's politicised. Okay, you couldn't hear much because of all the rock – but still, that wouldn't happen in England. (Great address, too: 'I'll see you at the rock bar on Hope Street.' That's the sort of thing you'd like to find yourself saying more often.)

The new dawn came and went. It was quite grey. Was a nation being (re)born? Er, sort of: the SNP had secured one single seat more than Labour. Alex Salmond could rule the Parliament but only by relying on Liberal and Tory votes. The Voice Of Scotland appeared to be saying something like: 'We'll give Salmond a go. It'll be a laugh to see Broon's face.'

Never one for understatement, Salmond could barely contain himself, declaring: 'We have felt the heavy Hand of History blow past on the winds of change, accompanied by the voice of the people. Ringing in the changes of a new dawn of a new era of change for Scotland.' Some shit like that, anyway.

The SNP's win didn't strike us as a great victory for progress. But it was a bloody nose for Labour, richly deserved. Then we heard on the radio that, against the odds, Chris Harvie had been elected. This made us imagine Chris Harvie giving Broon a bloody nose – and we quite enjoyed this image.

But now what? All this election seemed to prove beyond doubt was that everyone hated Labour. The rise in SNP popularity hadn't seen much change in support for independence, so far. (Thorough polls on independence remained fairly constant with only about a third of Scots favouring full independence.) There had clearly been an increase in 'Scottishness' of a sort under devolution, but what were its limits?

The genie was out of the bottle. But how big was the genie? How big even was the bottle? *Was* there a bottle? Yes there was.

FOUR

CASH FOR HONOURS

THE NORMAN CONQUEST
FISH
A HANDBAG

THE IRONMONGERS' HALL, tucked beneath the Museum of London, is home to the Ironmongers' Company, a medieval guild concerned very much with iron, ironworks, working with iron, and furthering the secret, closely guarded interests of iron-people and their irony ways. The City of London might be famous for forcing newness on other people – new working practices or bizarre new forms of dodgy credit – but amongst their own ranks they like nothing more than a bit of archaic weirdness, bonding together in ancient closed shops with dizzying rituals.

The hall looks suitably old: a bit Tudory, all of stone and oak. In fact it was opened in 1925, and is something of a put-on designed to whisk up a spot of cheap awe. This made it an apt setting for the event we had come to witness. On this weekday lunchtime in late May, the hall was hosting an auction of ancient British titles by property consultants Strutt & Parker. Going under the hammer were five baronies and 33 lordships of the manor. These were the kinds of titles bought by City boys, carpet kings, footballers or anyone else with too much money and strange notions about self-esteem.

The winners wouldn't sit in the Lords (or bag any property), although there could be benefits – a few years ago, Chris Eubank became Lord of the Manor of Brighton, which apparently entitled him to 4,000 herring a year. Maybe that's why he needs that big truck? (Four thousand herring: that's too much herring, even if he really likes herring, which he may.)

The interior was all coat-of-arms wall-hangings, portraits of the young Prince Phillip, capacious wood-panelling. At a desk in the voluminous upstairs corridor, we registered for the event (20 quid!) and were furnished with a handsomely tooled silver booklet on the titles up for grabs and a name badge with a coat of arms on it (the 'armourial bearings of Strutt & Parker'): nice.

We were here to get beneath the froth and consider real power. Old power. Aristocratic power. Britain's ruling caste. How William of Normandy landed on this land, turfed the Saxon landlords off their land, and dished out titles to the new lords of the land after generally knocking everyone and everything about a bit (so setting in train centuries of upper-class bad behaviour).

Before the auction started, we sat in the hall, a 60-foot affair with cascading chandeliers and stained glass, eating the free biscuits and quaffing complimentary coffee and juice, watching the title-hungry title-seekers file in: judging by appearances, older City folk on extended lunch breaks, plus the occasional country type and random oddball. (You'd have to assume the supremely rich or famous would be utilising the manned phone lines to the side of the auction block.)*

The refreshments table was buzzing. (No wonder. Yes, it was 20 quid to get in; but if you put your back into it, you could easily drink yourself up on the deal.) We kept off the sauce, for fear of rash bidding under the influence. One false wave of the arm in an exuberant 'More wine!' gesture and we might end up with an overpriced baronetcy.

Not that we hadn't considered the benefits. You could be called the Baron, for starters: 'Lisa, you say? Hi. I'm the Baron' . . . 'The Baron? Could you photocopy these documents' . . . 'Hello, is that the Baron? I'm conducting a telephone survey on behalf of a leading soft drinks supplier . . .'

The titles might not come with anything more than petty privileges, but they didn't come with any obligations either – viz. unquestioning military service to the monarch (which might stop even the most status-hungry carpet king in their tracks). And if we did get the right to graze sheep somewhere, that might come in handy if we ever got those sheep we're always talking about.

As the auction started, we retired to the large wooden balcony at the back of the room, and surveyed the bidders from above. These people didn't look like barons. No swagger. (Not even the couple who turned up clutching motorcycle helmets.)

The auctioneer, perched behind a lectern at the front – a besuited bespectacled chap in his fifties – was fleshing out each lot's history. Well, sort of. What was for sale was of course just a title: the lords of the manor titles were divorced from their original locale by a law passed in 1922. But the auctioneer kept talking about the *places*, at considerable length.

He told us that Carriglaine is 'famous for porcelain'. The place, that is. Of the house at Hamstall Ridware he revealed: 'Jane Austen stayed there and wrote some chapters.' Yes, in the house. Which you are not buying.

---

* All that complimentary fizzy water necessitated a visit to the gents. There were six washbasins in there, each with a bar of Imperial Leather soap – all with the little black rectangular logo sticker entirely intact. The soaps were in various stages of use – from very light, to light-moderate or thereabouts. But each – against all the soapy odds – had a pristine logo. Quite sinister, that; and a small insight, perhaps, into the true power of this shadowy ironocracy.

The lordship and feudal barony of Castle Knock, County Dublin, was, the auctioneer explained, 'near Lucan, famous for the lord of that name . . . disappeared . . .' Yes, after murdering his children's nanny at the home of his estranged wife. (Those lords, eh?)

This title, perhaps unsurprisingly given its now explicit links with a celebrated homicide, was greeted with apathy from the room.

But what were these people buying into, hoovering up Norman-bestowed feudal titles? The Normans were professional rampagers, Vikings who settled in northern France in the tenth century. Something of their general attitude and ethos can be garnered from how they dispatched the English king, Harold, at Hastings. Harold is on the floor,

A LORD.
Photoshot

having possibly been shot in the eye with an arrow. Seeing this, a bunch of Norman knights fight their way over to the prostrate English leader. Then, according to the Bishop of Amiens: 'The first Norman split Harold's chest, driving the point of his sword through the King's shield. The gushing torrent of blood drenched the earth. The second knight struck off his head below the helmet . . . [Harold was quite possibly dead by now, but . . .] . . . the third stabbed the inside of his belly with a lance. The fourth [possibly a bit of a joker, this one] cut off his leg and carried it away.'

Well, who hasn't brought home a souvenir of a successful south-coast trip? 'Remember that time we went to Bournemouth and you chopped that man's leg off? Great days.' The bishop failed to mention that Harold was also castrated. In short, they were quite violent.

And so it was that the English were put under the Norman yoke – handing over land, service, tribute, anything so they wouldn't chop one of our arms off. The Norman yoke. What an image is evoked here: under their *yoke*. We were their beast, their bitch, dragging their cart or their shitty French plough, or bearing 'a frame fitting the neck and shoulders of a person, for carrying a pair of buckets or the like, one at each end'. Carrying their buckets! For shame!

We wanted to shout from the balcony: 'You're buying your own oppression! You're buying your own oppression!' But we thought this might look a bit mental. So we had another biscuit, and just thought it.*

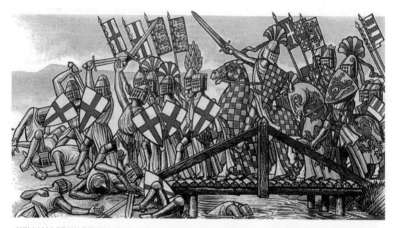

WILLIAM OF WARENNE, THE NORMAN EARL OF SURREY WAS RECENTLY CALCULATED AS THE RICHEST BRITON EVER. THAT'S TAKING OVER OTHER COUNTRIES FOR YOU.
The Bridgeman Art Library

The auctioneer was a bit of a comedian. He also kept trying to tell jokes. When he got to Lot 28, lord of the manor of Bracknell, he told us it was 'made famous by Oscar Wilde's portrayal of Lady Bracknell in *The Importance of Being Earnest* . . .' He paused . . . Everyone knew what was coming, even though we hoped it wouldn't, for we feared it . . .

'A *haaandbaag*?' he screeched. The whole room flinched. No amount of complimentary biscuits is worth this, we felt, even genuine butter ones with real chocolate chips. (The lot went for £7,000: £3,500 below the guide price.)

In truth, we were getting a little bit bored by now. The proceedings were proceeding pretty slowly. There was no manic

---

* On the plus side, the Normans properly introduced rabbits to Britain. Ah, bunnies, though, eh? They only did this so they could kill the rabbits for their fur and meat, of course – grinding their fluffy bunny faces into the cold, dead earth.

auction frenzy, no screaming in the aisles; it was all a tad sedate. *Cash in the Attic* this was not.

But then all of a sudden things picked up. The climax of the bidding, the penultimate lot, was for the lordship of the manor of Bermondsey, in south-east London. Bidding for this did get quite frantic, the title eventually going to a phone bidder for £55,000.

As of today Bermondsey had a new 'lord of the manor'. Perhaps, flushed with their success, they would visit some pubs in the area to proclaim their newfound status, or announce it on the terraces of the New Den at the next Millwall home game. That would be good.

Perhaps because of all the Bermondsey excitement, or because it was everyone's last chance, the final lot went for way over its guide price too: the lordship of the manor of Plumpton, in Sussex, netted a very respectable £29,000, from a bidder in the room.

Afterwards, as we waited in the voluminous corridor for Strutt & Parker PR woman Charlotte Lewis to see if the 55-grand Bermondsey phone bidder was prepared to divulge their name (Jade Goody? Theo Paphitis? Barrymore!?), a small media scrum formed, possibly one of the weirder media scrums that has ever existed, consisting entirely of: BBC London radio; *Optima* magazine (whatever that is); the *Mail on Sunday*; and the *Shropshire Star*.

They weren't having much luck: most of the successful bidders didn't want to reveal who they were. In a further blow, Charlotte Lewis came back and told us that the lord of the manor of Bermondsey wished to remain anonymous too.

This was quite common, said Charlotte. Some people buy the titles to give as wedding gifts say (whatever happened to steak knives?), but 'one person who bought a title told me they did it to actually hide their identity. It would mean they didn't have to sign their actual name any more, and they'd been "hounded by the press".'

No one was being hounded by this press, that was for sure. We started to feel sorry for the women from BBC London and *Optima* magazine (whatever that is), but not the one from the *Mail on Sunday*. We felt particularly for our new friend from the *Shropshire Star*, what with him having come all the way from Shropshire.

Just then, as they were all about to give up, a woman called Susan Reese said she was willing to talk – and the man from the *Shropshire Star* hits paydirt: she'd bought one of the Shropshire titles. This was gold.

Susan lives in Wigan and bought the title 'for purely historical reasons', being generally interested in genealogy. Whatever. The man from the *Star* was home and hosed, and we saluted his perspicacity.

We grabbed our things. Just as we were leaving, we overheard the press throng bag the winner of the Plumpton title. He was self-made property magnate Mike Holland, owner of the eighteenth-century country house to which the title once belonged, Stanmer House on the edge of Brighton. We hoped he wasn't now planning to ruthlessly subdue the local area.

SOLD – TO THE GENTLEMAN WITH TOO MUCH MONEY.

The Normans subdued everything of course. For generations following the invasion, they – 1 per cent of the population controlling virtually 100 per cent of the land – refused to intermarry with their subjects, in what has been dubbed a 'medieval apartheid'. Imagine that: signs up all over England saying: 'No English'. The English forced off the pavement. English pavements! In England!

But irony was to have the last laugh. In 1204, Philip II of France muscled in on Normandy, and gave the Normans a choice: come back to Normandy and keep it, under his overlordship; or stay in England and forfeit Normandy. There was no contest: France is warmer, and has all that runny cheese and fine booze. Amazingly, though, the Normans chose to stay in England, and became English. It probably started raining at that exact moment. That's not in any of the sources. But it probably did happen.

Later that week, an item on *BBC South Today* showed Mike Holland back at Stanmer House, actually a hotel and conference/wedding venue he opened with the help of David Van Day out of Dollar.

The female news reporter walked into the entrance hall, past a suit of armour in the hallway, talking of a new lord of the manor . . . 'but while he has a coat, it's not a coat of arms, it's more a coat of fur . . .'

Yes. Mike had conferred the title on his pet white Alsatian Dillon.

The news reporter entered a side room to meet Dillon, who was barking loudly and trying to escape, perhaps perturbed by the cameras and also the lordly ruff he was wearing. The reporter asked Holland: 'People might say you're barking mad, you've spent £29,000 on this title for Dillon. Why?'

Holland replied: 'I think we're all barking mad here. That's part of the fun of the place . . .'

Christ, what's going on over there? Everyone all mad? A dog in charge? That doesn't sound like fun, that sounds like an apocalypse.

Still, at least they haven't cut anyone's leg off, to the best of our knowledge.

SUMMER

FIVE

SUN-SEEKERS

THE MAN
THE KIDS
THE A303

WE ARE TREKKING, in darkness and wearing our thickest coats, along the side of the A303, seeking Stonehenge. We have come to commune with the spirits of Ancient Britain, but it seems we're more likely to commune with an oncoming lorry. There is no footpath. We are walking through thick roadside weeds with massive lorries roaring past with headlights glaring in our eyes and baleful, primal horns wailing in our ears. It does not instil a calming or beatific frame of mind with which to infuse the midsummer. Will we ever reach the top of the hill, the stone puzzle from the past, the pre-digital transmitter of The Vibe?

Finally achieving the summit, we catch sight of the immutable stones, and are filtered by officials – along with other questers (better questers than us, ones who seem to have discovered routes involving pathways) – off the road through a field towards the blue arc-lit monument, repetitive acoustic beats drifting across on the breeze. One group is already off the other way, warning some friends: 'There's too many police there, man . . . we're going to Woodhenge.'

Woodhenge is the remains of an ancient wood structure a few fields away, part of a network of megalithic stone and wood structures stretching across Salisbury Plain. Woodhenge? It's okay – but here's Stonehenge. Ancient and inscrutable. Constructed of huge stones. We've all seen the pictures. No offence to Woodhenge, wood, or smaller henges generally, but Stonehenge is *much* better. Stonehenge pisses on Woodhenge.

Despite all the years of conjecture, scientific investigation and outright madpants fantasy, the Henge has kept its meaning close to its stone chest. All we really know is that we are here for the moment the stones were made for, the summer solstice, when the sun rises and its beams align between the hele stone and the altar and enlightenment floods around. This we know: Stonehenge is aligned with the solar system, but we know not why. (Some people say it doesn't even do that, that the alignment is out, and always has been; but this was 2000 BC, so give the Ancients a break, for fuck's sake.)

The stones are only available to us tonight under English Heritage's Managed Open Access scheme. The rest of the year, you can see the stones but at a price and from a distance. This happened because The Man got scared of people taking drugs and dancing with their tops off, and wanted to take control of the astral pathways, lest the dancers bring down The Man himself. Which could have happened. But for this night, the stones are our stones. We are going to touch them. We are going to stroke them all night long.

On the train down, we had met a man from English Heritage who was working as a steward. We wanted to tell him that he was unfortunately The Man, out to Manage the British people, a proud people who would not be Managed by No Man. But he seemed like quite a nice man. Like us, he had a room booked at the Amesbury Travelodge a mile down the A303. We were sleeping with the enemy. Or sleeping in the same Travelodge as the enemy.

The Man – that is, English Heritage generally, not the man we met – had issued rules to ensure The People at the Henge were Controlled. We must use the Portaloos provided: 'Do not desecrate the Monument or surrounding area.' You must not – and this cannot be stressed enough – shit on the Henge.

No sleeping bags either – sleeping bodies would constitute a 'trip hazard' – and a *big* no to 'garden furniture, large rucksacks . . . trolleys . . . wheelbarrows and any other form of porterage'. (After much heartache, we deposited our wheelbarrows at Left Luggage in Salisbury.)

As evening fell, we supped at a pub in Amesbury. In one corner, King Arthur Pendragon could be seen imbibing some solstice spirit. (That's the self-styled Arthur Pendragon, a freelance druid/motorcycle enthusiast and veteran of the free festivals and anti-roads movement.)* Having lucked into this encounter, we had hoped to plug King Arthur for The Code. But no sooner had we arrived than he was on his way – the King of the Britons, having to momentarily hold on to a wall for support. King Arthur was pissed again.

* So committed is Pendragon to free access to Stonehenge (once holding a months-long vigil at the perimeter) that, during a pre-Managed Open Access experiment with an invite-only solstice, he managed to get arrested for breaking through the fence even though he was in fact invited. He once sent his Warband knights to 'invade' the old floating *This Morning* weather map over the issue, where they claimed squatters' rights. (The four 'knights' only withdrew when given the model dragon that signified Wales, which they used to raise money for the homeless.) Arthur's vigil at the Henge was a boon for tourists because, as Andy Worthington points out in *Stonehenge: Celebration and Subversion*, they could get their picture taken with a bloke in a tunic called King Arthur waving a fucking great big sword about.

In the gents, a smartly dressed middle-aged local reminisced fondly about the free festivals that began in the sixties. 'It was drugs everywhere,' he recalled with jollity. 'Blokes with signs around their necks saying "Get Your Heroin Here"!' What would English Heritage think about that, we wondered? They would presumably be firmly against it; even though it is in some senses traditional.

At around ten, we stocked up on supplies of crisps and biscuits and swung back to the Travelodge to pick up our John Smith's for a ritual we had devised called The Sacred Ritual of the Drinking of the Britishness Tinnies. This involved drinking cans of John Smith's left over from Christmas while thinking about Britain, In the Shadow of the Stones (you need to say that last bit quite portentously: you know, *In the Shadow of the Stones*).

Through the windows of the Little Chef adjacent to the lodge, a lone diner could be seen bathed in orange light and surrounded by empty tables – a scene of Hopper-esque melancholia. This eatery was not a happy eatery, the whole Travelodge campus providing a miniature of the alienated modern life we were aiming to get away from – and a stark contrast to the shamanic revelations that awaited up the road.

Back at the Henge, we headed for the spotlit field on the other side of the dip. Stonehenge is famously ill-served by its surroundings – the crappy visitor centre, the A303. At this point, plans were still afoot to dig a tunnel very near the monument, burying the road under Salisbury Plain, in the process totalling a vast swathe of unexcavated archaeological gold. Environmentalists, historians, the local population – basically anyone who isn't a fucking moron – opposed the plan. Well, except one faction of British druidry. Philip Shallcrass, of the British Druid Order, said he had consulted the 'spirits' of the Henge and the spirits ('of the land and of our ancestors') were actually 'in no way opposed' to the road tunnel. 'Go ahead' – that was the message of the spirits: 'Dig it.'

A303 notwithstanding, over the dip on the arc-lit crest of a sloping field, Stonehenge didn't look too shabby. You sometimes hear people say it's 'too small', but when was the last time these people shipped any very large stones over from West Wales on a raft?

At the entrance gate, people were being formed into orderly queues to have their bags inspected by security looking for glass and grass. The Man was taking away The People's glass bottles again. Many of the security were Eastern European. A few lines of police hung about nearby, counting up their overtime.

Wandering around the monument used to be The People's right. When the first fence was put up in 1901, and the landowner started charging admission, there was a demonstration by local people. Animals grazed between the stones. In the nineteenth century, the butcher in Amesbury even hired out hammers, so you could chip pieces from the stones and take them home. Wander in with a hammer now, and English Heritage would shit down your neck.

We were in! Past the Portaloos, and the tea stall, and the people selling heroin (not really), we walked through the crowd towards the stones, following the line of burger vans up to the monument. This was a gathering of tribes. Goths, druids, hippies, scallies, security . . . all together again! It was like the arc, the Convoy, Hawkwind's *Earth Ritual* . . . There were people everywhere, spilled all over the monument, and filling the spaces in between. Some knelt down and worshipped the Henge. One woman stood vacantly swinging a glowstick hula-hoop. Others hugged the stones, splayed wide to touch as much of the surface as possible. Some rested their foreheads on them to hopefully transport the stones into their brains. Music played everywhere, competing groups of drummers hammering out circular beats to whooping, gyrating disciples.

Having visited before and been kept back from the stones by ropes (not actually tied up, just made to stay on the other side of a rope), walking through a lintel and into the circle was quite a thing. Imagining the vastness of time since they were put here stretched the mind in ways that could be described as, well . . . cosmic. And we hadn't even started on the John Smith's.

After half an hour, though, it was starting to feel more like Glastonbury after the bands had finished. There's only so much milling about getting vaguely high on the atmosphere you can do. The focal point was, after all, a bunch of rocks, and they were doing the same thing they'd done for the previous few millennia: hardly anything at all.

As we neared midnight, we pulled back to a less populous spot – near the outer cordon, affording a full view of the stones full of revellers – and cracked open the John Smith's. It was the Sacred Ritual of the Drinking of the Britishness Tinnies. What is more British, we had surmised, than leftover tinnies out of the shed that were bought for your dad at Christmas but your dad never drank them. Whose dad? It doesn't matter. Is there any nation on earth with as much leftover bitter as the Brits? Is there fuck. In this, we lead the world.

We saluted Stonehenge with our tins, holding them aloft to the ancient circle within circles, and to the dead of many ages. Then we drank deep of the bittery brown brew, and jammed open our doors of perception.

We waited. Stonehenge poses deep questions. To everyone, inside everyone, it

Picnic time is Guinness Time
—that's the secret of a really good time

ALL RACES to the picnic. Out come the cold cuts, the boiled eggs, the lettuce and tomatoes. Good show? Somebody's opened the Guinness. Doesn't it look wonderful. Foaming, creamy, refreshing, there's nothing like a cool dark Guinness to make a meal so very appetising. When you've finished that long and satisfying drink, how much better you'll feel. Life is worth living after a Guinness.

IT'S THE APPETISING TASTE OF GUINNESS THAT GOES SO WELL WITH FOOD

A PAGAN FEAST.
Advertising Archive

prompts one special question. Even long since back, before they even knew that the stones had been brought from so far, people were wont to stand on Salisbury Plain, consider the ancient edifice, and say: 'What the fuck are these huge stones doing here?' (And other people would say back unto the first people: 'We don't know.')

There have always been theories, of course. Oh, the many, many theories. Was it an astral observatory, a palace, a ring of ancestors turned into stone, a giant stone computer for predicting eclipses, the physical representation of the lady-bits of the Goddess, leftovers of the Biblical flood, a landing pad for flying saucers? Or, as recent research favours, a healing site for prehistoric tourists after a touch of stoney Welsh magic?

Classicists of the seventeenth and eighteenth centuries decided that as Stonehenge was so impressive, it could not possibly be native and must have been the work of the Romans. (Bit racist, that, really.) The twelfth-century fabulist-historian Geoffrey of Monmouth thought it was all bound up in the great mythic Matter of Britain story, with Merlin bringing it back from Ireland using only his special magic.* The eighteenth-century druid revivalists started claiming it for themselves of course. Ironically, the modern druids started using Stonehenge for their rituals at the exact time archaeologists confirmed it pre-dated their predecessors' arrival in Britain.

We could see why Stonehenge has always proved such a mystery: we'd been there for ages and even *we* didn't know what it was all about yet. The author and rural activist Rodney Legg called Stonehenge 'a moment from the national dream'. This seemed vague and trippy enough for us, so we went back to join the throng, the thousands who were trying, in the words of Andy Worthington, recording the modern pagan/free festivals/New Age traveller take on the Henge, to 'discover the relevance . . . by the physical experience of spending a lot of time there'.

We'd love to say we were up all night, dancing semi-naked on a trilithon, plastered in woad, but really the whole thing

NEO-DRUIDS GET ROUND SALISBURY PLAIN'S LACK OF ANCIENT GROVES BY DRAWING SOME IN. 'LOOK, THERE *WERE* GROVES!'
Charles Walker/Topfoto

* This story is featured prominently in the classic children's history of Britain, *Our Island Story*, by H. E. Marshall, still adored by right-wing pro-Britain educationalists today. Stories about made-up wizards whisking bits of masonry hither through the heavens: how's that going to stiffen up the nation's youth? Haven't they heard enough lies about wizards already?

BRONZE AGE NOUVEAUS

Built in three main stages, the Henge took an estimated 30 million labour hours to build.

Stage 1. Neolithic tribes build a timber henge and earthwork around 3100 BC as part of 'a world of stone and wooden circles connected by lines of posts, stones and ditches' all across Salisbury Plain. The ring enclosed 56 small pits. We don't know what they were for. Things may have been placed in the holes. Justin Pollard says the third millennium BC was a time of 'virtuoso, interconnected monument building', but a big circle made out of mud is a bit rubbish. Unlikely to have become the world's foremost henge.

Stage 2. Around 2550 BC, the Beakers bring the inner bluestones (not the bigger buggers, but still big enough) from the Preseli Hill in West Wales, which is quite a long way away. The Beaker People may have brought metallurgy to Britain, as well as lots of beakers. The lavish grave of a Beaker chief, the Amesbury Archer, was found nearby in 2002. Called the King of Stonehenge by the newspapers, this nobleman was found to originally hail from the Alps. His hair was laced with gold; archaeologists concurred that this made him look 'a bit eighties'.

Stage 3. In about 2000 BC, the large sarsen stones arrive. This is what we're talking about. This is the Henge. Each needing 500 men dragging them with leather cords from the Marlborough Downs 20 miles up the road, the stones would have been highly coloured; lichen has greyed them over time. Amazingly, stone circle expert Julian Cope reckons this section is all flashy and nouveau, 'a fashioned Bronze Age power statement'. Still, he also thinks that goalkeepers are 'the ultimate shamen' because they guard the gates of the otherworld 'wearing the No 1 jersey in a different colour and not seeming to be part of the team', so let's not get too hung up on that.

To put this achievement in perspective, it was in 2570 BC that the Egyptians built the Great Pyramid of Giza, which is obviously bigger but definitely not better. Well, not *necessarily* better. Anyway, it's not a competition. It's easy to get caught up in all this mists of time nonsense, but at the same time as 'we' were putting up Stonehenge, in the Middle East they had art, law, etc., whereas the Brits were probably still eating each other.

was a bit like a shit rave. Now, we all know what makes a shit rave interesting, and it isn't out-of-date tinned bitter.

So we had a kip. You may wonder how. We wonder how – given that it was fecking cold. But sleep we did. We slept In the Shadow of the Stones. In fact, all round the main circle, a carpet of people was disregarding the danger of becoming a trip hazard and sitting, lying or snoozing. So we also fell asleep, thinking about those big rocks on a plain in Britain, which is a big rock in the sea on earth, which is a rock in space, which contains other rocks and also ether. We knew all this before. But we didn't *know* all this. You know?

We woke up an hour and a half later, as cold as Neolithic man himself, stood up, brushed ourselves off and tried to fight off some quite violent shakes – proper Scooby Doo shakes – with a cup of tea from the food stall. Food stalls do not occur naturally in nature. At this point, we liked food stalls more than nature. We ate the biscuits we'd bought in Amesbury. Good old Amesbury Spar, we thought.

Soon, strips of pink signifying the sunlight were arriving. Dawn was nearly here. (The good thing about the shortest night is that it's quite short.)

We walked over to the hele stone. As dawn breaks, sunlight is supposed to stream across the monument, splitting the circle symmetrically, aligning with the hele stone. That's the theory anyway.

The sky brightened. Everyone turned expectantly to the east. Would there be a dramatic breakthrough, celestial shards shooting powerfully through the cloud-cover and burning off the mist so that in an instant we were bathed in the summer and the new? Of course not. It was very cloudy. Thousands had come to worship the sun, but the sun? It wasn't bothered.

When even was the dawn? With no actual dawn to speak of, everyone was reduced to looking at their watches and mobiles. But a random sample of watches and mobiles will never be synchronised, so there was a series of cheers, most of them fairly listless. Given that everyone had stayed out all night to see a cloud get slightly brighter, unalloyed rejoicing would have felt wildly inappropriate. Some people over at the trilithons just carried on partying. 'Dawn? Is it?' they might have said, if they'd had greater control of their jaws.

At the hele stone, Arthur Pendragon led a pagan service,

IN WILTSHIRE, A NEW DAY BEGINS.

'hailing' the sun that was not there. A few more horns went off. A man with a grey beard and straw hat blew a trumpet. The woman with the fluorescent hula-hoop was still going. She was definitely on drugs.

As we turned to begin the knackered trudge back to the Travelodge, King Arthur was telling someone a motorbike anecdote that involved making 'vroom!' noises.

Back down the A303, the man at reception asked if the sun had come out. When we told him the sad news, he shrugged: 'I moved to the area in 1971, the day before the solstice. You could see the sun that year, but it's never come out since to my knowledge.'

After a snooze, we bounded outside to enjoy the new summer and were instantly enticed inside the Little Chef by the banner outside promising a 'Great British Breakfast'. Like the Henge the night before, it was a gathering of the tribes: some of the same tribes, in fact, plus some other bemused tribes who just happened to be passing on the A303, clearly wondering who all the saucer-eyed tired people were, and why the car park contained so many old vans.

Sitting down at the table amid some surreally cold air-conditioning, we pondered our experience. Did this mean anything? Was this place more special, or more British, than other places? The Little Chef menu prompted our own theory about the area's energies, offering as it did 'outdoor-reared sausages', which sounds like some hideous GM experiment at Porton Down, the chemical weapons centre just down the road. The Man is frantic to regulate the Henge, in the shape of English Heritage. But of course The Man owns the freehold all across the plain, in the shape of the military. Ironically, the military presence has meant that much wildlife and fauna has prospered in the absence of agricultural chemicals. (This is doubly ironic when you consider Porton Down's terrifying nature-bending missions.)

Maybe The Man is keeping careful mitts on the Henge so they can get their biological warfare specialists in there at night, dancing naked in the moonlight with spooks and breeding a new generation of genetically enhanced warriors out of the soil – really fucked-up ones whistling 'Colonel Bogey'. This is what we read in the sausages.

It's merely conjecture, of course. But in our search for meaning, to learn from the past, to see how the past informs our present and the future, perhaps we had found at least one thing we can truly share with ages gone: not knowing what Stonehenge is for.

BRITAIN'S FAVOURITE ANIMALS

British people have always loved animals, as evinced by an eighteenth-century London fayre promising: 'a mad bull to be dressed up with fireworks and turned loose in the game place, a dog to be dressed up with fireworks over him, a bear to be let loose at the same time, and a cat to be tied to the bull's tail, a mad bull to be dressed up with fireworks to be baited'. Bulls covered in fireworks are fun, but which are truly the nation's all-time best-loved beasts?

GREYFRIARS BOBBY: The great Victorian terrier who loyally stayed by his owner's Edinburgh grave for 14 years, until his own death. There have been numerous film versions of his story, all of which have faltered due to the lack of drama inherent in seeing a sad dog lying next to a grave.

DOG.
Rex Features

GUY THE GORILLA: A gentle giant. Not indigenous to Britain.

But still British. The pride of London Zoo. Big in the seventies. Almost became the first gorilla in space.

A GORILLA.
Rex Features

DAREDEVIL SQUIRREL FROM *WILDLIFE ON ONE* CLIP: Who can hear the *Mission: Impossible* theme without imagining that plucky squirrel taking to the assault course to get the nuts? Used by the SAS in the Iran Embassy siege, apparently. Safely retrieved all the Embassy's nuts.

DESERT ORCHID: Dessie. The great grey. A hero to many. There's even a fan club. Which is mental. Did a lot of work for charity. Didn't like to talk about it. One wheelchair-bound young fan took a piece of Dessie's mane into his GCSE exams and gained seven passes. Not that students are recommended to take pieces of horse into the exam room. Imagine if everyone did it.

THAT DOG THAT FOUND THE WORLD CUP: South-east London mongrel Pickles succeeded where a nationwide hunt had failed by finding the Jules Rimet trophy in a garden after it was stolen in 1966. The story was turned into a TV film 40 years later; faltered due to the lack of drama inherent in seeing a dog find a trophy.

SEALS: Ah.

THE KESTREL IN _KES_: In reality, there were three kestrels. Many people have been saddened by the final 'killing' scene. This was a very sad scene. In fact, no kestrels were killed, but director Ken Loach allowed the actors to believe they had been. He said this was so The Kids would find out at a young age about imperialism grinding their dreams into dust. Well, he didn't actually say that, but he definitely thought it.

SHEP: The _Blue Peter_ dog. John Noakes got to keep Shep when they both retired, even though he belonged to the BBC. Then the Beeb stopped paying for his vets' bills, which made Noakes get in a big huff. The ungrateful twat.

DONKEYS, GENERALLY: Donkeys are verifiably British, by dint of having to hold a passport (FACT). As a testament to our great love of the domestic ass, the British public gives more in charity to the Donkey Sanctuary in Sidmouth, Devon, than it gives to the Samaritans, Age Concern and Mencap. The money is sorely needed, as the number of people buying donkeys (but then having second thoughts and abandoning them when they think through the implications of actually having to look after a bloody great big donkey) went up massively following the success of donkey-based film sensation _Shrek_. Oh, for fuck's sake.

PHAROS: The Queen's oldest corgi savaged to death by Princess Anne's bull terrier Dotty. The Queen was apparently devastated and so was the nation . . . wasn't it? Dotty had also just attacked two children in Windsor Great Park, so perhaps the name Dotty doesn't really do her justice. Unless her full name was Dotty the Fucking Mental Case Who Is Likely to Attack Anyone and Anything at Any Time. Should have been put down years ago, the mad bitch (that's the dog, NOT a sexist way of describing Her Royal Highness Princess Anne).

SIX

IT'S ALL TOO BEAUTIFUL

POLO
LOVELY BOOZE
PRINCE WILLIAM GETS AN AUDIENCE
WITH ALAN

COWORTH PARK IS 'Britain's most luxurious residential polo estate'. We'll take Coworth Park's word for that, what with it being the only residential polo estate we have ever visited.

It was a glorious summer afternoon and we were here to sample the posh English summer Season in all its pomp. To get within spitting distance of the elite. Not to spit at them, that would be unsanitary. But to gain their confidence and hopefully their assistance in our quest. Mainly, we were here to see the King. Well, the future King.

This was, it must be admitted, not proper polo. We're not on The Circuit and don't really know what The Season is (we do know what seasons are), but we did get a sniff of a corporate-sponsored charity royal polo match on a pukka English polo field on a proper country estate amidst deep-pile forestry on the Surrey/Berkshire border. It turned out we knew somebody who knew somebody who in turn knew someone else. Knowing people: it's what the elite is all about.

Not that we wish to sound churlish. On a divine July afternoon, relaxing on some decking outside a marquee in the company of the sort of people who might conceivably get their photo in *Grazia*, it was quite the place to catch a few chukkas. Rachel Stevens swished past, exchanging a nod with Natasha Bedingfield, and Ash Atalla entertained a huge posse of laughing ladies. People held hushed conversations like: 'Is that Pierce Brosnan?' 'Don't think so.' 'Was he the best Bond?' 'No.'

Doing this vital research for the good of the nation, we tried to blend in by drinking any free booze that came by and generally giving off the illusion of enjoying ourselves. In the event, we spent most of our time trying to catch the wine waiter's eye, being the sort of gauche herberts who believe the free booze might run out.

Then the polo started. But it was okay: we very quickly established that they were going to continue serving drinks throughout the game.

Out on the pitch by the marquee, the players warmed up on their ponies. They're not really ponies; polo players don't come out on to the pitch on tiny Shetland ponies, their feet dragging along the ground. No, they're horses. That are called ponies. And one of these riders was the King. We couldn't work out which one most of the time, what with those helmets and the size of the pitch. But he was definitely out there somewhere in a red top, chucking up (that might not be the right terminology).

THE FUTURE MONARCH IN ACTION. JUST LOOK AT HIM!

William's team was called Umbogo, for reasons that are unlikely to ever become clear. The other team was sponsored by Audi, the German car firm. So yes: here was our King literally taking on the Boche. On a horse. Old school!

Polo is the sport of kings, of course. Albeit Eastern ones. Invented in Persia some time between the sixth century BC and the first century AD (sorry to be so vague), it caught on as an effective means of training cavalry and by the Middle Ages was played from Constantinople to Japan (that's different matches, obviously, not one huge match played over that whole distance). The Army brought the sport back from India and formalised the rules (naturally), connecting it forever with bloody good blokes hacking chunks out of lawns to prove their ruling class prowess in riding and, indeed, ruling.*

William's team won, just. He's not a brilliant player, but he can ride a mean horse – which is important, for the country. To our untutored eyes it looked very much as though, as the game reached its climax, William was accidentally on purpose teed up to score the winning goal. What a climax to a Royal charity match, what a memory to take away: your actual HRH

* The sport of British kings is horse-racing. Of course they don't actually ride the horses, so it would perhaps be more accurate to say that the sport of British kings is betting on horses.

sealing the game by personally banging in the winner – snatching victory from the jaws of defeat at the hands of Germany once again. He missed. But one of the pros was on hand to tap it in for him. England 3, Germany 2.5. Come on!

Then there were speeches. We ducked out of those, but returned to the fray to find William chatting to his people. At the edge of a roped-off presentation area (a sort of royal pen), he was being waylaid by four gals in flowery dresses, while his minders (big chaps) kept trying to usher him away. With the posh gals competing for who could giggle most and loudest, it's a wonder the poor chap didn't go deaf. There was quite a twinkle in those twinkling royal eyes. Was he on or off with Kate at this point? Who cares?

We saw our chance to go mano-a-mano with the monarch. (Not to flirt outrageously, that would have been terrible, but to enquire of his mind.) We had, frankly, been drinking.

The full exchange with His Royal Highness went thus:

ALAN: Excuse me. Sorry to keep you, but I'm writing a book about Britishness. Can you tell me what it is?

HRH PRINCE WILLIAM: Erm . . . Britishness . . . that's a tough one.

[Minders do some quite hard staring at this point.]

HRH PRINCE WILLIAM: [Smiling] Hmm . . .

ALAN: Just the first thing that comes into your head. A sentence, a couple of sentences . . .

[Minders communicate using only their eyes that, yes, they are carrying weapons.]

HRH PRINCE WILLIAM: [Smiling] Er . . . One sentence? Or more than that?

ALAN: The first thing that comes into your head. A sentence . . .

VOICE FROM THE CROWD: Yeah, a sentence! [You know in films of the olden days, when the mob get excited about a medieval poll tax or a beheading or something, and one of them shouts something. Well, it was a bit like that.]

ALAN: I know it's tricky, but just the first thing that comes into your head. Anything at all . . .

[Minders appear to be trying to make the Prince move using only the power of their minds, but no need . . .]

HRH PRINCE WILLIAM: [Large, satisfied grin] The best.

[Crowd smile and go 'Aaah.' They like it. HRH has

carried the day for the second time today. No one throws their hat in the air, but clearly they did think about it. Hurrah for the King!]

And there you have it. The future monarch of the Brits says the Brits are 'best'. There was more we wanted to ask him. Would he be a Good King? Or, like so many others, a Bad King? Or did he think all that was an anachronistic absurdity that makes fools us of all, despising with all his being the fatuous fetid swamp of privilege, the backroom deals, the corporate clubability, the lies, the lies – that sickens him to his very soul so he wants to tear his way out of the edifices of power and cry 'Freedom!'? But he had to go.

Interestingly, we were about five miles from Runnymede where that baddest of Bad Kings, King John, was in June 1215 forced to sign the Magna Carta, perhaps on a day like this one. Maybe they had some drinks and rode around on horses. Maybe Rachele Stevenes was there.

Fans of Britishness love the Magna Carta. They say it was the birth of liberty, banishing tyranny from Britain forever, and all sorts of other things that don't seem to be all that true. But among its myriad clauses about wood allowances and stuff were a few that limited the powers of the king, particularly in regard to locking up opponents and leaving them to fester without putting their case before a court.

PRINCE WILLIAM IS ACCOSTED. WHAT A DISH.
Ian Tucker

Even though royalty systematically ignored these clauses for generations, and the populace largely forgot about its existence, in a very real sense Magna Carta is the reason that today royals cannot on a whim clap in chains anyone who, say, collars them at polo matches to ask unanswerable questions about Britishness. Real in the sense of not all that real.

Anyway, you just want to know how dishy he is, don't you? You're like, Magna Carta? Whatever. Is Wills a hottie? Well, considering how many of his family look like horses, he's doing okay. The hair loss is a bit of an issue, but yes, he's definitely better-looking than his dad. He is, we can confirm, a bit of a dreamboat.

It had been an odd day out. The event wasn't really about the polo. It was about PR for the car company. (And charity, of course.) A few dozen celebs had bodded around alongside the King in the hope of getting snapped for the next day's papers. But on a fine July afternoon you do have to wonder whether they haven't got any real friends they might want to hang out with. It was different for us of course, we had a purpose: we were there to see the King. Not like all these other people.

Anyway, the highlight of the day had not been meeting Prince William, even though that had been an intellectually exhilarating experience that had nourished all concerned. The highlight of the day was meeting Kenney Jones, drummer out of the Small Faces (and the Faces and, briefly, the Who). Now this we could get into. For a few golden minutes we were once more youthful, uncynical, unbent and unbroken by the cares of life and the suffocating grip of the pan-Thatcherite junta.

We are not ones for false idols. But this was Kenney fucking Jones! Fortune was shining on us, providing the chance to fleetingly genuflect before the drummer out of the Small Faces, the band Ron Wood called 'our Booker T & the MGs', and assure him that he is A Legend Who Will Never Die.

IT'S ONLY KENNEY JONES!
Nils Jorgensen/Rex Features

He seemed pretty happy to be discussing the Decca years versus the Immediate years, but maybe we were flattering ourselves. It's certainly possible. Anyway, we had our picture taken with him. We were going to frame it in sweat and tears and give it to our grandchildren, and say: 'That's Kenney Jones, that is.'

Then we looked him up on the internet the next day and found out he's a polo-farm-owning Tory supporter. Aarrghh!

NEVER have heroes. NEVER! Because it all gets broken and ruined and destroyed and you are left weeping in the dirt with NOTHING. Nothing.

Still, focusing on the positives, we had peaked beyond the velvet rope. We had seen the glass menagerie that lies behind the iron curtain. We had had a look 'inside', if you will. Pretty quickly we wanted to go back outside again. In fact, almost immediately after going inside we were most keen to get ourselves back outside. Then the dancing started.

If you've ever wondered what you're missing out on not having a first-class ticket for the corporate-jolly gravy express, it is this: middle-aged executives, ties abandoned, collars undone, sweating their alarming stuff to Rick Parfitt Jnr and band belting out 'Teenage Dirtbag'.

That really happened. We went home at that point.

SEVEN

SOUNDS OF ENGLAND

SWAN OF AVON
A MILLPOND
TINA HOBLEY
CHEESE

ENGLAND IS BACK back back, with polls showing people in England suddenly feeling more 'English' than 'British': *Telegraph* leader writers, white-van men, Billy Bragg . . . all together, getting weepy over the end of *The Railway Children*.

We needed to go to England. But this presented us with a problem: where is it? We know there will always be one, but where will it always be? It can't just be the bits of Britain that aren't Scotland or Wales – that would just be rubbish. It's England – England, our England, all of that. But what represents it? What signifiers are English rather than British?

We knew in our souls that, sadly, we would have to go to the countryside. Bizarrely, for a country that includes Tyneside, London and the Midlands, England and Englishness is almost always framed in ways that are rural, elegiac, a bit posh. Think John Major misquoting Orwell to evoke warm beer, old maids cycling to communion and, of course, the thwack of leather. And before him, 1930s prime minister Stanley Baldwin's 'sounds of England': the tinkle of hammer on anvil, the scythe against the whetstone, the corncrake on a dewy morning. (Corncrakes make quite an unpleasant raspy noise. But of course you knew that.)

But which particular countryside? Englishness historian Edwin Jones says it is 'certainly arguable that there is a no more quintessentially English area than the Cotswolds . . . This whole area is rightly an essential part of the itinerary for visitors from abroad who wish to breathe the atmosphere of genuine "Englishry".' We had severe doubts over whether 'Englishry' was even a word, but it certainly sounded like exactly the sort of thing we ought to be breathing the atmosphere of. So we had our destination, our end-point, our limestone peak: the Cotswolds.

But first, to Stratford, to see the most patriotic lines ever written by William Shakespeare, Bard. Late of England.

The great thing about Stratford-upon-Avon is that, yes, Shakespeare was born there, but they don't like to make a fuss about it. It's a self-confident little town that knows it has many other attractions. Ha! Only joking; they in fact never shut up about Mr Swan.

All over town, it's Shakespeare this, Falstaff that. Even the coach station is called the Birthplace Coach Terminal (many exciting journeys begin there, after all).

Mr. WILLIAM
SHAKESPEARES
COMEDIES,
HISTORIES, and
TRAGEDIES.

Published according to the True Originall Copies.

LONDON
Printed by Isaac Iaggard, and Ed. Blount. 1623.

WILLIAM SHAKESPEARE: ENGLISH/BRITISH.
Corbis

It wasn't ever thus. When Shakespeare's own company, the King's Men, tipped up in 1622 to perform in a Stratford in the grip of Puritanism, they were paid to go away, the borough chamberlain recording in his accounts: 'To the King's Players for not playing in the Hall: 6/-.' 'Shakespeare? Here? Are you out of your fucking minds?' the elders might have said (if they weren't Puritans).

It was nearly always thus, though, travel historian Ian Ousby likening the nineteenth-century town to 'the medieval Catholic Church' – powered by 'solemn reverence', 'blatant hype' and bogus relics. The birthplace became a tourist trap, with many writers, including Sir Walter Scott and Thomas Carlyle, scratching their name into the window frame. That's responsible writerly behaviour, is it – defacing historic buildings? (Scott carved: 'Byron is a twat.') Not that anyone knew Shakespeare had been born in this particular room; the eighteenth-century actor David Garrick just decided he probably had been. 'Trust me,' he might have said, 'I'm an actor.'

Having checked into the Shakespeare Hotel and taken a stroll down Shakespeare Street, we headed for the river. This was the week after the Heart of England – the loose tourist brochure area stretching from the West Midlands down to the Cotswolds – had been covered in water by the worst floods on record. For a few days, the Heart of England really wasn't what it used to be. It was under water. The banks of the Avon had burst, covering the centre of Stratford. By now the flood waters on Waterside had receded, with only The Works stationery/art shop being closed for repair. (Any budding scribe would have to go elsewhere for their sheafs of lined A4.)

The play's the thing, of course, and *Richard II* was being staged at Stratford in an RSC season featuring each and every one of the History Plays. We limbered up for the theatricals at the thespian pub, the Dirty Duck, admiring over stiff gins the wall of framed pictures of great actors like Derek Jacobi and Mark Rylance, imagining them all sitting here relating anecdotes, roaringly letting off steam after another triumphant performance. Thank God they're not in here right now, letting off steam, we agreed. That would be terrible.

Safely installed at the Courtyard Theatre, we eagerly anticipated a rich hit of literary patriotism. Shakespeare is of course English/British (he often melds the two, like an American tourist), but bagging him up with nationalist sentiment is tricky: being one-sided is very much what nationalism is all about, whereas plays tend to require a spot of dynamism. So when the government requested a propaganda film of *Henry V* during the Second World War, Laurence Olivier had to take out the scenes with English troops being infiltrated by traitors, English soldiers committing war crimes against the French, and Henry shrugging off the nameless dead in his own ranks – plus the general tenor of war being a fruitless waste of life. 'Loving your work, Larry, loving it – but I wonder if we might tweak it a little by taking some of the central themes and completely reversing them. Yes, you still get to ride the horse . . .'

But one speech does unequivocally stir up 'we're the best' passions: the 'sceptred isle' speech in *Richard II*: 'this other Eden . . . this happy breed of men . . . this precious stone set in a silver sea . . . this tophole place that everyone knows, deep down, is the dog's'.

According to trad history: Richard II started off well, bashing the hopes of his people by ruthlessly repressing the Peasant's Revolt aged just 14. Shakespeare takes up the story when the young Plantagenet had gone to cat-crap with arrogant self-regard (this seems harsh: he was an absolute monarch . . . these days, people get arrogant and self-regarding if they know someone who's directed an advert) and by having 'favourites' – history's word for effeminate guys, or 'gays'. This performance, starring Jonathan Slinger, ramped up Richard as a powdered ponce just asking to be usurped by propah blokes' bloke Henry Bolingbroke. The subtext: England cannot have a leader who can't take his ales. It's just not natural.

To be honest, John of Gaunt's great speech more or less came and went. We're not saying people should have stood up and cheered. That would have been too much. (Or would it?) But it did still provide one important insight into Englishness: Gaunt followed his ruddy litany by detailing England's present dereliction and decay. Thanks to Richard, England was now 'bond in with shame'. The country 'that was wont to conquer others/ Hath made a shameful conquest of itself': Richard had screwed England so much that it's now screwing itself. England should be screwing other countries! But it's screwing itself! Remember England before the king started screwing us all and making us screw ourselves? Those were the days.

So England has been going to the dogs since *at least* 1399, which is over 600 years ago. That's a lot of dogs.

Afterwards, we head for a curry at the Thespians Indian Restaurant. Thankfully, there were no thespians in it.

Next morning, the plan was to go north, to the northernmost tip of the Heart, then trace a line down to the Cotswolds, taking in Tolkien's Shire, the Archers, and the odd flooded abbey along the way to find the guts of the heart at the Heart of England. This whole area – Warwickshire, Shropshire, Gloucestershire – is a sentimental repository of Englishness, a Deep England where, every lunchtime, ploughmen tuck into their ploughman's. Where shepherd's pie is eaten by shepherds. And where cottage pie is also enjoyed.

Collecting our rental car, something mystical happened. We got an upgrade. But not just that . . . for our odyssey into the world of Worcester Woman, we were given a Mondeo, Middle England's own winged chariot. But this wasn't just any Mondeo: this was a lunatic, souped-up, metallic-blue turbofied beast of a Mondeo. We were not merely Mondeo Man. We were Mondeo Superman. Broom broom.

In suitable style, it was time to cut this town and discover the real demi-Eden, the real precious stone set in the silver sea. Yes, we were heading for Birmingham.

The Lord of the Rings was written by J. R. R. Tolkien as a 'new English epic'. Tolkien was so into English stuff that he would spend hours solely speaking Old English, the ancestral language of the English. He didn't get invited to many parties.

Tolkien's epic told of humble Little England types in an unlikely fight for national survival, going off to fight wars and giant spiders to defend their green and pleasant little lives of parochial content. He based his Shire on the village between Birmingham and Solihull where he spent his childhood called, slightly unfortunately, Sarehole. 'It was a kind of paradise lost,' Tolkien said. 'I loved it with an intense love . . . I took the idea of the Hobbits from the village people and children.' (So, it's true. Hobbits are Brummies.)

This hamlet has long been subsumed by the Birmingham suburbs but there is still a Sarehole Mill preserved by the city council. Approaching on the A24 Stratford Road, we passed a gargantuan Harvester modelled on a Greek temple. A burnt-out speed camera reared up on the right.

Turning off this thoroughfare towards Moseley, there it was: Sarehole. In all its glory. A pretty little mill and a field surrounded by twenties suburbia. Site supervisor Kevin Lynch explained how the mill has become a stop-off point for Tolkien fans, even staging some mock battles, with Eastern Europeans often coming up to him talking Elvish. 'I have to tell them: sorry; I'm not fluent.' He opened the back door to show us the millpond, an ineffably still pool, the odd duck and dragonfly the only sign of movement. It was as smooth as a millpond. It *was* a millpond. 'You wouldn't think we were three miles from Birmingham city centre,' Kevin reflected. Only the thrum of traffic from the nearby road gave away that, in fact, Sarehole was lost and gone and ruined.

Like all true Englanders, Tolkien was obsessed with England disappearing. When he returned here after the First World War (he witnessed the Somme), he was upset to see Sarehole swallowed up by Brum, saying: 'I always knew it would go – and it did.'

That's the trouble with England: where once were harvesters, now there are Harvesters, and this can make people sad.

We went down the road, through a small council estate of bungalows where two large skinheads were sunning themselves on plastic chairs while an old lady brought them tea on a tray, to Moseley Bog, a nine-hectare dell that was the basis for the Old Forest, the primeval woodland in which the Hobbits became entangled after leaving the Shire. In this unlikely wilderness, the summery stillness was slightly unnerving and it was not hard to imagine the roots and tangled undergrowth coming to life and grabbing at our limbs. (Not that we thought this might actually happen, but you know, inner child and all that.)

FE FI FO FUM, I SMELL THE BLOOD OF A GERMAN

A question we often find ourselves asking is: who the fuck are the English? It's a knotty one. This question in fact hides a darker question, with a dark heart, relating to the Dark Ages. The question is this: are the English actually German? (We told you it was dark.)

The first people to be called English were the Anglo-Saxons (or Angelcynn), the collective name for the Angles, Saxons and Jutes, Teutonic peoples who came to Britain from the fifth century AD, after the Romans had gone. (They weren't a collective, though, and set up shop as a variety of different tribes and kingdoms.)

As to how the Anglo-Saxons came to run everything, the Dark Ages were very dark (don't listen to the revisionists who claim they were actually quite light), so experts disagree slightly on the answer – the two mildly divergent schools approximating to: 'Race war! Rah!' and 'Race war? Nah!' The first camp claims the Angles and Saxons came over in a heavy-metal blitzkrieg and fought the romantic natives back into Wales; and points to all the battle poems and books bemoaning 'The Ruin of Britain'. The second camp says the Germans came over and settled, inter-married and brought some nice new words (well, a whole language), pointing to the lack of mass graves or other evidence of ethnic cleansing or movement of Jah Peoples that a full-on race war would presumably entail: less warrification, more gentrification.

DNA studies can now finally shed light on this darkness. And what do these tests, taken from people in villages across the UK, show? Well, it's tricky. A genetic difference between English and Welsh does exist, with West Wales well Celt and East Anglia mostly Saxon. But most areas show a hotchpotch of both. About 80 per cent of the DNA in 'indigenous' Brits goes back to the prehistoric settlers stuck here when the Channel arrived 400,000 years ago (and who may have come from Spain). So it might not come as the greatest surprise to realise that any distinction between 'English' and 'Celtic' ethnicity is at best shaky, at worst a waste of a life even thinking about. Blood nationalism, then, is a fucking stupid olden-days idea: if it's not going to work in Serbia, it's not going to work in Surbiton. (Or Barking.)

SAXON.
Redferns

The English population was not politically unified until the tenth century, by Aethelstan (grandson of Alfred the Great). The Anglo-Saxons had been organised at first in petty kingdoms, over time coalescing into the so-called heptarchy of seven powerful states. In fact, Aethelstan was trying to make Britain: he tried to conquer the whole island, but the Scots and Danes got in the way.

The Norman Conquest finally imposed a reasonably fixed England on the English. Initially the Normans were legally referred to as French, and the pre-invasion natives English; but this distinction soon passed away, and everyone in England became English. Hurrah!

So, to sum up: the original 'English' were German, whereas 'England' was properly invented by the French (well, the Normans, who were French Vikings). The idea of the English as being completely distinct (and superior) people to those of mainland Europe has been attributed (by Edwin Jones and others) to the Tudors. Who were Welsh.

Tolkien would play here for hours till his mum called, 'JRR! Your tea's ready!' He'd reply: 'There I was having an idyllic time of things and you come along with your offer of tea and ruin everything . . . I knew it would go – and it did . . . What is it, spaghetti hoops?'

Back in the Mondeo, we were now entering Worcestershire. Land of plums.

The sacred area bordered by the M4, M5, M42 and M40 is truly the Heart of England. Surrounded by motorways, but also untouched by them. This northern edge was once covered by the vast Forest of Arden. (Shakespeare borrowed the name for the French forest setting of *As You Like It*.) The forest was a vast carpet of green in the geographical middle of England. It was largely cleared in the Middle Ages (it provided the beams for many of Stratford's buildings), although we do spot a sign for the Arden Forest Industrial Estate, so all is not lost.

We had been from Shakespeare Country to Tolkien Country, then back through Shakespeare Country. As we piloted the Mondeo past Tamworth-in-Arden, the village where deified songwriter Nick Drake spent his childhood and is buried, we pondered the Englishness of his sad songs about sheds, leaves, harvests and being born to sail away into the land of forever.

Leaving Nick Drake Country, we stopped off in Ambridge for lunch: Archers Country. *The Archers* isn't lost and gone, of course. We knew that much. We'd just heard that unmistakable theme tune start up on the radio, and quickly tuned to another station. But Ambridge is changing: at Inkberrow, the village that producers at the BBC's Pebble Mill studio took as their model (it was originally intended as a piece of Ministry of Agriculture propaganda for new farming practices), a new village was being built on the side of the old – a soulless identikit 'executive' estate. Betjeman might have written a poem: 'Ambridge has turned corporate now/ With lacquered boards and shiny taps.' Some bollocks like that. (Betjeman was German, you know.)

They didn't serve the Ambridge beer, Shires, at the Old Bull (the model for, yes, the Bull). Nor much in the way of lunch, either. We wanted a ploughman's, like the ploughmen used to eat: Baldwin said England was 'the sight of a plough team coming over the brow of a hill'. We had no great desire to see

THE OLD BULL AT INKBERROW OR THE BULL AT AMBRIDGE. OR BOTH. OR NEITHER.

a plough team, but we would certainly enjoy a spot of their lunch. In the event, the most English option was battered fish and chips freshly pulled from the freezer.

Outside, as we took photos of his pub, the landlord drove off in his massive Jag: 'The *Daily Express* called it England's most sought-after village,' he informed us out of the window as he went past.

That's great news. Wouldn't have killed you to do a ploughman's, though.

Next up was Tewkesbury, Gloucestershire. En route, we briefly joined the M5, which took us past Worcester, home of the Worcester Woman, a Middle England figure of mythical importance who speaks oracularly for the British people, telling us what they are thinking, and how their leaders should act. Like some Tolkien figure, she 'holds the key' to electoral victory. Do not anger the Worcester Woman, for she is wrathful and all-powerful. (In the Hollywood version, she would be played by Cate Blanchett, doing a very convincing accent.)

Before this month, Tewkesbury was most famous for its War of the Roses battle – held, as the name suggests, on the Bloody

Meadow, within sight of the abbey. According to some sources, the victorious Yorkists came inside the abbey and slaughtered cowering Lancastrians in cold blood, the resulting bloodshed causing the building to be shut for a month. ('Closed due to blooding,' the signs might have said.)

But the floods had made Tewkesbury a picturesque totem of climate chaos, a newly created island adrift in muddy waters. Being built on the confluence of the rivers Avon and Severn, and once abuzz with trading barges, the town has always been prone to flooding. But not like this. There's English gardens wet with summer rain. Then there's being deluged with 10 billion tonnes of water – the same amount as in all the lakes in the Lake District (that's what fell on Gloucestershire in one month). This was biblical.

The water had by now receded, but an air of wound-licking quietude pervaded the town. Firefighters were pumping out water from basements into the high-street gutters. The smell of damp carpet emanated from the houses near the abbey; we passed a junk shop that positively reeked. Outside many houses were piles of unwanted items ruined by the flood: despoiled books about shrubs and cooking with citrus, a discarded fax machine. We couldn't help thinking that someone had probably just taken the opportunity to throw the fax machine out; you know, while we're at it. Faxes? Like England, they are gone now.

The abbey is massive, larger than many cathedrals. We stood admiring an immense red-leafed tree, the thick leaves of which cast a deep shadow on the grass below. An elderly lady helpfully came to tell us it was a copper beech, probably planted in around 1600. We were standing talking about a massive tree with a really tiny old lady.

Our new friend led us round the side and into the abbey, telling us a little about the history of the place, and the flooding. Of the recent events, she explained: 'Oh, the vicar's had a terrible time getting everything up and running again. But the vergers have worked like blacks.'

We tactfully put this choice turn of phrase down to her being quite elderly. And a bit racist.

Inside the abbey, the verger recalled the previous week with genuine horror; how some visitors were completely cut off and had to stay the night stranded inside the abbey pews, sleeping in blankets as water edged up the floor. 'Look, you can still see the line,' he said. 'And it was sewage water, so it wasn't too pleasant.'

Back outside in the town, we hunted for great local cheeses. For our next stop, we needed provisions. We were seeking an English epiphany, and that always involves going up something high and looking down. Visionary mystics often go up mountains, but the Heart of England doesn't really do mountain. The Heart of England does hill. We were going up Bredon Hill, the name of which breaks down as 'hill hill hill' in three different languages. A hill called Hill Hill Hill. To us, that just screams 'hill'.

And not just to us. A. E. Housman, a particularly English poet, wrote the very English summer poem 'Bredon Hill' about being up Bredon in the summer. At the top, we planned to eat cheese and see how English England could get.

Cheese is pretty English. Ideally we wanted some Cheddar, which is a very English cheese. It's even named after somewhere in England: Cheddar. But Tewkesbury offered little in the way of curdled dairy goodness. There was a bargain booze shop ('Great deals!') – and considering the past week's events, you could definitely see the appeal of bargain booze – but no cheese shop that we could find. We remained cheeseless until we gave in and went to the M&S food shop, which only sold little individual portion sticks of Wensleydale and cranberry. Is Yorkshire English? It's a moot point. But it would have to do.

Cranberries, though. Aren't cranberries American? Surely we wouldn't have to spit them out?

Housman had Englishness bad. The Worcestershire poet decided to build a cycle of 63 poems around an imaginary English rural idyll, which he decided was in Shropshire. He had never been to Shropshire, it just sounded like the sort of place he'd be into. *A Shropshire Lad*, based around his childhood in Worcestershire and Gloucestershire, is kind of the Bible of lost Englishness, its 'blue remembered hills' a bucolic idyll to set against the reality of young men disappearing to war. (Housman, by the way, was probably that most English of characters: a closeted homosexual. Lots of strapping young farm labourers with their tops off, that sort of thing . . .)

Bredon Hill, which is not in Shropshire, is one of the few places Housman describes accurately, probably because he had actually been there. Imagine loving England so much you decided to write a poetry cycle about the idea of Shropshire,

A COW EATING SOME GRASS ON BREDON HILL: ENGLISH.

the mythical ideal of Shropshire. A Shropshire of the mind. Now that's loving England. Anyway, the poem 'On Bredon Hill' has it all: church bells ringing out clearly across the quiet, memories of sweet lazy days with loved ones, death taking away the loved ones, making the memories really quite painful, the skies filling with larks. All of that.

We parked up in a layby on a tiny lane. The sun was heading towards late afternoon. We walked past cows, who reared around us curiously. Roughly a rambler a year is killed in Britain by stampeding cattle. Being trampled by cows upon Bredon Hill would be a poetic way to go. Bittersweet, even. But still quite unappealing. Cows look bovine, more than any other animal, and this bovine blankness can be a cover for great evil.

At the top, the view of the Vale of Evesham was outstanding. We listened for some corncrakes or some church bells or other sounds of England. A cow went 'Moo'. Which isn't so much English as just the international language of Cow. But still, a row of trees stood on the crest of the hill silhouetted against the golden glow of the fading day. A mild breeze came up from the south, blowing through the hay in the field on the top of the plateau. It rippled. This was it all right. We unwrapped our cheese sticks and tucked in. The cheese was quite sweaty by now. It didn't matter.

Turning back to the Vale, the light green slope in front of us gave way to a valley floor patchworked with fields of green and ochre, then some way away the land rose again, irregularly, as bumps spreading off into the distance, deep green trees on top, the start of the Cotswolds. The sun was golden and warm, and the scene evoked a great nostalgia for how it all used to be around here. Of course, we had no real idea how things used to be around here. We had never been here before. But in a way, Worcestershire has always been with us. We'd just never realised this before. Any Englishman worth his salt has to love Worcestershire like a dead lover. Remember all those great times spent here? Not actual real times, obviously. But still, great times.

This was back in the golden age of course, the golden days of old. Before the war took all the strapping young men away. The golden age. With the golden sunshine and golden hay and golden retrievers. A scrumped apple that tasted never so sweet. The smell of a plough. A stolen kiss with a milking maid. All those bees. Why did it have to go? Why did you have to take it away? Mummy, why did you send us away? Oh England, England, our England.

Perhaps we'd had too much sun. Perhaps it was the cheese. Perhaps it was *England*.

Back down in the Vale and in the motor, we put on *The Lark Ascending* by Vaughan Williams ('the man who set England to music') and, as if we hadn't already gorged ourselves on landscape, headed into the Cotswolds: Vaughan Williams Country. England didn't really need evoking considering it was right there outside the window. But still, just in case England was not evocative enough of itself, then here was *The Lark Ascending*, evoking England.

This was, assuredly, balming stuff; the dipping, undulating violin line echoing the lark

A LARK. GET A GOOD LOOK, BECAUSE THEY'RE ALL GOING TO SOD OFF SOMEWHERE ELSE.
Corbis

scanning the ages-old network of meadows. Larks, incidentally, may soon be a thing of the past, due to global warming. (Although there'll still be the Birdsong channel on DAB.) We were enjoying fields out of the window and drifting away with the music – with the lark – when the car stereo went over to local radio: 'Things not looking too bad on the roads tonight.'

Indeed they were not. We arrived at Stow-on-the-Wold in no time at all.

We needed to unwind, to relish the peace and tranquillity of rural England in the past. And where better than at England's oldest inn?

The Royalist Hotel on Digbeth Street dates from AD 947. This town was, we learned, the scene of another bloody battle, this time in the Civil War. Yes, nearly 200 years on from Tewskesbury and Englishmen was still ripping huge chunks out of Englishmen in the Heart of England. Eventually the Royalists were defeated and over a thousand men were imprisoned within St Edward's church. The streets that had latterly been awash with floodwater were then awash with blood. Digbeth Street, meaning 'duck's bath street', is allegedly named because so much blood flowed here after the fighting that ducks could bathe in the pools. You do sort of wonder whether ducks really would bathe in pools of blood rather than just run away, but still: gory stuff.

Was the Royalist really England's oldest inn? Call us cynical, but we've been burned with this kind of crap before, so we had to ask: were there any other claimants for the title?

'Yes, there are a few,' admitted the receptionist. 'But we're the only one mentioned in the *Guinness Book of Records*.'

This was acceptable to us.

We wanted to keep up our researches, but were tired and required sustenance. In the handsome central square, the mellow, honey-coloured Cotswolds stone looked, in the evening sun, especially mellow and especially yellow. But this was not the only colour in evidence: there were Union Jacks flying everywhere. The whole place was dripping with Union Jacks. Many, many more than we have seen in one place at least since the Queen Mum died.

Strolling around the square, we came across the village shop, Stars Newsagent. In the window was a proud display of patriotic items: Union Jack mugs, pens and lighters; a red phone-box teapot; a sour-faced toy bulldog in a Union Jack vest . . . all sat proudly alongside a selection of golliwogs. Golly.

In the Queen's Head, a pub on the square (framed picture of the British Empire resplendent above the fireplace), a jolly middle-aged man with a moustache sought to initiate us in the ways of the locals. He was really very keen to educate us in the ways of the locals. We were not going to get away with not being genned up on the locals and their ways. As we looked at the beer options, he informed us that 'locals' always – *always* – have 'that one'. He also told us that when it comes to bar snacking, 'locals' eat Nobby's Nuts. A great Cotswolds tradition: Nobby's Nuts.

But when we asked him what 'locals' have from the dinner menu, he clammed up. 'That's different,' he said, gnomically.

We concluded that it would be best to sit at a table quite a long way from this man. There we met two fanatically QPR-supporting cabbies down from London on a jolly. From a country life research perspective, the whole evening would have to be put down as 'inconclusive'.

Over warm beers, we considered Englishness. We were doing well. Rural idyll? Check. Evocative music? Check. Stirring literature? Check. Flags? Check. Warm beer? Check. Old maids on bicycles? Not one. Not that we'd noticed. That was it. It must be. Clearly, we needed to consult some perambulating aged virgins.

It's a moment of realisation that comes to everyone eventually, if they drink enough warm beer. We resolved to get onto it in the morning.

You can tell Chipping Campden is in your actual proper countryside as there was a tractor going up the main street. Albeit jockeying with an oncoming Jeep 4x4. Followed by an old man in a dinky open-topped sports car, then a Mercedes estate. It's not that rural England is lost and gone; we'd passed some of it, and it looked remarkably intact. It's just not all that *rural*. The farm workers for this area are bussed in from as far away as Birmingham, country folk generally being unable to afford to live in the country.

We were off to Cirencester, to hear the oldest church bells in England, at the Church of St John the Baptist, and consult with any old maids we found around and about. But we headed first to Chipping Campden, the home of shin-kicking, a sport that signifies like nothing else the rougher end of English ruralism. According to Edwin Jones, the high street is 'the best example of its kind in England'. And who doesn't like a nice high street?

We picked up a copy of *Cotswold Life*, a magazine about . . . oh, you know. It was all property ads, Princess Anne on eventing, property ads, and lots of picture of Laurence Llewellyn-Bowen and posh gals at drinks parties. There weren't many small ads for second-hand farm machinery. TV's Tina Hobley said that arriving at her weekend Cotswold home 'feels like . . . opening a gift'. She also said that people were not snapping up homes in the Cotswolds for speculative reasons. Her house in London is 'ten times the value' of the one she has in the Cotswolds, so that would just be foolish. So that's *Cotswold Life*, then.

Maybe, then, this England, the England of the mind, is more about what people are escaping from: your actual England, the one that's not of the mind, but of the body. Historian Peter Mandler claims the rural-nostalgic strain was invented by the dominant classes towards the end of the nineteenth century to 'thwart the tendencies towards urbanism, democracy and modernism'. Yes, we're talking about those fucking working classes again: the people who don't doff their caps enough and who have always been, and probably still are, most of the English. England for the English? England for not that much of the English, thank you! (Late nineteenth century? That's almost last week.) Whatever: only the old maids could help us now.

COUNTRY FOLK.
Ida A. Battye

Cirencester turned out to be a little further from Chipping C than we'd allowed for. Time was getting tight if we wanted the full, on-the-hour effect of the bells – well, not without sitting round for an hour and risking hitting traffic on the M4. And not wanting to hit traffic on the M4 is one of the few things that genuinely unites the nation.

We stepped on the gas, negotiated the one-way system and

looked out for a large church tower. Think *Starsky and Hutch*, only trying to find a church in time to hear the bells. Pulling up outside the church with seconds to spare, we got on the lookout for old maids. The bells chimed. They sounded like church bells. As the last dong dinged its last, we cast about this way and that for the aforementioned elderly females. This way, only parked cars. That way, a tailor (a real one, not Burton's). And here, an outlet of the West Cornwall Pasty Company, and Boots. A fine-looking town, all in all.

No old maids were forthcoming. We did talk to an elderly lady in the church shop, about the bells, but she was wearing a wedding ring. She might not even *have* a bike.

None the wiser, we set fair in the Mondeo – for Swindon and the M4.

BRITAIN'S MOST DISSOLUTE MONARCHS

WILLIAM THE CONQUEROR: By middle age, William the Bastard had become William the Fat Bastard (Philip I of France said he looked like a pregnant lady – 'a woman in child-bed'). At his funeral, as aides tried squeezing his huge corpse into the coffin, it exploded, releasing a foul stench that cleared out the church (and funerals are awkward enough, without that).

HENRY I: Couldn't keep it in his medieval trousers. Except they didn't even have trousers. Holds the record for the most illegitimate children of any English monarch. One medieval manuscript shows him in bed with Welsh mistress Nest, naked apart from their crowns. Their repose suggests they have just 'done it'. Quite porny sometimes, history.

HENRY VIII: Got so fat in his final years that a special trolley had to be constructed for him to be wheeled around Hampton Court by servants. He used to pretend it was the *Mary Rose* and shout: 'Land ho!' Also, had six – yes, six – wives. Not a lot of people know that.

CHARLES II: According to Samuel Pepys, while the Dutch set fire to the English fleet in the Medway, Charles was in the chambers of his mistress Lady Castlemaine all day, 'looking for a moth'. They were probably just at it, though.

GEORGE I: Installed as king in 1714, the first of the Hanoverian dynasty (he was about 787th in line to the throne and ghastly, but at least he wasn't a Catholic) brought with him two mistresses: one very fat and one incredibly stick-thin. Soon nicknamed 'the Maypole' and 'the Elephant'. George had them with him in his coach as he went to his coronation. 'Who wants a piece of George?' he used to ask. In German.

GEORGE II: 'An obstinate self-indulgent miserly martinet with an insatiable sexual appetite.' Well, according to his own son, Frederick. The feeling was mutual and George could barely contain his glee when Frederick was killed by a wayward cricket ball. By the way, following government measures to reduce gin consumption, a mob attacked the royal coach screaming: 'No gin, no king!'. Now *that*'s a demonstration.

GEORGE IV: The king of the dissolute monarchs. Got his marriage to Caroline of Brunswick off to a bad start when he spent the wedding night passed out drunk on the floor. He was not the first, nor the last. But he also had his mistress on hand. Which isn't even trying. Oh, and he was already married to someone else.

EDWARD VII: Involved in an illegal gambling scandal and enjoyed the 'social companionship' of actresses including Winston Churchill's mum and Camilla Parker Bowles's great-granny. Called as a witness in a divorce trial, it was shown that Edward had indeed visited MP Sir Charles Mordaunt's house while he was away at the House. Asked why, Edward replied: 'Why, I was giving his wife one.' (He didn't really say that.)

EDWARD VIII: Britain's most esteemed alcoholic Nazi.

ELIZABETH BOWES-LYON: Consort of George VI, aka the Queen Mum. Keen follower of

EDWARD VII: SEX MACHINE.
Popperfoto/Getty Images

horses. Looked *EastEnders* in the eye. Pissed all the time. Royal gossip claimed her favourite tipple was gin and Dubonnet. Bloody hell, that's boozing! According to royal-watcher Thomas Blaikie: 'In Venice in 1984, the Queen Mother remained utterly serene and unflappable as her launch began to take in water. In fact, her lady-in-waiting had the greatest difficulty getting her out before it sank entirely.' She was doing her duty and going down with the ship. Implication: the old girl was totally shitfaced.

EIGHT

ENTER THE
DRAGON

MOUNTAINS
MEN OF HARLECH
DOG

THERE IS HUSH in the marquee housing the main event of the 2007 Eisteddfod – the Welsh festival of Welshness. This is the Gorsedd Bard, an ancient rite celebrating the finest traditional poets of Wales. The 2,000-capacity arena is packed with fans of Welsh stuff: mainly, but by no means exclusively, middle-aged and elderly women, from Wales. The stage is filled with vast rows of druids dressed in white and purple robes, incanting. A line of children dressed in green stands silent, having just completed a dance. The head druid steps forward. An announcement is made. A couple of hundred rows away, near the very back of this vast auditorium, we shift uncomfortably in our seats as the head druid motions to where we are sitting – and there is a light.

The audience – expectant, excited – turn their heads in our direction. We haven't done anything. We're not even Welsh. But still the spotlight moves towards our very seats . . . finally coming to rest four or five places away, as the man occupying the seat (early forties, dark hair) stands up. The crowd erupts. The man in our row smiles beneficently, modestly acknowledging the adulation – for it is nothing less. He is the Chosen One, the one everyone is turning in their seats to get a good look at, while also clapping and grinning. They really love him. This man. This bloke in *our* row.

We have absolutely no idea what is going on. Everything is in Welsh (fairly obviously). But we do understand one thing: this guy – he's the King of the Eisteddfod. And he's right next to us. We practically know him. He's, like, right there. He is our friend, and everyone loves him. Given the adulation he is currently receiving, it seems highly likely that he is currently the most celebrated figure in all of Wales. You would have to be almost definite about that.

Druids process down the middle of the auditorium, proffering before them a purple cape, and a shiny thing – a crown. After an eternity of clapping, they are almost here. The bloke in our row starts to move along the aisle. We stand to let him pass. We are close to greatness. So close we could touch him. Actually, we do sort of brush him, by mistake. That's how close we are. Go, bloke in our row! Go!

The druids place the crown upon the head of the bloke in our row, and the clapping gets louder still. He is led in a triumphant procession to the stage, surfing an undulating wave of goodwill. He ascends to a wooden throne – while druids

THE GORSEDD OF BARDS:
STANDING UP FOR WALES.

make speeches about our man and joyful songs are sung – to be master of all he surveys. Teenage girls give him bouquets ... Go, bloke in our row!

So, we enjoyed the Gorsedd Bard. We'd earlier accidentally got involved with watching a clog-dancing competition, which we hadn't been so keen on, but our enjoyment of the Gorsedd Bard was possibly even enhanced by the fact that we didn't understand the first thing that was going on. (At one point earlier on, a Celtic brother from across the sea did a speech in Breton. We didn't understand that either.)

This ancient gathering of Welsh talent is a tournament, but a tournament of bards, which isn't as exciting as tournaments with people being thrown off horses but does test the competitive mettle of poets and bards, people who otherwise tend to lack a competitive ethos of any kind. This travelling circus of Welshness pitches up at a new Welsh location every summer, this year taking over a few fields near Mold, which is barely in Wales (it's on the English side of Offa's Dyke). Although it is more in Wales than Liverpool, which had asked to host this year's festival, causing offence to those Welsh people who thought Wales's foremost cultural event really should take place in Wales.

Little is known of the original Eisteddfod ceremonies that flourished between the tenth and twelfth centuries before being silenced by bard-hating English king Edward I (the Hammer of the Scots could also have been called the Hammer of the Bards, which doesn't sound nearly as hard). But then, in the eighteenth century, the cultural Welshists recharged the batteries with some new Eisteddfod gatherings taking place in that great Welsh city of London. The leading light of one notable ceremony in 1792 on Primrose Hill was a stonemason from

Glamorgan so homesick for Wales that he changed his name from Edward Williams (only mildly Welsh) to Iolo Morganwg (very Welsh).

Seeing the new England-based druidic orders, he thought that if anywhere should play at being ancient Celtic spiritualists, it really should be Wales. So began the Gorsedd Beirdd Ynys Prydain, or the Gorsedd of Bards of the Island of Britain, a vibrant order similar to the English ones but which has also bagged a place at the top table of Wales's official culturefest.

Morganwg was an ideal figure to forge this revived national identity: he was a forger. That's in the sense of 'forever making forgeries'. Indeed, his dedication to forgery was so complete he often missed the essential difference between genuine antique poetry and poetry he had written himself, a real psychological advantage in fooling others that can probably be put down to his lifelong addiction to laudanum.

Outside, the Eisteddfod site felt like a summer fete, but a summer fete not for a small town but a small country. You could have a go sitting in a police car, or get advice on eco-bulbs, and take leaflets about them home in branded carrier bags. A hopper bus ferried the elderly around. The young had their own area, Maes B (Field B, a camping site), which hots up later on with some typical Welsh young people's activities like getting pissed.

It all seems a long way from the (now defunct) Welsh *Mirror*'s rabid front-page denunciation of a FESTIVAL OF FEAR AND HATRED (because people were speaking in the secret, racist code that is Welsh). The politics probably hardens up after a few meads, but we didn't see much blood-and-soil brimstone. Where they saw hate, we saw handicrafts.

And Welsh versions of toddler classics like the Spot books. Maybe these translations incorporated violently anti-English messages, Spot getting fucked up on laudanum and telling Helen the hippo he's the reincarnation of Merlin, but it seems quite unlikely, what with the copyright laws being what they are.

Having seen the most enduring image of the day, some old people watching a live folk band next to a stone circle constructed all of plastic, we made for the car park. Enough with the made-up bardic ceremonies. It was time to get real. Real Wales.

*

We were off to Harlech on the west coast, skirting Snowdonia, to investigate the question: 'When was Wales?' This politically charged issue has vexed historians for generations. 'Where is Wales?' That's pretty easy. We'd passed a sign saying 'Welcome to Wales' earlier on. Having hired a car at Crewe station, we'd headed straight for the border. Hitting this border didn't carry the same desperado charge as, say, hitting the Mexican border with saddlebags full of mail-train booty. It was the border to Wales. But still, another country. Or principality. Or something. (The second we passed the sign, it started raining.)

So when was Wales? Whenever, or wherever, it was, we knew it had something to do with Owain Glyn Dwr, the last independent Welsh prince, and his dream of a Welsh nation, centred on his stronghold in Harlech, before that dream was all battered up by the English. Harlech even has its own heroic song. Sometimes called Wales's unofficial national anthem, 'Men of Harlech' is a stirring battle song decrying the 'Saxon foemen' with their nasty prancing steeds and bastard sunbeams glancing off their shitty fucking helmets.

The tune features on Radio 4's *UK Theme* (a fantasia of British folk) alongside other songs less concerned with slaughtering Saxons, like 'Greensleeves'. Charlotte Church did a version that ended with her commanding her compatriots to show the English no mercy. 'Grind them in the dust!' she roared, before going off to get pissed on a beach.

Whichever version you hear, it always evokes the Welsh defenders of Harlech Castle, defending themselves and also the dream of Welsh nationhood. 'Death is glory now!' It's stirring stuff. Or just quite mental. One of the two. We were now heading for this richly symbolic medieval stronghold, rich symbol of the dreams of a Welsh nation. Confusingly, it also symbolises crushing the dreams of a Welsh nation. Built by the English after Edward I following that brutal invasion in 1276, it is one of the so-called Iron Ring of imposing fortifications that impose themselves on the landscape of West and North Wales. We would stop at Edward's castle, we had decided, and get a good look at his ring.

Rejecting the A55 dual carriageway across North Wales – which is probably tainted with the stench of imperialism; who can say? – we went across country. Mountainous country. Real Wales.

We had started drawing inspiration from an article by novelist Niall Griffiths written for the Committee for Racial Equality, and republished in the *New Statesman* under the heading 'Wales: England's Oldest Colony'. The writer, sometimes described as the 'Welsh Irvine Welsh' (he claims this description is lazy; bet he likes it really), eulogises this Wales, a world away from the 'citified south' or the arcaded and promenaded north, a Wales that is utterly 'other' to the Anglocentric mindset, that is in fact 'alien and threatening to the suburbanised soul; it's the cancer in the Little Englander's body politic'.

The 'real Wales', he says, is wild, untamed and untameable. Feral. Foreboding. Sexual. In a word: mountains.

'It suited the Enlightenment to present such a place as serene and beautiful, where men and nature lived in harmonious interaction, but the reality is what confronts you here every single day: mud, bone, shit, blood, rot, hawks hunting overhead, death always adjacent.'

That's right, the Wales you see on *Bobinogs* isn't the half of it . . . where's all the shit and rotting hawks, for a start?

Griffiths got the tag the 'the Welsh Irvine Welsh' because of his novels about people doing skag in Aberystwyth. Anyway, he is proud of his Welsh heritage, having been raised in that fine Welsh city of Liverpool. We headed for the coast, admiring his beloved Real Wales in its late-afternoon glory. A good valley. A great lake. A marvellous forest. And, ah, the mountains, the rightly famous mountains: big buggers, the lot of them. Not many people, though. Is that what Real Wales is all about? No actual Welsh people.

Harlech stands high on a rocky outcrop above Tremadog Bay, a smaller inlet of the massive Cardigan Bay (how can Cardigan Bay be a bay? It's *all* the coast). It's not an overly modernised town. People here don't moan about all the new coffee chains coming in and squeezing out the little guy. We checked in at the Castle Hotel. It's opposite the castle, affording an excellent view of the castle. In a passing nod to the post-1980 world, the hotel offered a bar menu of paninis. They didn't have any actual paninis, just the menu, but it's progress of a sort.

Guess what. There's not a lot to do in Harlech on a Monday night. In a tiny restaurant next to the hotel (yes, it was called The Castle Restaurant), we were confronted by a restaurant empty but for a long table of noisy English holidaymakers – an extended posse of parents, in-laws, children and children's friends. Oddly enough, the blonde mum in the middle of the table looked just like the newly appointed home secretary Jacqui Smith. We soon realised the reason for this: it was the newly appointed home secretary Jacqui Smith. (For their holidays, the new Brownian ministers were seeking to present themselves as sober Roundheads replacing the gallivanting Blairite Cavaliers – hence West Wales rather than, say, the West Indies.)

Something we should say on Ms Smith's behalf is that she was not noticeably strung out on weed. The previous month, the tabloids had dubbed her Jacqui Spliff after she revealed that, yes, she did inhale, then exhale, then inhale some more. But we didn't see her skinning up, popping outside to lug on a huge bong – coming back into the restaurant with wild, dilated saucers where her formerly sunken and blitzkrieged eyes had been, reeking of sinsemilla. We didn't see Home Secretary Jacqui Smith smoking that weed at all in any way. To the best of our knowledge, that didn't happen.

She may have gone to the loo at some point, but only briefly. Certainly not long enough to get too fucked up on da herb.

After the lively party piled out, we pointed out to the young local waitress that she had just been serving the new home secretary. 'Oh, was it? I didn't see,' she replied, indicating that she could not even begin to care less. Maybe they get senior members of the government in here all the time.

In the morning, we stormed the castle, climbing the spiral stairs of a tower to overlook the bay. It was a castle, ruined, but not so ruined you couldn't imagine standing on the ramparts and planning how to smash the dreams of a Welsh nation. Those Plantagenets really knew about imposing oneself on the landscape. In a word: castles. They really are quite imposing, aren't they?

Back on the ground in the keep, medieval cannonballs were scattered in piles, dating from the English siege of Glyn Dwr in 1409. The actual cannonballs used by the English to smash the dreams of a Welsh nation. You could touch them. Feel their power.

In the gift shop, we bought a *Sounds of Wales* CD with 'Men of Harlech' on it. We momentarily considered driving round town with it blasting out of the car-stereo with the windows down, just to show our solidarity with all the townsfolk, or at least the ones who weren't English, but then we thought that might be stupid. So we kept the windows rolled up. (That was still pretty weird, though. It's too much bombast for one small car.)

As it transpired, the song never did refer to Glyn Dwr's defence of the budding Welsh nation, but to later in the fifteenth century, when the budding Welsh nation was budding no more and the brave men defending Harlech Castle for seven long years were fighting for the deposed

HARLECH CASTLE: 'MEN OF' NOT PICTURED.

King and Queen of England in the Wars of the Roses – basically a schism in the English royal court. *Smash the Saxons!* Except the ones whose side we're on. *Grind them to dust!* No, not those ones, *those* ones . . . Yes, we know they all look the same.

Even more weirdly, the song's modern popularity stems from its stirring rendition, in the film *Zulu*, by the plucky Welsh Guards posted at Rorke's Drift in 1879. The plucky Welshmen were outnumbered by the Zulus (there were thousands of them, apparently). But really, in this particular conflict, who best represented heroically oppressed nationhood?

We drove back into the Snowdonia National Park, to stop off at Beddgelert, on the hunt for the Red Dragon. Wales is a land of dragons. Dragons festoon buildings and public squares. Fluffy dragons for kiddies festoon tourist shops. It's like one big dragon's den full of dragons. The red dragon – or Y Ddraig Goch in Welsh – is the main feature of what is apparently the oldest flag in the world. It's a flag that throws the prosaic

WHEN WAS WALES?

A recognisable Welsh border has existed since Offa built his anti-Welsh dyke in the late seventh century. On this side of the border you're Welsh, on the other side not. But you can say the same for Yorkshire, and that doesn't make Yorkshire a nation. (Like Wales, Yorkshire is also split and different between its south and north. In another parallel, Yorkshire also has its own language: straight talking.)

So what's Wales's greatest claim to independent nationhood? There have only been six welsh kings/princes – that is, who ruled/claimed to rule all or most of Wales. The first was Dafydd ap Llywelyn, who declared himself such in 1244. But his domain hardly included South Wales, which is a lot of Wales. He died in 1246. So that lasted two years.

His nephew Llwelyn ap Gruffydd (Llwelyn the Last, who died in 1282) had a more extensive domain in North and Central Wales. In 1274–5, he repeatedly refused demands to pay homage to Edward I, a notably hardcore monarch with a tough respect agenda. Edward launched a 'textbook campaign' of invasion, divide and then rule (what textbooks are these: *Smashing the Welsh, Stage 1*?) and decreed that Wales 'never be separated from the crown, but should remain entirely to the kings of England for ever'. (Nine thousand of Edward's 15,000-strong force came from South Wales.)

So was that the end of Wales? Not a bit of it. For the next hundred years, parts of it were united by people proclaiming themselves overlord of Wales. Then came Glyn Dwr. Owain Glyn Dwr. In 1400, a regional dispute got out of hand and this borders gentryman proclaimed himself prince of Wales. By 1404, with a court in Harlech and Parliament down the road, Wales was at its height. The English were on the run. The fightback was escalating. Welsh students in Oxford were abandoning their studies to fight. It was all looking hot for Wales. For a bit. But it was fading by 1406, with Harlech falling after a siege in 1409 and Glyn Dwr literally disappearing from view after 1412. (He was only really deified as a national figurehead from the nineteenth century onwards.)

After Glyn Dwr, hopes rose when the Welsh Henry Tudor came to the English throne in 1485. But the Tudors proved to be the sort of Welshies who really prefer being in England and speaking English (a bit like Sir Harry Secombe, only more ruthless), and when Henry VIII passed the Act of Union of 1536, the Welsh ruling class became virtually indistinguishable from the English.

So when was Wales? This was the question posed by the late Gwyn A. Williams ('the rememberancer of Wales') in his book *When Was Wales?*. One of the most erudite, rational and learned advocates of Welsh nationalism, he said that Wales has never been a nation. (He thought it could be and should be; he wasn't pushing the concept of being a nationalist quite that far.) Excepting, perhaps, Glyn Dwr's 15 minutes of fame: 'Owain Glyn Dwr was the first, indeed the *only* Welsh prince to command wide popular and spontaneous support from every corner of Wales.' The revolt was 'a lightning-flash vision of a people that was free'.

OWAIN GLYN DWR: SITTING ON THE THRONE.
MEPL

So, imagine a lightning flash. Six hundred years ago. You could have gone on a reasonably long holiday and missed the whole thing. Unless, of course, you were holidaying in Wales. Which you should: it's cool.

nature of other flags into stark relief: it's got a bloody great dragon on. If we do need flags, they should surely all feature deranged creatures of fantasy. For the new Union Jack, we propose a giant ladybird with tusks, or Buffy.

The *Mabinogion*, the collection of ancient Welsh folk tales that's among the most treasured repositories of literary Welshness, claims that this very Welsh dragon lies slumbering under a hill outside Beddgelert – a small slate and stone tourist town surrounded by brooding peaks – along with a white dragon embodying Wales's eternal foes. (No, not the Zulus, the Saxons.) The town's Tourist Information sold maps of Wales illustrating where the various tales supposedly took place. Oddly enough, the book was written by English writer Lady Charlotte Guest, a nineteenth-century aristo who fell out of love with her Welsh industrialist husband and, in bizarre consolation, fell right in love with Wales. (Many of the tales are classics of world mythology and have been traced to as far away as India – still, it's a Welsh classic.)

When we asked in the Tourist Information shop for directions to the hill where the dragons are, a passing cleaner nodded at her better-paid colleagues behind the desk and muttered: 'The only dragons around here are behind that desk.'

Or are they? Apparently, legendary King Llud found his kingdom harried by the monstrous cries and screams of a ferocious melee between two dragons and did what anyone would do when faced with fighting dragons: he got them pissed. This he achieved by digging a large pit in the middle of Britain, filling the hole with mead and covering the mead lake with cloth. The dragons didn't know what was going on! They fell in, supped up and fell asleep to be dragged over and imprisoned inside this hill for what must now feel like eternity. (You're probably thinking: 'Where could he have got that much mead from?' But this was the olden days.) This tale probably pre-dates the Saxon invasions but, cometh the hour, the two fiery foes symbolised the Briton/Saxon face-off perfectly.

Before the dragons, all visitors to Beddgelert must check out the grave of Llewellyn's dog. The signs take us out of the village, along the banks of the river and finally across a field to a tree under which sits a small pile of stones and an engraved sign. The story sees the great prince hunting without his faithful hound Gelert. On returning, he finds the hound stained in blood and his son's cot empty. Believing his supposedly loyal hound has killed his son and heir, he slays him with his sword. Only then does he hear his son's cry, finding him next to a wolf slain by the good, and now sadly dead, dog. Llewelyn never smiled again, which must definitely have had an impact on the ongoing father–son relationship. The lesson here is plain: don't kill your dog unless you're absolutely sure that it has killed your son.

Happily, this story is not a true story. Probably also Asian in origin, it was nabbed for the area by an enterprising manager of Beddgelert's Royal Goat Hotel in the nineteenth century to get the murky locale on to the tourist trail. On this bustling if overcast weekday in August, it certainly seemed to have done the trick. It's a strange feeling, standing at a grave, a small clump of stones under a lone tree in the middle of a field surrounded by bleak brooding peaks, paying homage to a dead dog that was never alive in the first place. Still, keeps us out of trouble, eh?

After snacking on Welsh teacakes, it was time to meet the dragons. Driving a mile north towards Snowdon, we pulled over by a precipitous dome of tree and rock surrounded by much greater peaks. There it was: Dinas Emrys. This was a site rich with myth, figures like Briton King Vortigern, who first enticed the Saxons over to work as mercenaries (which turned out rather like the Stones employing Hell's Angels for security at Altamont) and the wizard Merlin. It was Merlin who told Vortigern of the dragons below, their presence explaining why every time he built up his castle walls, they crumbled ('Who've you had in? Some joker's put dragons in down there . . .'). He also predicted that, after a long period of adversity, the red dragon would ultimately overcome the white invader. Let's hope he wasn't lying, for Wales's sake.*

Climbing over a wall into the farmer's field to get a better view, our first thought was: if you're going to concoct a myth involving dragons slumbering in a mountain in Snowdonia, surely you'd choose not a medium-sized hillock, but one of the adjacent brooding slate behemoths? Unless of course there really are dragons in there.

Still, it did finally feel like we were closing in on the heart of

---

* Big on Merlin, the Welsh. Owain Glyn Dwr wrote Merlin's prophecies into his diplomatic correspondence and peace treaties. The French responded: 'You know that guy trying to stitch up the English? Well, he's mental.'

'SNOWDON FROM LLYN NANTLLE' BY RICHARD WILSON, MAJOR INFLUENCE ON TURNER.
BUT IS THIS REAL WALES? IS IT *REALLY*?
The Bridgeman Art Library

the Welsh nation. Okay, so there was no one else about. No line of Welsh pilgrims patiently snaking down the road to pay homage. Just a small flock of sheep hanging out on the sloping field at the bottom. The more we examined Dinas Emrys, the clearer it became that if only the English and Welsh dragons could put aside their differences, then everything would be okay again.

Imagine having two dragons at your disposal. That's strong.

We drove north towards the coast, hoping to answer the question: how Welsh is the Welsh dragon? Some believe it was originally Roman, a griffin on the standard of a legion head-quartered here – making the red dragon a symbol of another occupying force, albeit one that had definitely left. Or had it? It was time to head to the garrison port of Abergele to find out.

We joined the A498 passing under the shadow of Snowdon, down to Betws-y-Coed and on towards the coast. It was stunning. Awesome. Mountainous. Brilliant. Although we didn't get out of the car for fear of all the mud and death infecting our Little Englander body politic. No one wants that. Plus we didn't have time.

Our guru Niall Griffiths says of this landscape: 'Superficially, it resembles the Lake District, but where that has been widely gentrified and prettified and twee'd down towards the tourist quid, this place stays filled with that brooding wildness which tends to characterise lives lived in the shadows of colossal waves of rock.' (Of course, Wales has never fallen for the 'tourist quid'. Could you even imagine a world where people went on holiday to Wales?)

Just before we leave real Wales, as we wait at a STOP sign, a truck roars past in the direction of Snowdon. The word CYMRU is stuck in individual letters above the windscreen. There are two big dragon stickers on the front bodywork. Behind the driver inside the cab hangs a huge Welsh flag.

He likes Wales, we think.

Abergele. Being in this part of the world offered us a golden opportunity to dabble in a spot of science. Many of the core ideas of Welsh culture are to do with ancestry: speaking the oldest language, having the oldest flag, being the last true Britons undiluted by Anglo-Saxon blood. That's the general idea. It's the land of our fathers, or rather their fathers. Modern Welsh nationalism is clearly not all about racial purity (Plaid Cymru preaching a form of inclusive civic nationalism), but Welshness is not *not* about that either. ('Land of my Fathers' hails 'This pure, dear land'.) And it's part of lots of other mixed-up ideas about other identities, too: the supposed Anglo-Saxon Englishman, the Vikings still holed up on some of Scotland's remotest northern islands.

But dig below the surface – or rather, take a swab from someone's cheek off to a laboratory – and the picture becomes more complex. In Abergele, a resort in Colwyn Bay, DNA tests found the population to have a high proportion of African DNA: genetic marker e3b (found at its highest concentrations in North Africa at 75 per cent but in northern Europe generally at less than 5 per cent) was found to average at 38.97 per cent in male Y chromosomes in Abergele. This dates from the town's role as a Roman trading centre (most Romans in Britain came from the Middle East, North Africa and Eastern Europe). But would we be able to tell the difference?

We had pledged that, while researching this book, we would

never reduce ourselves to driving round in a car, staring at people out of the window and making wild generalisations. But we were pushed for time in Abergele (we had a date to keep in Llandudno, as you do), and how else can you get a sense of someone's DNA? It's a bloody stupid thing to do, whichever way you slice it. So we drove round in a car, staring at people out of the window. From this exhaustive research process we concluded that the people of Abergele looked pretty 'Welsh'. More Welsh than African, on the whole.

So the people of Abergele have different DNA, but are ostensibly exactly the same as all the other Welsh people we had seen. For this reason, DNA as a determinant of nationhood is, it's fair to say, not wholly reliable. Still, it's kind of great to know that, in this land of our fathers, with its occasional rather wearying obsession with ancient bloodlines, at least some of those fathers' fathers' fathers' fathers' fathers' fathers' fathers' fathers' fathers' fathers' fathers' fathers were black.

Abergele had more to tell us. It was the site of a moment that had the potential to really shock the nation. In 1969, two members of Mudiad Amddiffyn Cymru (the Welsh Defence Movement) apparently planned to plant a bomb under the train carrying Prince Charles to his investiture in Caernarfon. Charles's investiture was a politically charged event, coming against the background of parts of the Welsh countryside being flooded to create reservoirs (to supply cities like Niall Griffiths's native Liverpool).

Welsh activists were put under constant surveillance, and the secret services were accused of intimidation. When the bomb accidentally went off, the pair were killed. The families of the Abergele Martyrs (as they became known) said the men had not intended to kill anyone (innocent train-drivers, say, or passers-by). But not intending to kill people is definitely better achieved by planting no bombs under trains, rather than some bombs under trains.

We went to Abergele train station, on the coast by the beach, the very spot where Prince Charles might have been sent skyward. Well, more or less: they don't put up blue plaques for this sort of thing. We looked up and down the railway tracks. It was good to see a wind farm churning round out to sea, generating clean power. Prince Charles would, at least, approve of this development, we thought, in stark contrast to, you know, the other business.

Violent struggle to achieve Welsh independence has obviously been very much the cause of a small minority. But Welsh independence generally has always been a minority cause, too. As Gwyn Williams says: 'Since 1410 most Welsh people most of the time have abandoned any idea of independence as unthinkable.'

So, painting Wales as some kind of nation in chains – a Tibet with tenors – is possibly a stretch. The soul of Welsh Wales is in the west and north. All the actual Welsh people are in the south. There is no major road from North to South Wales. There is no train. This is not so much an English conspiracy to keep the nation split as just neither side being all that bothered. (And there's all the mountains.)

THE VERY TRACKS ON WHICH PRINCE CHARLES WASN'T BLOWN UP.

But what about 'the English'? In his book about English attitudes to Wales, *Neighbours from Hell?*, Wales-loving writer Mike Parker (who is actually from the West Midlands, the ones in the middle of England) gives the game away somewhat when he talks of Victorian propaganda against 'the Welsh' as 'anti-working-class' and directed against anything that was not 'middle-class England'. Yes, 'the English' oppressed and exploited the Welsh, but they oppressed and exploited the English too. And you know what? The Welsh oppressed and exploited the Welsh. There was a lot of it about.

Thinking about the last few days, we became vexed. We had sampled it all: dragons, dead dogs, teacakes, bombing campaigns. We like Wales as much as anyone . . . okay, not as much as anyone; we weren't going to join those other English writers who dedicate themselves to writing about how great Wales is and how Welsh it makes them feel. But we liked the thing it's got going on. Nonetheless, we were slightly puzzled by Welshness: its sacred texts, its rituals, its martyrs, the veneration of ancients, the driving sense that, if only Wales could be fully Welsh, then everything would be okay. You have to ask: is this a culture, or a cult?

If Snowdonia is real Wales, we must have ended our trip in unreal Wales: the altogether less tricky, less wild, less mountainous, less misty nineteenth-century coastal resort of Llandudno. More docile than desolate, and momentously sunny on our visit, it's kind of like Eastbourne, but surrounded by mountains in North Wales.

This was once a rather grand resort, attracting the likes of Napoleon III and exiled Romanian princesses. Today, women dressed as sequinned Vegas showgirls were walking along the pier handing out flyers. Some spectacularly aggressive local seagulls were eyeing up holidaymakers' food lasciviously.

Suitably armed with a 99 each, we took our places in a 50-odd-strong throng at the entrance to Llandudno Pier, to enjoy Britain's longest-running Punch and Judy show, Professor Codman's. An Italian street puppet tradition imported in the 1600s, Punch and Judy has been part of the British seaside experience since the nineteenth century, and four generations of Codmans have run this show since the 1860s.

Neither of us had seen a Punch and Judy show since childhood and the details were hazy. We were in for a treat. By the end, though, we were in a state of advanced shock. That Mr Punch? He's a menace. First he's beating his wife. Then he's knocking the baby about. He's a fucking liability. He can't even say 'sausages' properly. He hits his wife again (with a stick!), throws the baby down the stairs, then chins some crocodile who's nicked his (mispronounced) sausages. Fuck knows where the crocodile came from, or why it likes sausages. Next up, he's twatted some copper and tricked the hangman into hanging himself. He even gives the devil a slap. What a cunt.

It's all a bit of fun, though, and the whole audience – child and adult; Welsh, English, even a French chap – is laughing, no one being noticeably traumatised by all the diabolism and slaughter of innocents. And perhaps this is the message: are we really so different that we can't all enjoy a big-nosed puppet smacking his wife around?

Afterwards we spoke to puppeteer Jason Codman-Miliband. Jason, who recently took up the reins from his sick father after jacking in a 'very corporate' job in England, summed up the appeal of Punch: 'It's a straightforward storyline; it's daft. There's no political correctness. I have heard of a PC Punch and Judy show that's toned everything down, but you never see any glowing reviews for it, if you get me . . . Kids can tell the difference between a puppet show and reality. And this isn't the worst by a long shot – I've seen some where the dead body won't fit in the coffin and the kids are shouting "Cut his legs off!"'

Cut his legs off indeed.

In a newsagent's, we spotted the King of the Eisteddfod on the front of the *Western Mail* – our good friend the bloke from our row. He was wearing his crown and beaming. That's our boy. The article revealed him to be Tudur Dylan Jones, a teacher from Llanelli who had won the Eisteddfod Crown for writing a poem on the given topic of 'Copaon' – 'summits' or 'peaks'. (Proper Welsh subject-matter, that.) We can't say we weren't a little disappointed to have our reverie punctured by facts. Perhaps it would have been better never to know; there's just so little mystique in modern life.

We headed back to Crewe. We were homeward bound. Oddly enough, Crewe station was where a homesick Paul Simon wrote 'Homeward Bound' during a solo tour of northern folk clubs in 1964. Or it might not have been. The historical truth of the matter is actually disputed. It might have been Widnes. Does it matter? It was a long time ago.

NINE

'NOW THAT MAY SOUND BRUTAL, LADIES AND GENTLEMEN, BUT IT DID IN FACT HAPPEN ON MORE THAN ONE OCCASION'

A CASTLE
A 'MEDIEVAL WEEKEND'
TIPS ON WAR

SO SAID THE self-styled 'wench' compering a re-enacted Wars of the Roses knockabout in front of Herstmonceux Castle, Sussex, as the ten-year-old son of a Lancastrian noble was dragged across the brick-built bridge over the moat to witness the execution of his defeated father.

For a second, it seemed like the radio-mic'ed 'wench', a sort of medieval Holly Willoughby prowling a large gravel area in front of the redbrick castle, was offering her profound summary of the historical experience generally. She probably wasn't, though. And anyway, this is what everyone had come for: the chance to kick back with a roasted hog bloomer and watch big chaps in funny costumes punching each other up the bracket.

We had arrived at the Medieval English Festival ('England's largest'), taking place on a sunny August Bank Holiday weekend, just in time for the main event from a violence perspective: Yorkists trying to seize the castle from the Lancastrians with a spot of full war. This was the Wars of the Roses – the epic in-house punch-up of the aristos that closed the Middle Ages (our battle was supposed to have taken place in 1470) – brought to

WAR! OF THE ROSES!

life before our actual eyes, incorporating scale replica trebuchet siege engines poised to launch huge wooden balls all over the shop, armour, shouting, and a spot of manly man-to-man combat with huge man-swords. Occasionally, the gunners would come forward to let off an almighty crack (apparently, these early firearms were so unpredictable the gunners would regularly get their faces blown off . . . it never pays to be an early adopter).

The War of the Cousins (not called the Wars of the Roses until later – after the red Lancastrian rose and the Yorkist white one) ended after a mere 32 years in 1487 with victory for Henry Tudor, at which point the Middle Ages ended and the credits rolled. Henry Tudor was crowned Henry VII. Within 25 years Jonathan Rhys-Meyers would be on the throne, and so began what historians call the modern age (no, it wasn't really that modern . . . but that's historians for you).

We'd arrived separately, and found ourselves on opposite sides of the battleground as the warring began. When the 'wench' compere (wenchpere?) urged the two sides of the crowd to cheer for either the Lancastrians or the Yorkists, text messages ensued: 'York's going home in a fucking ambulance'; 'Lancs no chance, m8'. People were really getting into the spirit. A small child yelled: 'Smash his head in!'

When the Middle Ages *started* is debatable: it's either 1066, when the Normans turned up, or c.500, when the Romans left. But what's 566 years between friends? You could lose that down the back of the sofa. The issue was probably not giving this event's organisers restless nights. Here, 'medieval' was defined as just, like, olden days; you know, knights and shit. Rarefied academic debate was not on the menu; hog was. Which, actually, was just fine by us. At the main gate, a colourful tent acted as a ticket hall. 'Who be nexteth?' asked the dressed-up cashiers, before swiping your debit card.

After the carnage, we checked out the shopping opportunities, at the open-air mall of a hundred or so tents around the roped-off falconry arena hawking medieval paraphernalia: snoods, pointy shoes, some spare parts for your armour . . . Celtic leather armbands . . . heraldic tabards . . . wizard stuff (that's as in items of interest to wizards, not as in retro-speak for 'really good') – it was a historical phantasmagoria (or an ahistorical phantasmagoria).

Inside the Robin Hood's Craft Cave tent, the Everest

Windows stall ('fit the best') was staffed by two monks and a Maid Marion, handing out leaflets for a never-to-be-repeated offer on ye olde uPVC replacement windows.

There was even a medieval-themed Mouse Town, which pleased Steve particularly, as he is a great lover of Mouse Towns.

All around the Herstmonceux estate, which rolls down a green hill to the redbrick and

ARMOUR. FOR SALE.

green-sandstone castle, sitting in a huge lake-like moat, and then back up the other side, there were medieval activities: falconry, archery, burger vans . . . Herstmonceux is an ideal place to have a historical festival that's a bit sketchy about history – not being a real castle. It was actually Britain's first brick-built mansion, constructed in 1441 by Sir Roger Fiennes, treasurer to Henry VI, as a showboating exercise (launch a serious attack on this gaff and it would fall to bits . . . Edward I would probably call it 'a pussy's castle' and storm it on his own, just to make a point).

Out the back of the castle, the Living History Camp was peopled by re-enactors, living in tents and endlessly roasting meat. Some of them did a spot of old-school woodwork; another spun yarn. We chatted to one pretend soldier who bemoaned the lack of proper jousting at the event. 'It's just impossible to get the insurance,' he said.

As we walked off, we overheard another soldier informing some punters all about medieval fighting techniques: 'It's one thing to kill a man,' he revealed, 'but if you can turn a horse mad . . .'

We kept walking. There was no way that whatever came next could possibly measure up to that introduction – no way on this earth – so we got while the going was good.

The Living History people were too clean for our liking. Where were the purple Black Death blisters popping all over their retching, wretched bodies? Why weren't they falling-down drunk, knifing each other in the back over a bit of bread? Presumably they would say it was a family day out and so hardly appropriate. But that's the trouble with people these days: they've been sanitised against mortal screams of agony and the stench of death. People just do not want to smell the stench of death. They are weak.

On the other hand, though, people on this isle have been reliving their own versions of the Middle Ages since . . . actually, the Middle Ages. People think of the Victorians as kicking off medieval kitsch, but in the fourteenth century Edward I's grandson Edward III hoped the legend of King Arthur might provide England with some national glue and had a huge round building constructed within Windsor Castle to contain a Round Table for a new order of 300 knights, who could live by the chivalric code of days of yore that never actually existed. 'We shall be like knights of old!' 'But aren't *we* knights of old?' 'No, I'm talking about the real olden days, when *magic* filled the air.' 'But . . . we all still believe in magic, don't we?' (He eventually ditched the whole Arthur thing as unworkable – you'd never get enough seating – and instead opted for another, even less likely national hero, a third-century Christian martyr from Turkey called George.)

Seven hundred years on, British tastes still veer towards the medieval. Coats of arms, pubs, suburban houses, Parliament – all somehow best at their most faux-medieval. This is despite medieval Britain being, to put it kindly, rubbish. Not some rompy Eden with Barbara Windsor serving nut-brown ales to Robert Plant, but a grim, dysfunctional backwater whose leaders were generally too obsessed with fruitlessly knocking lumps out of each other to particularly notice the civilisation taking root elsewhere. (The biggest battle to ever take place on English soil, the Wars of the Roses battle at Towton in 1461, killed off 50–60,000 soldiers in one go – 1 per cent of the entire English population. Now *that's* a battle.)

So, in a way, aren't we all medieval weekenders, out for our feudal fix without necessarily having to deal with all the attendant blood and shit? Obviously, some of us are more medieval weekenders than others. The ones dressed up in all the armour, for instance.

Things were a bit more authentic and earthy over at the kiddies' sword-fighting workshop. Here, at last, was a scene of abject chaos. Hollering children were running round and round and round in circles, bashing anyone and everything up with swords. This should surprise no one. However, it did seem to surprise the man running the sword-fighting workshop, who had presumably assumed that 20 small maniacs hopped up on candyfloss would sit attentively as he kindly passed on some worldly sword-fighting expertise. 'Will you PAY ATTENTION!' he yelled, batting a four-year-old around the head with a foam sword (he wasn't joking, either). 'If you don't LISTEN, you won't know what to do . . .'

According to the programme, this man had been James Bond's fencing double in *Die Another Day* (bet he doesn't like to talk about it). So he really shouldn't have had to take this kind of crap.

As we strolled away from this miniature Bosworth Field, we overheard a re-enactor announcing to a little boy, as his company marched past towards a bit of mock carnage: 'If you want to see some blood, son, follow us . . .'

Days like this really are for the little ones.

TEN

A DIANA MOMENT

BARRIERS

FEELINGS

SHE VOWED TO US HER COUNTRY

THE DIANA MEMORIAL service didn't lack for build-up. The papers were full of who was invited and not invited. That is, Camilla. Would Camilla come to the service in the Guards Chapel at London's Wellington Barracks? Should she come? Would it be better for her to be invited, but not come? Or should she come even though she wasn't invited, but just thought she had been? Maybe she should come at the start, but leave before the hymns? These were the questions that vexed the nation, via its third eye, the media.

There was also the televised concert in Hyde Park on what would have been Diana's birthday. Channel 4 stoked the flames with a hard-hitting documentary alleging she turned tricks for crack; some attention-seeking mad crap like that, anyway. And there was the drip-drip of news about the inquest that was due to begin its festival of the insane in October.

One thing was clear: on the day, the public would turn out. Our Queen was dead. Not our real Queen, she was still going. But our Queen of Hearts, the figurehead who showed us how to feel. She was lovely and wondrous and caring and fun. And hadn't she healed Africa and ended all those wars? It was now the tenth anniversary of her death: emotions would be running high.

Or maybe not. Coming up from St James's Park Tube on to the narrow Westminster thoroughfare Petty France, we could see no weeping, no flower mountain. No sense of mass hysteria whatsoever. Just

OUR LADY.
Corbis

a small trickle of figures entering the Wellington Barracks before a thin line of photographers. After seeing Elton and

David Furnish walking in (walking!), we headed to the front of the barracks, on to Birdcage Walk.*

Inside the park, a massive line of outside broadcast vans was parked next to the lake, showing that at least the worldwide media knew what was important. But compared to the massed ranks of 1997, this was a virtual no-show. Closed off for the day, with crowd barriers lining its entire length, this section of the park could have comfortably accommodated hundreds of thousands. But there were probably a thousand at most. Maybe fewer. And half of those seemed to be journalists and camera crew. Or tourists.

BIRDCAGE WALK: THE EXPECTANT, GRIEVING CROWDS.

On the news, the cameras would resolutely refuse to pan down the unmanned crash barriers, at crowds who were not there. ITV called the crowd 'significant' (as in 'large', not 'significantly small'). A nation was mourning again, after all, and to contradict that evident truth with mere facts would be a grotesque dereliction of duty.

Rounding the corner towards Buckingham Palace, a thin crowd, about two deep, manned the barriers, with a few more clambering on to the Victoria Memorial, waiting patiently to see the monarch go past. As we arrived, an argument was breaking out.

'It's insane – she was a serial adulterer,' said a grey-haired man to a group of women.

'We've got a right to be here,' one responded, her teenage daughter looking mortified at her mother's involvement with our new friend.

---

* Named after James I's nearby Royal Menagerie and Aviary, Birdcage Walk was once reserved for the exclusive use of the royal family and the Hereditary Grand Falconer. *Hereditary* Grand Falconer? What a world. If the film *Kes* teaches us anything, it's that jobs like these need to be decided on merit.

'I know you have, but I'm just here to tell you that you're wrong,' explained Martin Gwynne, the whippet-thin man in the black corduroy blazer. 'She was an adulteress, who committed adultery.'

The women had come for a parade, quite literally, and Martin was raining on it.

Just then an elderly man in a white suit, without a hair on his head, walked past holding a candle and a bouquet, with a rectangular sign around his neck. The sign bore pictures of the princess cut out from magazines, and handwritten keywords like 'Diana' and 'Shalom'.

'We're not insane . . . *that*'s insane,' muttered the daughter.

Martin believed this whole event was grossly immoral. 'It's an exhibition of unbelievable bad taste. Diana did nothing but cheat and lie, and then go round parading her good works: this is the morality that Britain has come to.'

Then a car went past. 'The Queen!' said one of Martin's victims. 'I saw the Queen!' In passing, someone else revealed that they were actually only here to catch a glimpse of Wayne Sleep. And why not? He was in *Cats*, after all.

Back on Birdcage Walk, the man in the white suit was posing for tabloid photographers, crouching on the pavement behind his bouquet and candle. 'Harmless nutter, but it's a picture . . .' said an *Express* photographer.

We idly chatted with this seasoned royal snapper, and he educated us in some relevant paparazzi slang. Kensington Palace is called KP. You know, like the nuts. There were some nuts hanging about outside KP today, he said, but not many.

Inside the Guards Chapel, the great and the good were belting out 'I Vow to Thee My Country', Diana's favourite hymn. This is a hymn so patriotic that, one verse having already been excised after the First World War for being too nationalistic and warlike, the Bishop of Hulme called in 2004 for the first of the remaining two verses to be removed, labelling it 'totally heretical'. He said it placed national loyalties above religious ones, and encouraged racism and an unquestioning support of governments. That's a pretty patriotic hymn, that is. Do you have a favourite hymn?

Many great people were squeezed into that chapel – Gordon Brown, Viscount Linley, Cliff . . . they were all there – and were now ringing out 'I Vow to Thee My Country's lines about Britain being 'entire and whole and perfect' and 'the love [of

God and country] that makes undaunted the final sacrifice'. Crivens.

Even Tony Blair. Blair? Him again? He was yesterday's chip wrappers by now – having finally had the decency to be forced out of office, his fingernail marks still visible on the Number 10 door frame. A footnote to Thatcherism, who also, incidentally, caused calamity in the Middle East. The kaleidoscope had been in flux. Then he'd dropped the kaleidoscope and broken the kaleidoscope and the kaleidoscope was now fucked.

Nineteen ninety-seven: that was his pomp. Had it really been ten years? A whole decade since He had come and She had gone? Well, yes it had.

For this new anniversary, *Guardian* columnist Jonathan Freedland challenged the idea that Diana '97 was a moment of collective insanity: in letting our guard down and creating a moment of communal tenderness, 'we' had 'nothing to be ashamed of'. At Kensington Gardens the night before the funeral, he recalled 'clusters of people sitting on the grass, chatting in a low murmur. Pictures hung from trees, flowers were everywhere, and the whole place was lit with 1,000 candles. A London park had become an outdoor cathedral, its congregation led by no one but themselves.' This moment remained among his 'most cherished London memories'. Okay, so it definitely didn't make you want to throw up, then?

Of course, Diana had been at the centre of public celebration even before that, with the 1981 Royal Wedding when the British public turned its back on economic turmoil and the streets at boiling point with a big pageant of flicky hairdos and street parties (the parties were usually held on different streets to the ones at boiling point).

Now the public appeared to have moved on. We were right in the middle of the mania surrounding the disappearance of three-year-old Madeleine McCann. Maybe the public was all used up being brought together by a different morbid spectacle. Maybe Freedland will claim that applying what we've learnt from watching *CSI* to a handful of facts and a bucketful of conjecture about the tragic disappearance of a child was good for us too.

In the media reports to come, the take on this memorial service would be that the wound in the royal family's prestige had healed; a line had been drawn under all the hysteria. This was a private event for the boys, albeit one with the world's media

THE QUEEN.
The Kobal Collection

invited. The Bishop of London's service caught the conciliatory mood: 'It's time to deify Diana as someone terribly, terribly nice who gave the unwell a lift – without at the same time thinking the Queen's a bitch. We've all seen Helen Mirren in *The Queen*, that bit with the stag where she's crying because she knows that she, like the stag, is a noble animal, hunted and haunted, just as Diana was, and she weeps for them both, for us all, weeping. So the Queen's human too. You've seen it with your own eyes. In that film. See Queen, think Mirren. Pretty soon you'll be looking at the Queen and thinking she looks pretty fit for her age. Perhaps, one day, white-van man will turn unto white-van man and say: "I'd do her."'

The white-suited man on Birdcage Walk was, it transpired, probably a Holocaust survivor from Austria – his strong accent made everything fairly unclear. He showed us his board, repeating the words: 'Shalom . . . Europe . . . Paris/London . . . The Rose of England . . .'

Then he handed over a candle from his stash, a symbol of her warm heart, and some photocopied press cuttings from Germany, grainy copies cut out with his own shaky hand.

He pointed to the word 'myth' and said: 'Myth.'

Then he looked up and asked: 'You see?'

Not really, to be honest.

BRITAIN'S SILLIEST TITLES

SILVER STICK IN WAITING: Were you to attack the person of the monarch, you would get hit with a silver stick and/or a gold stick, depending on what day it came in the very complicated job-share arrangement between the Gold Stick in Waiting and the Silver Stick in Waiting. Would you take notice of the precious metals being deployed, or just the fact that you were being beaten with sticks? The British aristocracy: the best aristocracy in the world.

ORDER OF THE GARTER: Not as saucy as it might be. Title held by John Major, so definitely not that saucy. Garters, though, isn't it? Eh? Not 'alf.

DEFENDER OF THE FAITH: A title still held by the monarch that was given to Henry VIII by the Pope for defending the Catholic church in England. Not renounced when Henry started destroying the Catholic church in England. Destroyer of the Faith? Weren't they on the cover of *Kerrang!*?

BLACK ROD: DO NOT put this formulation of words into Google.

COMMANDER OF THE BRITISH EMPIRE: Hard to imagine, but Simon Cowell CBE is actually in charge of our empire. Good job it's only South Georgia and Gibraltar or we'd all be fucked.

HIGH SHERIFF OF THE ISLE OF WIGHT: On this island, Alan Titchmarsh is the Law. So watch out.

TITCHMARSH: THE SHERIFF.
Rex Features

ORDER OF THE BATH: Not the bloke who holds up a towel for Prince Charles when he gets out of the bath. Someone else. The title was formerly the Most Honourable Military Order of the Bath, back during the ill-fated Georgian experiments in bath warfare. Crazy, wet, brutal days.

THE ROYAL SWAN MARKER: Marks the Queen's swans. Isn't that obvious?

MASTER OF THE QUEEN'S MUSIC: Keeps her CDs in alphabetical order. The position is currently held by Brian May.

MASTER OF THE GREAT WARDROBE: Anyone thinking the wardrobe in question isn't that great, think again. It is great. British wardrobes: best in the world.

ELEVEN

YOU'D BETTER BLOODY SAVE THAT QUEEN, GOD

THE LAST NIGHT OF THE PROMS
DICK & DOM
GAUL-BAITING VICTORY ODES

LET'S BE CLEAR about this. In the normal course of things, we don't tend to find ourselves down the Last Night of the Proms. Not lately, anyway. The Proms are all right . . . Mahler, that Venezualan guy, biggest classical music festival in the world; all of that. Last Night of the Proms: good God, no – have you *seen* those bastards? Waving their flags, bending their knees to bob up and down in unison. Man alive. But we wanted flags, passion, the nation coming together to give it the big 'we are'. So needs must. You can't write a book about Britishness and not go to the flag-waving totem of British triumphalism. Sadly.

We decided not to hit the Albert Hall – have you *seen* those bastards? Man alive. But we could handle the Proms in the Park in nearby Hyde Park. Less High Tory, more plain old Middle Britain. And much cheaper.

It was early evening as we strolled across the park to collect our tickets, and overcast – not the Indian summer we'd been promised. Everywhere people were turning up with sophisticated kit: rolled-up ground mats, flags (not a surprise, that one), bowler hats, wine boxes . . . Outside Stalag Proms, the high-walled temporary arena, a handful of people were pitching tents. This must be the equivalent of the Green Fields at Glastonbury, we thought. They're probably going to do some shrooms and fuck in the open air like rabbits. (Camping outside something that's on the telly, to watch a screen behind a makeshift wall from the comfort of one of those camping chairs with a drinks holder in the arm: that's a bit weird, we thought.)

Beside the ticket booth, we overheard one steward telling another about a woman who had just been duped into buying someone else's receipt off them for £23, thinking it was a ticket. She'd had to buy another one: 'I assured her it's worth every penny. Because it is,' said the steward. (So you can put a price on patriotism, and it's 46 quid.)

The place was buzzing, in a polite sort of a way. But then, a blow. We'd planned to sample the pre-Proms entertainment – CBBC favourites Dick & Dom compering the Tony Hadley Big Band and identical twin opera singers RyanDan – before retiring to a series of pubs, having devised an educational Britishness pub crawl taking in the Churchill Arms, the Prince of Wales and the Britannia, to fully anaesthetise ourselves before the Big Push. (We also planned a saunter through M&S on Kensington High Street, to really get us in the mood.)

But the stewards told us: once inside, you can never leave. (Well, not until the end.) No readmittance. If we went inside, we would be stuck in there for many hours. And that wasn't going to happen. So, for us, it was not Chico time. Bloody but unbowed, and with a newfound feeling of joy, we went to the pub(s), keeping up the patriotic vibe by ordering pints of Bombardier and Seafarer.

It was dark by nine, and time to head back to the Proms. We passed the Royal Albert Hall and Kensington Palace, heading for the giant corrugated-iron pen at the other side of Hyde Park. We girded ourselves. Entering the main arena, we passed from semi-darkness into bright light and were suddenly hit by a tidal wave of noise and colour. There were 40,000 people in Hyde Park alone. That's a lot of people. And a lot of flags: Union Jacks, Welsh dragons, lions rampant.

So we had come into a pen to rejoice for our country while people did the same in other pens in Middlesbrough, Swansea, Belfast and Glasgow. Britain together (with Northern Ireland, which is not Britain). Here we were: all rejoicing! In pens!

Before we knew it, we were right into some *Pomp and Circumstance*, as we began working our way down the front, along the side via the ample toilet facilities and chip vans. Revisionists claim that Elgar was aghast at his work being used for patriotic tub-thumping. Mind you, when challenged about all the tub-thumping, he replied: 'England for the English is all I say – hands off! There's nothing apologetic about me.' So maybe he didn't mind it too much.

ELGAR: 'TACHE, MUSIC.
Corbis

For the 'Land of Hope and Glory' climax, everyone started singing along. The *Telegraph* had recently sprung to the defence of this anthem, and of its flag-waving enthusiasts: 'The Union Jack is no longer seen as a symbol of the far Right, *Our Island Story* is now making a comeback, people want to sing "Land of Hope and Glory". This is not about jingoism. It is to do with being confident about who you are.'

Who we are, on this definition, is world-conquering imperialists: 'The blood a hero sire hath spent/ Still nerves a hero son.' Yes, your fathers spilled blood bravely taking over half the world, but don't just sit back and rest on their achievements: take more bloody land! (Implicitly, African land.) Spill more blood for the gloriously bigger Empire! And be confident while doing so.

By now, the flags were all waving wildly. Man, we had never seen so many Union Jacks. The crowd was waving flags while looking up at a massive videolink screen of people in a hall the other side of the park waving more flags.

There were St George's Crosses, Saltires and more. On the screen from the Albert Hall you could even see a Norwegian flag draped over the front of one of the boxes. Norway? There's always one, isn't there?

Mostly, though, it was all about the Union Jack. This was some flag: the invention of King James I/King James VI of Scotland after the Union of Crowns in 1603 and his accession to the English throne. James believed in Britain. He wanted to call himself the King of Great Britain, but the English wouldn't have it. The Scots, meanwhile, didn't like his flag, thinking their blue Saltire was obscured by the brighter

PEOPLE WITH FLAGS, SINGING LIKE BILLY-O.

red St George's Cross. Scots later built the Empire, as we know. But did they also invent Britain? Would that be a good thing in their eyes, or would it piss them off?*

---

* The St George cross, by the way, was probably imported from Genoa, being licensed by the English Navy in 1190 to gain protection in the Mediterranean from the vast Genoese fleet. So it might actually symbolise Genoa ruling the waves.

Next: a *Fantasia on British Sea Songs*. This would culminate in 'Rule Britannia', but in the meantime dawdled down some frankly unpatriotic byways (blame the Czech conductor): 'Born to be King' . . . blah blah . . . choirs . . . 'Danny Boy'. Forty thousand people waving national flags during 'Danny Boy': now that's just weird.

But here she comes: 'Rule Britannia', a 1740 missive from the heart of the 'second Hundred Years War' with the French (a single Hundred Years War just not being enough). Come on, everyone: ' Britons never never never shall be slaves.' Slaves? Never. Slave-traders? Of course!

Oddly enough, it's all connected: Britain ended up not being enslaved by 'French tyranny' partly thanks to the national coffers being filled with slave-trade booty. Still, no matter: we rule!

In a post-Britannia lull, we found ourselves chatting to some girls from Derby who were virtually drowning in Union Jacks. They had driven down from Derby. They have done so every year for the past five years. It's safe to say they're not from the rougher parts of Derby. We were curious about the flags. Where did you get them from? 'Tourist shops,' they revealed.

One of them started taking her jumper off. This made us shift about awkwardly, hoping she wasn't going to strip for Britain. That wouldn't be a very Last Night thing to do. Luckily, she was just showing off a home-made T-shirt saying 'Cool Britannia'.

'We just really love England!' she said.

'Britain!' chided her friend.

England or Britain? Let's get this sorted.

She paused, then repeated, half-apologetically: 'England.'

Bloody hell, it's 'Jerusalem'! With words from visionary English poet William Blake. He was mad. At a party he once asked a woman, 'Have you ever seen a fairy's funeral?', before describing the one he'd seen in his garden earlier that day. Not cease from mental fight? He was fighting mentally till the end. Still, always good to have a few 'mad' people at a party.

Blake probably wouldn't have liked the Last Night of the Proms. Once arrested for sedition, he thought all barriers and boundaries leave us in dismal darkness and that only the liberated imagination can throw off the shackles of class, money, exploitation, division and property. His lines about 'England's green and pleasant land' urge us to struggle against inequality and injustice, possibly to the death. Not a Last Night guy at all.

At last, 'God Save the Queen', the first ever national anthem in the world ever (the 1740s). The Albert Hall guys were really roaring now. Albert would be proud. And the people in the park were roaring too.

BLAKE'S JERUSALEM: MAD SHIT.
The Bridgeman Art Library

Dum-dum-de-dum dum-dum! Come on, God – get a shift on with the saving. Or you'll really be for it.

Save her from whom? The French, of course! It also righteously lays into all the other enemies of mercantile naval-supremacist Great Britain. Knavish popes? Coming at ya. And the, er, Scots . . .

Some Scots don't like the national anthem very much, taking offence at the rarely sung fourth verse: 'May he sedition hush and like a torrent rush,/ Rebellious Scots to crush,/ God save the King.' It's not really about crushing *all* the Scots. Only invading Jacobite Highlanders intent on restoring the (Catholic) Stuart dynasty. Still, you can see how Scottish people might find it strange singing a national anthem that includes lines about them being crushed.

After the national anthem came the closedown. The lights came on and we felt a little dazed. All the people – all *our* people – were packing their flags into their flag-bags and ambling towards the exit. Hey, don't go! We had a big old gang thing going on here. The songs? The flags? Don't you remember? Let's stay a bit longer – do that one about slavery again. Yeah? Back to mine? No? You sure?

As all our new friends headed for the coaches lining Park Lane (or their tents), we wandered hungrily over to a burger van, and chatted with the young Polish woman serving us. She hadn't been mad keen on the Proms either: you can certainly see how, having started life under Stalinism, then coming to 'liberal Britain' to escape the stultifying clutches of reactionary Catholic nationalism, you might find being presented with this lot shouting along about roughing up eighteenth-century foreigners a tad bewildering. She gave us free curry sauce, which we took gladly as a true offering for internationalism, and we stood munching chips as the stragglers filtered out and people started cleaning up the detritus of 40,000 picnics.

Funny business, patriotism. Everyone understands the need to belong. But why would you want to belong to something that is all about sticking it up the fuzzy-wuzzies? It was like some sort of nationalist Sing-a-Long-a-Rocky-Horror-Show in there; standing in a pen, waving flags before a giant screen, bellowing allegiance to slave-trading exploiter forebears with terrible breath. (The sort of thing that even voice of Empire/prophet of imperialism Rudyard Kipling had second thoughts about when his son was killed in the First World War.)

KIPLING: 'TACHE, POEMS (PATRIOTIC).
Corbis

These people were not, generally speaking, rampant nationalists champing at the bit for ethnic bloodlust. Their lives are probably not dominated by thinking up new and ingenious ways to stick it right up the French. They'll have a standing order to Comic Relief. But the line between even mild patriotism and reason is a blurry one. Because patriotism is about feelings, and feelings are, by definition, not thoughts.

John Hadfield, in his introduction to *A Book of Britain*, a handsomely tooled treasury of picture, prose and verse of yore, wrote: 'Love of country has certain parallels with the love of a man for a woman. Beauty is an element of it, but not an all-important one. A man may be drawn to a woman by perfection of feature or figure, as he is attracted to the Wye Valley by the view at Symonds Yat. It is doubtful, however, whether men want to make their home by Symonds Yat. Just as the enduring love of man and woman is stirred by a mere turn of the head or a footfall on the stairs, so the deep attachment of man to his native place can be reawakened by such homely sights as the mist rising from water meadows or the first blush of apple blossom in a suburban street.'

Patriotism, then: it's very much like making love to a beautiful woman.

AUTUMN

TWELVE

ROOTS

ROBIN HOOD
ACORNS
MIGHTY OAKS

'ARE THERE ANY druids here?' asked the Sherwood Forest ranger.

Sniggers from the 20-strong crowd gathered on a Saturday evening around the visitors' centre near Edwinstowe.

'Well, there's usually one or two,' he shrugged.

This was the Autumn Equinox Walk in Sherwood Forest Country Park, and, as we know, druids like equinoxes. For once, though, they were elsewhere, making this the first quarterly festival of our quest not spent in the company of any druids. We sort of missed them. There were two pagans in Iron Maiden T-shirts. They would have to do.

Sherwood Forest. The very name evokes a forest. Sherwood Forest is mighty. The oak of oak forests. The forest all the other forests would bow down to, if trees could bow. It's the medieval forest island of legend, and actually also a real forest. It is the best forest. Okay, the Amazon rainforest *looks* good. But is it really that good? Really?

Guiding us and other enthusiasts of nocturnal nature around this famous wood as darkness fell about us was Andy Boroff, an avuncular man who strongly resembles the mustachioed TV scientist Robert Winston and has tended the forest for 30 years. Sherwood – and the mythical greenwood generally – is natural Britain incarnate, home to Britain's most persistent fictional hero, and some of its greatest trees. As we set off, the ancient deep dark greenwood closed in around us, with gloriously gnarled hunks of oak bursting out of the bracken undergrowth. There's something very British about Britain in the autumn, we agreed.

Autumn: the twilight time; a time of wistful melancholia; a time of brown leaves. The time when our thoughts naturally turn to trees. Leaves on trees. Leaves falling from trees. Thinking about trees is very British. The pornographer D. H. Lawrence (who was born ten miles away in Eastwood) once declared: 'I would like to be a tree for a while.' (Not sure if he ever got round to it. Probably rubbed his bits up against one or two, the mucky little dog. D. H. Lawrence: a dirty man.)

We were told to expect owls and bats engaging in mind-games. 'Owls around this time start battling for territory, not actually fighting but screeching and flapping and making quite a scene,' said Boroff. (Might interfere with feeling melancholic, we thought, all the screeching. But this is British nature all right.)

Andy's colleague took out a bat detector, which picked out and amplified the sounds of the bats in the treetops. Before long, a noctule bat emerged and swooped around the hollow. We watched it for a while and then walked on, hoping for owls. Boroff approximated an owl call: 'It sometimes works,' he shrugged. 'Or maybe they're just going, what a rubbish owl call.'

Owls are good, big eyes and that – but they weren't the main event for us. We were here to summon the ghost of Robin of Sherwood. Fair-minded, brave, dishy (except when played by Kevin Costner), a dab hand with the old longbow and swooping across castle great-halls hanging on to the curtains . . . By the time of his first known mention – in *Piers Plowman* by William Langland, a 1377 poem that is no one's favourite bit from an English degree course – Robin Hood was already an outlaw superstar, known to all through since-lost popular ballads.

All down the ages, people have warmed to the good outlaw robbing the rich and giving to the poor. We love that redistributive shit. Although, with the earliest audiences, just robbing the rich was fine. Robin seems to have come from the thirteenth century, and become popular in the fourteenth (there was lots of thirteenth-century detail in the ballads). But that all-important giving to the poor aspect only appears later. Medieval peasants were happy enough just to see it stuck up the bosses and the church: 'He keeps all the stuff at the end? Ach, he deserves it . . .'

The ultimate source for Robin is unknown. Invention? Real person? Archetype? Common pseudonym for a robber ('robbehod' or suchlike)? No one really knows. We know how aspects of the story were blended in over time – new characters introduced, like Friar Tuck or Maid Marian, or changes like Robin being promoted from yeoman to displaced noble in the seventeenth century – but the ultimate source remains an enigma. And the myriad film versions, for all their scrupulous efforts at medieval veracity, have only raised more questions than they answer, like: whatever did happen to Michael Praed?

Some candidates for an original, real hooded man have been tracked down: a Robert of Loxley, even a Robert Hood of Wakefield, with his 'merrie men' clearly based on the brigands preying on travellers on the Great North Way, the future A1 that ran through Sherwood from London to York (wonder if it had a big sign pointing to 'The North'?).

Back in the woods, we were, put simply, walking in the woods. But we were also looking for spirits. We don't actually believe in spirits, of course, not literally, so in a sense we were walking round somewhere real in order to conjure things in our own minds. So it was kind of like drugs, only it was woods.

BEING A FOREST OUTLAW PUTS HAIRS ON YOUR CHEST.
Rex Features

So we considered the trees and the myths. The past. Robin Hood, swooping across the castle great-hall hanging on to the curtains to save his poacher mates from The Man; ripping off the king's tax collector who's taken all the people's swag, storming the armed wagon train in a dewy glade; giving Keith Allen a slap . . . Later on, the Merrie Men at some stage in the evening going well past 'merrie' and instead turning into drunk men: Robin Hood and his Drunk Men. Maid Marion: she'd had a few also.

Whatever. Maybe it's time for a new Robin. A real new one – properly up-to-date. Robbing the rich may be the only way forward now, seeing as no one seems prepared to tax them. (Why does this bring to mind the image of a man in Lincoln green (which, by the way, might have been red . . . or blue – but let's not even go there with that shit) kicking in the door to the Dragon's Den? 'Out of my way, Davis!') There would be complications, of course – it wouldn't all be knockabout firing-longbows-at-the-rich fun. These days, we don't see poverty in absolute terms, including things like a cultural life as part of the minimum standard of living. So maybe our new Robin could rob the rich and then set up some adult education centres. Are you listening, Hollywood?

We traipsed along through the dark, trying to follow the torch at the head of the line while not tripping over the person in front. (This was quite difficult while also trying to maintain a greenwood-inspired reverie.) Rounding a corner, we came face to face with a very big tree.

This was no ordinary big tree, although it was certainly a very big tree. This was no less than Britain's favourite tree.

Well, at least according to a 2002 poll (hope you voted). Here was the Major Oak, a 23-ton world of wood with gargantuan drooping branches supported by scaffolding (as they have been since it was a Victorian tourist attraction). We beheld its oaky immenseness. It is a very big tree. It is one of the 50 Great British Trees named by the Tree Council to mark the Queen's Golden Jubilee. Irritatingly, the Tree Council refused to put these 50 wood patriots into numerical order of merit, so we can't judge if public and critical tastes coincide on this one. Fence-sitters.

Around 800 years old, the Major Oak has gone past middle-age spread and would now be considered thoroughly obese, with a waist size of 33 feet. If it was human, it would be the subject of its own *Bodyshock* documentary on Channel 4, called 'The Tree That Ate Its Own Head'. Something like that.

The public is kept back, even on the autumn equinox, but the hollow trunk contains a sizeable chamber where, according to legend, Robin Hood stored his treasure and hid from the sheriff's men. (Bet D. H. Lawrence would have liked it in there. He'd have probably started thinking about a quick bunk-up, the filthy sod.) We thought about Robin Hood hiding in the tree.

The tree is named after the eighteenth-century Major Hayman Rooke, who chronicled the great oaks of Sherwood – which is a job for a real man. So the name's more of a coincidence than a description. But there's no doubting that this is one major oak. Did we touch it? We did. Then we thought about Major Rooke sitting inside his oak, even though we don't know what he looks like.

Is there a more British tree than the oak? There is not. It's got roots, like we've got roots. It is strong, like we are strong. Arthur's Round Table was made of oak. Okay, it didn't exist. But it was still made of oak. That's the thing about oak: strong, mighty, symbolic – but you can also make furniture out of it. You can even sit on oak. Okay, people more usually have pine now – but this is often unreliable Scandinavian furniture. Not British furniture. Not really.

Softwood: it's all right. But if you're going to rule the world, you require hardwood. The great ships that conquered the world were made of it; the Navy anthem is even called 'Hearts of Oak': 'Heart of oak are our ships, jolly tars are our men . . . We'll fight and we'll conquer again and again.' Who doesn't like pubs with oak beams? Or oak panelling? Who wouldn't panel their whole house in mighty oak given half the chance?

A big green oak silhouette was of course recently chosen as the new Tory symbol. Cameron's Tories chose the oak tree for its solidity, tradition and Britishness. A party official told *The Times*: 'We consulted members across the country about our new identity . . . We tested a large number of different images. The tree logo proved the overwhelming favourite.' British people fucking love oaks: simple as. (What the Tory spokesperson didn't say was that the other images on offer were a swastika or a Father Christmas strung up on a noose. A noose shaped like a gaping anus.)

In the clearing before us, another bat circled above the heads of this little band of nature-lovers. That was good. That was nature. But where were the owls? What was their problem exactly? This was night-time, they were owls. Maybe they'd sorted out all their border disputes, which would be good news for the owls, but what about us? We wanted blood. Or at least some owls freaking each other out in the head.

Still, owls or no owls (and it was no owls), seeing Sherwood Forest – the ferns, the bracken, the *oaks* – was proving undoubtedly good for the soul. Okay, we couldn't actually see it. The sky was now pitch black. But we could definitely feel it.

We felt the forest's pain. For the oaks are dying. The medieval forested island – that thick blanket of mystery and myth – is just that, a myth: the ground under Sherwood's trees is furrowed, meaning round here it was once all fields. But the oaks that are here, the ancient oaks sucking national life-nutrients out of the earth for us, are dying out.

Today, most of Sherwood's trees are conifers planted in the early twentieth century to satisfy the new demand for softwood. People get angry about conifers. They are a foreign tree, considered an alien. Not that the oak is madly 'indigenous' – it actually moved up from Africa (just like people, really).

'The oak comes from the equator and is at the north of its territory here,' Boroff explained. 'With global warming, it's going to be moving further north.' (We think he means that trees will start growing further north, not that these actual trees will up sticks and start moving. Hope not, because if the trees start moving, things will have reached a pretty freaky, apocalyptic level and we'll be really fucked.) Anyway: fans of oaks in the Orkneys should be over the moon.

SHERWOOD FOREST: FEEL THE DARKNESS.

And what about Hood's existence in Sherwood? Boroff was interested in the reading of Robin as mythical Green Man figure, a perpetual spirit of British nature: 'The Green Man is a figure dressed up in green, who is there and who isn't there, who goes in and out of trees, and what does Robin do?'

In times of environmental uncertainty, this is a nice idea: Robin the eternal people's hero as nature's protector, an enviroforest sprite of justice. Maybe the spirit of Robin Hood could pop out on people visiting the country park and say things like: 'Remember: always turn the lights off in rooms you're not using.' Stuff like that.

The spirit of Robin hadn't popped out while we were here. Maybe we were looking in the wrong place. Most of the early ballads actually place Robin 50 miles up the road in Barnsdale, South Yorkshire. His home got moved to Sherwood later on. Not sure why. (Maybe no one could believe in a bunch of Yorkshiremen being merry all the time?)

And what about the Major Oak being an outlaw's hideout? Boroff scoffs, in a way you rarely hear people scoff: 'It's a well-known meeting point. It's a massive landmark and an obvious hiding place. If he was on the run, where were they going to look for him?'

We were going to ask Andy if he'd ever met Michael Praed – whether he comes to, like, hang out here and stuff – but you know . . .

We'd enjoyed our communion with the trees. It's good to free-associate once in a while, let your mind wander a bit. Everyone was leaving now, our temporary band of brothers drifting off to the car park. We followed them, not giving up on the idea of Robin Hood imbuing the area with some eternal rebel yell, an outlaw spirit drifting across this forested land of mythic outlaws and mythic trees.

As we left via the small town of Edwinstowe (where Robin and Marian were supposedly wed), we spied some young people hanging out and getting merry on a Saturday night. It sounds unbelievable, but some of them were actually sporting hoods. Strange hooded garments seemingly designed for the wearer to blend into their environment, perhaps even hiding their identities from the forces of the law.

Clearly, the spirit of Robin lives on. We almost composed a ballad.

TOP BRITISH SAUCES

BROWN: A truthful, if not particularly appealing, descriptor. Britons are great lovers of brown sauce.

HP: Much the same as brown sauce. Called 'Wilson's gravy' when wife Mary claimed British PM Harold Wilson drowned everything in the stuff. It later transpired this was common-man spin and he actually preferred the hoitier Lea & Perrins, a superior brown sauce. Lea & Perrins Worcester sauce is like brown sauce, but runny rather than sticky. Well, it is sticky if you spill some and let it dry. You'll want to be wiping that bastard up double-quick. See also: Daddy's, OK, and Branston Rich & Fruity – all essentially brown sauces. HP is made in Holland these days, of course: ruined.

BREAD: Another well-named sauce. Made from bread. Only the British would consider it a matter of culinary excellence to make a sauce out of white bread.

HORSERADISH: Not so accurately monikered, this one. It's got the word 'horse' in it, but it tastes nice with 'cow'. Although it might taste nice with horse . . . Ask the Belgians.

SALAD CREAM: A sauce, not a cream. But is it British? Yes. Top chef Marco Pierre White said it was 'one of the greatest culinary inventions of the twentieth century'. And he wasn't wrong.

Except it was invented in the nineteenth century. So he was wrong about that. And about the other bit.

BRITISH.
Advertising Archive

REGGAE REGGAE: Never underestimate the appeal to Britain of a smiling black man singing a happy song about sauce.

MINT: The British are quite particular and prescriptive about their sauces, as befits a people who take their sauce seriously: mint for lamb, apple for pork, horseradish for beef. If a British person catches you eating the incorrect sauce with your meal, he will cuff you.

MASALA: A gravy, essentially, added to dry chicken fresh from the tandoor to satisfy the insatiable British lust for gravy. The late Robin Cook hailed Chicken Tikka Masala as 'a true British national dish' and said it was 'a perfect illustration of the way Britain absorbs and adapts external influences'. Rather, it's a perfect example of how Britain absorbs external influences and adds sugar, food dye and trans-fats.

THIRTEEN

NOT TO PUT TOO FINE A POINT ON IT, WE CUT THE KING'S HEAD OFF BEFORE THE FRENCH DID

CLASS
WAR
CLASS WAR
PUTNEY

IT WAS A time of turmoil and tumult. Of apocalyptic ferment and also foment (which is similar but not quite the same as ferment). The most turbulent years of British history. A conflict that touched everyone, when loyalties to either King or Parliament divided families: father against son, neighbour against neighbour, girl on girl.

This was the English Civil War, the conflict that ripped through the heart of the seventeenth century. But was it English? Not really. The turmoil encompassed England, Scotland, Ireland and Wales – that's why the 1638–60 period gets called the Wars of the Three Kingdoms (that's presumably Wales they're not counting as a kingdom . . . sorry, Wales).

But how could one get a sense of it all, this tumultuous period of tyranny and terror, of tantrums and tiaras? Well, how about by recreating it all? This period attracts people who like dressing up and re-enacting things like re-enacted sharks to fake blood. The Sealed Knot are the original, and still the best, re-enactors. You know that well-known brand of baked beans that everyone likes? Well, they are like that, only with Civil War re-enacting.

The Knot closed their summer season of battles, we learnt, with a memorial service in Ripple, Gloucestershire, dedicated to their deceased founder, Brigadier Peter Young – a bona fide Second World War hero who dedicated his post-military life to dressing up as a Civil War military leader and directing mock battles from the nation's greatest internal conflict, from atop a horse. This would, we reasoned, be a side of the Sealed Knot the world never usually sees. The world thinks it's just all battles and stuff. But they don't know.

Church services start quite early on Sunday mornings, we discovered. Which, given that Gloucestershire is a long way from where we both live, meant another early start. We met in the shadow of Windsor Castle. And we met at dawn. (Which gave the whole meeting-up thing a sense of drama that it really didn't merit.) We had chosen Windsor for its frankly excellent transport links, but it was ironic that, on our way to investigate the war that ended with the declaration of a British republic, we met outside just one of the opulent palaces owned by the present monarch. (Speaking of transport, Windsor Castle is right under the Heathrow flight path. There was plane after plane after plane coming down over the roof, raising once again the question of the royal family: how do they sleep?)

Windsor had also played an important role in the Civil War. The touch paper for the war was lit in January 1642 when Charles I, backed up by 500 troops, tried to arrest a group of five MPs leading opposition to him in Parliament: by storming into the Chamber only to find that, in his words, 'the birds have flown'. (He was neither the first nor the last bloke to go Up West looking for 'birds'.) Charles – his carriage surrounded by a jeering mob (even under seventeenth-century monarchist tyranny you could demonstrate in Parliament Square) – fled first to Hampton Court, and then to Windsor, before claiming Oxford as his new capital and declaring war in Nottingham (this is, it should be noted, a stupid way of getting to Nottingham).

THE TRIAL OF CHARLES I: GUILTY – OF MONARCHY!
MEPL

After Charles's deposition, Windsor Castle became the headquarters for the New Model Army. Here, on the eve of the Second Civil War of 1647–9 (Charles, the monkey, was trying to give the whole thing a second go), Cromwell finally resolved to kill the King. 'I've had it up to here with that floppy-haired twat,' he might have said. (Charles I is buried at Windsor.)

Ripple is on the Severn about five miles from Tewkesbury. We had recently been in these parts before, when we visited England. As we got closer, this caused us to reminisce. 'Have we been round this roundabout before?' 'Yes.'

Arriving in this well-preserved, Sunday-morning-deserted English village, we followed the signs for the Village Hall. In a gravel layby up a lane, lots of people were putting funny helmets on, and screwing the points on to pikes.

Sealed Knotters were still arriving, and hailing each other

lustily. They were meeting once again to relive those times, those times of Cavaliers, who laughed, and Puritans, who didn't, of a world turned upside down, and then turned back again, before being turned slightly on its side. A turquoise Japanese people-carrier rocked up with a load of wenches in the back.

The Knotters formed up and marched double-file towards the church to the beat of a drum – banners and flags at the front, women at the back (so conveying a great truth about almost all British history). A portly chap with proper seventeenth-century long hair and goatee walked in front giving orders. Some of the women chatted amongst themselves about the recent postal strike (another national conflict).

IF IT WASN'T FOR THE CAR, AND THE FACT THAT IT'S A PHOTOGRAPH, YOU'D THINK IT *WAS* THE OLDEN DAYS.

We followed at a safe distance (about 20 feet seemed safe enough), and once inside the church, we took a pew. The flag- and banner-bearers went up and presented their 'colours' to the vicar, who placed them behind the altar with all due ceremony. The other Knotters chatted and caught up with each other. A few were wearing their hair long, in keeping with the seventeenth-century vibe. One chap in his mid-sixties had his own solution: a lustrous mousy wig cascaded down to his shoulders. It was – we firmly believe – a woman's wig. A lustrous, cascading woman's wig that contrasted sharply with his grey moustache and silver-framed glasses. Imagine Arthur Lowe in a woman's wig. It was a look of great tumult.

Soon all the flags were stashed and the vicar commenced this special service. The subject of the Founder's Day Commemoration Service, the Brig, as his followers affectionately refer to him, was awarded the Military Cross after leading a team of commandos on a raid that involved climbing up a cliff at Dieppe before turning military historian and teaching at Sandhurst. (According to his 1988 obituary in the *Telegraph*, he would show cadets the cliffs he climbed: 'They looked at him disbelievingly. "See if you can do it yourselves," he said – and beat them to the top.')

The Brig formed the Sealed Knot in 1968 after a one-off battle to publicise a book he'd written about the Civil War. From these humble beginnings, the whole craze for re-enactment grew rapidly. The vicar, Reverend Geoffrey Moore, gave a fulsome eulogy for Young, who had lived locally: 'His seed has grown, his creation has given pleasure to thousands, if not hundreds of thousands.'

Then came the hymns, all rich with turbulent warrior imagery: 'And when the strife is fierce, the warfare long/ Steals on the ear the distant triumph song/ And hearts are brave again, and arms are strong. Alleluia, Alleluia!' And: 'Christ, the royal Master, leads against the foe;/ Forward into battle see His banners go!' (Let's be honest, Christ would have been a rubbish military leader. 'We're getting slaughtered here! What are we going to do?' 'There were these pigs . . . and a shepherd . . .' 'We're fucked.')

'We bless the Sealed Knot,' the vicar continued. 'We pray for our Queen.'

This was not a gathering suffering from any loss of deference. The Knot was established as a highly Royalist re-enactment society (they had to let in some Parliamentary regiments later, what with, you know, not really having anyone to fight) as a conscious riposte to the sixties left who had taken to their hearts the crazy radical groupings thrown up in the tumult like the Diggers and the Levellers (a loose coalition of writers and organisers). It can be hard leaving the armed services and fending for oneself in the outside world. People miss the camaraderie, the sense of purpose, the other people doing what they tell them to do. What better way to ease the adjustment than to start your own army? And so much the better if you can give the finger to the Reds at the same time.

After the service, the Sealed Knot formed up once again in the churchyard and marched round the back . . . for another service.

At the south side of the church, by some plaques set into the earth, decorated with flowers, they formed three sides of a square on the grass by the transept. The vicar then gave another eulogy as the Yeoman Ensign laid a wreath next to the plaques, one of which we assumed to be dedicated to Peter Young.

In fact, the plaque was dedicated to his wife. At which point, we slightly despaired. We were standing next to a made-up military-style ceremony being performed with great solemnity by a made-up army, in honour of a self-appointed commander who died in 1988. And he wasn't even buried here. It wasn't even his plaque. Not that the moment didn't have a certain poignancy, but . . .

After the service – the second service – we chatted to the Sealed Knot's current chairman, Tertio Commander Arthur Jackson, who jovially recounted anecdotes of the Brig's wartime derring-do, telling us about the time he got the Nazis to turn back from trying to take a bridge by putting a cardboard box made up to look like a bomb on it.

We also chatted with long-time member Sam Eadle; he's been a member since 1977, having been recruited, somewhat appropriately, at a street party for the Queen's Silver Jubilee. Sam related how the Knot's actual battles would be followed in the beer tent by idea battles – ribald tussles about who was best, over beers.

'The Civil War is a microcosm,' said Sam. 'It teaches you

THE LAYING OF THE SOLEMN WREATH.

how England is ruled: King, Commons, Lords . . . Of course there will be conflict, but you need all of them for it to work. You tinker with it at your peril.'

'The Parliamentarians didn't realise how flexible the constitution was,' beamed Arthur. 'When the Sealed Knot was formed, there was this thinking about what wonderful people the Parliamentarians were. Oh, democracy, Levellers, socialism . . . they drew this line, but that's just sloppy history.'

We couldn't help feeling like exactly the kind of the people he had in mind. But we didn't want to kick things off again. They had sandwiches to eat. And we weren't the ones with all the pikes.

The Civil War provokes arguments. The Civil War provoked argument then – to the extent of provoking a civil war – and it provokes argument today. Today's argument is essentially this: was this a bona fide British revolution or not? This same argument has prevailed, then not prevailed, and then prevailed again, roughly according to whether various historians like class war or not.

In the class-war reading of events, it probably helps to imagine John Cleese as the Royalists (led by King Charles), Ronnie Barker as the Parliamentarians (eventually led by Cromwell) and Ronnie Corbett as the newly radicalised common soldiery (coalescing around the Levellers). Now imagine Ronnies Barker and Corbett defeating Cleese in the Civil War and confining him to the Isle of Wight, only for Barker to find he is now getting it in the neck from both sides, so deciding to give Cleese the final heave-ho before – with the help of Cleese's old supporters terrified of the unleashed power of Corbett – smashing Corbett's power-base in the army and sending him, profoundly disillusioned after his brief taste of democracy, to the Tower.

Barker then establishes himself as military dictator of his own republic before unleashing genocidal hell on Ireland (obviously, Ronnie Barker himself would have done nothing of the kind). Simple, really.

There are complexities, of course. People also look to the religious divides, with many old-school Protestants supporting the Royalists against Puritan zealotry. Others hail the ethnic question, how the Parliamentarians' devotion to 'England' alienated the Scots and Welsh. Charles I's idiocy can't be ruled out of how and when things kicked off, and why they kicked

Druids!

Here we go round the 10-foot-high horned man-beast personifying evil.

Early (genuine) designs for the Union Jack. A bit shit.

George Cruikshank's 'Loyal Addresses and Radical Petitions'. George IV as Prince Regent greets post-Peterloo radical petitioners with his arse-gas.

Polo: is this British?

Tewkesbury, summer 2007. People laughed when he bought the canoe.

We found golliwogs to be surprisingly ubiquitous on our quest (this one is in the Cotswolds).

The longest-running Punch & Judy show in Britain. Diabolic, psychopathic family fun, Llandudno.

Living history, dead pig: Herstmonceux Medieval Weekend.

Proms: patriots.

The Major Oak: a very big tree. Some people are moved to sit and stare for hours on end.

Gibraltarian cuisine, on top of the Rock. De-licious.

Eid, Manchester: cars, kebabs, coppers . . . cool. It's even inclusive for the disabled.

Get stuck in! World Pie-eating Competition, Wigan. Former world champion Brendan Brockbank pictured on the right. Dog pictured on the left.

He's not watching you, this is just wartime propaganda (he is really).

John Major, member of the Order Of The Garter. Gives the orders. Wears the garters.

off this way instead of another way. But whichever way you slice it, a different class was in the driving seat at the end of the period than at the start, which would seem to suggest fairly definitively that a revolution had gone on. Absolute monarchy was holed below the waterline, and Cleese was never the same again.

Our new friends from the Sealed Knot were both firmly on the side of the King. They'd been very affable, and we'd enjoyed our chat, but we couldn't really fathom what inspired them to pick the Royalist side. It's like someone proposing a re-enactment of the signing of the Magna Carta, and then going: 'You know what – I'd really like to be Bad King John.'

A couple of weeks later, we went to a very different sort of civil war re-enactment. We were off to see Corbett's 'Red' element in action (in fact, the Levellers colour was sea-green – FACT – but still . . .). Another re-enactment was being staged to relive this time of explosive muskets and explosive pamphlets, both equally explosive (okay, not equally explosive): a dramatic restaging marking the 360th anniversary of the Putney Debates of autumn 1647. These took place at the Church of St Mary the Virgin in Putney, when radical 'agitators' from the Army's rank-and-file debated with Army leaders like Cromwell and Ireton the rank-and-file's new ideas about the rank-and-file having a go on some of the power.

This meant going to the posh South London suburb of Putney on a Saturday night, another place we rarely find our-selves. The Sealed Knot were here too, a Living History encampment of thin white tents inside the church grounds by the river, sitting enjoying their Civil War ales (fermented apoc-alyptically) from plastic cups. It looked a very, very cold way to spend the night. We had a quick look at the pewter smithing display by the Worshipful Company of Pewterers (it was Saturday night, after all), then made our way into the church.

The Putney Debates were truly extraordinary. By autumn 1647, the King was defeated (for the first time) but the vic-torious side was splitting and there was a new power in the land: the Army. Unlike most armies, this army had real intel-lectual clout, threatening to disband unless Parliament redressed its grievances and those of 'the people at large'. Now, at Putney, the Army leaders were forced to debate with repre-sentatives of each regiment – the 'agitators' – the contents of

the radical Levellers pamphlet: *The Agreement of the People*.
This was little short of the prototype of a written constitution,
calling for freedom of religious practice; equality before the
law; and, most revolutionary of all, an almost universal male
franchise. It was, clearly, good.

Inside the church, the actors sat along the back wall beneath
windows that looked out at the night sky above Putney Bridge.
These were at the perfect height to see the top half of passing
buses coming over the bridge, so moments of high political
drama were accompanied by the sight of the top deck of an
idling 74. No matter. Because there's nothing like dramatising
something to really bring home the drama. And nothing evokes
the interior of Putney church quite like the interior of Putney
church (are all churches full of English Civil War re-enactors?
we wondered).

To the left, behind a table, were the Army leaders; 'the
grandees', as writer John Lilburne – whose ideas partly
inspired the *Agreement* – mockingly dubbed them. To the
right, the agitators and Leveller writers/activists were looking
pretty radical in their black hoodies under leather jackets.
Chairing the debate, 'Cromwell' also had a leather jacket – but
the longer overcoat style, with a black jumper underneath,
gave him a certain Stasi vibe.

As the drama unfurled, the debate was strong and swift,
Ireton trying to bat away the soldiers' demands. Occasionally,
Cromwell sprang to his feet to boom things at the Levellers,
including once exclaiming: 'Would it not make us like the
Switzerland country?'

Christ, we all thought: not that.

But the debate shifted in the Levellers' favour with the
famous intervention from Colonel Thomas Rainborough calling for government by and for the people: 'For really I think
that the poorest he that is in England have a life to live, as the
greatest he.'

These lines could not fail to resonate around the church and
also, in a way, around the world outside. Mainly in the church
though, really.

The debate's core ideas – that all men are equal, that only
elected government is legitimate – usually get nabbed by the
French or American revolutions. But the first attempt to create
a written liberal constitution happened here, in Putney. This
was revolutionary. *British* revolutionary. This was nothing less

than the birth of modern politics (not tonight, before). In Putney!

In Putney, the people in power had not won the argument, but then again people in power don't necessarily need to win arguments. As we know, democracy did not immediately ensue. The Cromwell who gave the floor to the Levellers at Putney, the self-taught military genius who brought down a king, later decided that the best way to win any debate was to lock the other side in the Tower and leave them there to rot.

We left considering the fact that there were no simple answers; that in this time of experimental government and experimental haircuts, of revolting bourgeoisie emerging, and declining monarchy revolting, there were no clearly delineated goodies and baddies. Oh, except the people inventing democracy. They were the goodies.

Outside, it was Halloween, and on the high street, revellers in ghoulish costumes mingled with hen parties wearing twinkly head-dresses and waving wands. Strangest of all, one side of the bridge was just being reopened by the police, while the other direction remained closed. While we'd been inside getting a dose of righteous revolution, outside a man had been threatening to throw himself from the bridge.

There wasn't really any great symbolism here, but it was all making us feel very differently about Putney.

THE FUTURE'S WILLIAM OF ORANGE

The 1688 Glorious Revolution is an event absolutely central to British national identity. It was Dutch, though.

For the great Whig historians (the optimistic nineteenth-century school that put Britain at the centre of liberal progress), and for modern-day Tories, 1688 is an event of almost mystical importance, stopping the pendulum at just the right 'not too hot, not too cold' point between absolute tyranny and mob rule. In his big speech on Britishness, fan of Britishness Gordon Brown pointed to 'a golden thread' of liberty running from 'that long-ago day in Runnymede in 1215 to the Bill of Rights in 1689'. He didn't point to anything in between those two things, so it was a very long thread. And, as we say, it was Dutch.

The 1660 Restoration of the Monarchy had gone tits up when the borderline Catholic Charles II was replaced in 1685 by his utterly Catholic brother James II, who wanted his absolute monarchy ball back. Soon, the new political class of Tories and Whigs were banging their heads against the wall at their mistake in kick-starting the Stuart revival. Then James had a Catholic baby – thus dashing hopes that the crown would pass to James's Protestant daughter Mary – and they really went mental. And so they phoned James's son-in-law, William of Orange (who was actually of Holland), inviting him to invade. (People who stage successful invasions of Britain are always called William. Or Aulus Plautius.)

WILLIAM OF ORANGE: SPORTING A GENTLEMAN'S MUFF, NO LESS.

MEPL

William wanted to secure Protestant England's support in his war with Catholic France. He was offered this in exchange for the invasion. He'd also get to be King of England (bonus!) – ruling jointly with Mary, the couple having signed up to a deal that gave Parliament the whip hand against the monarchy (the basis of the 1689 Bill of Rights).

On 5 November 1688, William landed with 500 Dutch ships full of

20,000 Dutch soldiers (a force four times the size of the Armada) to send his father-in-law packing. ('And you can take that shitty bread-maker. Call that a wedding gift, you Papist tightarse?') William deliberately landed in the far West Country and made slow progress towards London – avoiding all but small skirmishes, as James's officers went over to the new order. In the small hours of the morning of 11 December, James slipped out of London, and headed for France. Irritatingly for William, some Kent fishermen caught James and sent him back to London. William 'accidentally on purpose' let James escape again, and he nipped off to Ireland and France again (not Holland, though).

The invading Dutch soldiery occupied London, and until 1690 the English Army was not allowed within 20 miles of the capital. William and Mary became joint sovereigns. Constitutional monarchy was born (more or less). Everyone's happy!

So this 'sensible revolution' was a great British compromise. Mind you, the compromise only happened after loads of civil warring and a king getting his head chopped off, which doesn't sound all that compromising. And then, with the Restoration in 1660, Charles II having Cromwell's corpse exhumed, hung in chains and then decapitated, with the body thrown into a pit and the head stuck on a pole outside Westminster Abbey for the next 14 years. Which doesn't sound either that sensible or that compromising. (Fourteen weeks, maybe, but that would be the absolute limit of propriety on this one.)

Also, where exactly was the compromising for the emerging merchants and rent-seeking landlords in the middle? The monarchy had to compromise its interests to match those of the merchants. The commoners had to compromise their interests to match those of the merchants. The merchants also had to compromise their beliefs with those of the merchants. Oh, hang on . . . You can see how this could work out well for the merchants. They had basically used a foreign army to reorganise the state in their favour – finishing off what the civil war had started.

But at least it was 'bloodless'. Well, apart from the toe-to-toe civil war, bloody suppression of the Monmouth rebellion (Charles II's illegitimate son, flying the Levellers flag of all things, staged an invasion in 1685, which was popularly supported in the West Country and met with savage repression), the aforementioned skirmishes, and proper, protracted, brutal war in Scotland and Ireland after William came to power – including of course the Battle of the Boyne, which is quite famous and still a source of conflict today. Glorious!

FOURTEEN

THE LAST BASTION

THE BRITANNIC NAVY
THE BRITANNIC MONKEYS
EMPIRE
WEE

LOOK AT ANY decent, British map of the world and there it will be, coloured all in red: the Empire. The British Empire. All 13 territories of it. There's Anguilla, Bermuda, the British Virgin Islands (of course), South Georgia and South Sandwich Islands . . . A stirring panorama of very small, widely spaced red dots. Once, the sun never set on the Empire. And it still doesn't; it just has considerably less shining to do than before.

We knew we had to visit the Empire. To stand on British soil that is not in Britain, but which is British nonetheless. British soil that is British spiritually, but not British actually, not really, by dint of being far away. But sort of British actually, what with us being in charge and everything. Even though, as we say, it's not actually in Britain. We chose, of course, Gibraltar. We thought about going to the Falklands. We thought about this for approximately two seconds. Too cold. Too far away. No monkeys. To the rock! To the rock!

The *Rough Guide to Spain* describes this outpost of Empire as '300 years of concentrated Britishness'. Imagine that. Like Britain, but pickled. Pickled Britain: cracking. Or pureed. Pureed Britain. Britain mousse. Foam of Britain. (The *Lonely Planet* says it's like 'Britain in the 60s on a sunny day', which sounds pretty cool, even though they probably mean a sixties high street rather than sixties Carnaby Street; they're not saying that Gibraltar is, like, a trip.)

The GB Airways flight from Gatwick to Gibraltar spanned the length of Spain from the Bay of Biscay to Andalusia, right down to the tip at the bottom. For the Spaniard, there must be few more despised daily intruders into their country's airspace. Perhaps some patriotic Spaniards checked their watches, turned skyward and shook their fists at this most hated of scheduled flights. We got into the spirit by singing our new holiday tune, albeit quite quietly: 'We're not off to sunny Spain. Y viva Britannia.'

When the Royal Navy (with some Dutch assistance) shoved Spain off the Rock in 1704, Britain was living under perpetual threat of becoming a French puppet state under a Stuart king. By the time Nelson's corpse was brought ashore in Gibraltar following the Battle of Trafalgar in 1805, preserved in a barrel of booze, the waves could consider themselves well and truly ruled. (Imagine being a puppet on strings held by the French. Imagine all the dirty things they'd make you do.)

The first thing you see when you arrive in Gibraltar – the

very first thing – is a hand-painted board detailing the local meeting arrangements for the Rotary Club. Well, it's the very first thing you see in the terminal: the very first thing you see in Gibraltar is of course the bloody great rock. The bloody great Rock of Gibraltar. A very big rock.

THE BRITISH EMPIRE.

In fact we disembarked into the Mediterranean warmth (pretty hot, actually) to be struck by the dazzling sunlight bouncing off the Rock's iconic cliff-face. You might imagine this sharp jut of chalk faces south towards Africa – sort of like a mini White Cliff of Dover, a raised hand saying to anyone thinking of heading northwards from the Dark Continent, 'Hang on a minute.' But the famous vision of white actually looms over the airport, a bit like a chalky white middle finger forever pointing at the Spanish mainland.

When Byron called Gibraltar the 'dirtiest and most detestable spot in existence', he might have been going too far (he often did), but as we were deposited by taxi next to the pedestrianised Main Street, the place – a bizarre collision of Mediterranean town and sixties provincial Britain – was certainly keeping its appeal well hidden.

Along one side of the main Casements Square were well-preserved eighteenth-century stone barracks; along another was the kind of sixties municipal building possibly copied from Basingstoke or Crawley. Chairs from drinking establishments spilled across the square. As we passed one cluster of wicker chairs, a ruddy-faced Brit was apparently starting a fight with his own friend. 'I'm sitting here having a fucking drink,' he snarled. 'What does it fucking look like I'm doing?'

Walking down the narrow, high-sided main street, the sense of claustrophobia was immediate. Everything felt poky. This town was a poky little strip of poky streets huddled pokily at the bottom of a long lump of cliff. And that's pretty poky.

Just off the main drag we found a hotel, a few shitty storeys high, built around a cramped central yard, and then hit the town. Gibraltar Town. A town that is also a country. Any idea that this might resemble a sunnier Isle of Wight, forever a Britain before the evils of chain stores and wheelie bins and smoking bans and people wanking off pigs on reality telly, was soon banished. It's weirder – and harder – than that.

Walking about the town, it soon became apparent that cannons were all around us. Just when you thought there could not be more cannons, there were more cannons. They really had us surrounded, with cannons. You don't realise how few cannons other places have until you come here.

The names of businesses and amenities tended to be quite literal, we found. The hotels are called things like Rock (after the rock), Castle (after the Moorish castle – Union Jack above it now: no Moors no more) and the Cannon (after all the cannons). Cannon is quite a popular name for Gibraltarian business ventures. There's even an estate agent called Cannon Real Estate, which is sort of genius.

In one newsagent, the owner, an Asian man of about 50, enthusiastically grabbed a massive box of fag packets and waved it in our faces. This was, he was successfully conveying, a veritable smoking mecca. Obviously, cigarettes are a terrible blight on humanity and all that, but 90p for a packet of 20 Camel Lights? At prices like that, it would be actively immoral not to smoke yourself silly. Our new friend also made a huge point of telling us – six or seven times, possibly more – that he opened until 9.30. Nine thirty, we thought. Phew.

Also available was alcohol: the high street was filled with glittering windows full of bottle upon bottle of strange spirits from all the lands of the world, an empire of booze: Ballantines, Saint Brendan's Irish Cream Liqueur, Wild Africa

Cream, Kahlua, Drambuie, 100 Pipers Whisky, Gold Napoleon French Spirit, Captain Morgan Jamaica Rum, British Navy Pusser's Rum . . . We briefly considered staging a Trafalgar drinking game – with Napoleon French Brandy and Lamb's Genuine Navy Rum – right there in the pedestrianised high street. Briefly. But we are professionals, and can't go staggering round the back streets of the Empire like a couple of particularly jolly jolly jack tars on shore leave.

The collision of signifiers is slightly dizzying. Here is an Olde English pub with a fox-hunting theme. Here is a villa that's distinctly Mediterranean. The police were dressed like bobbies, but they stood around speaking Spanish. Down the road from the BHS was a shop selling the kinds of proper big Continental blades that would cause so much infamy on school trips. You could wander along the street and pass a couple of middle-aged men in suits chatting in Spanish, then see a gift shop window containing a golliwog in a Union Jack vest. It's all part of the magic of the place, and it's deeply, deeply confusing. It looks like a freak storm has relocated bits of Reading in Alicante, taking the people with it; only weirder than that. It's like someone sneaking up and putting a magnet next to your cultural radar.

Exploring some back alleys creeping up the side of the Rock, we did start feeling properly abroad: there were Greek kebab shops, a Moroccan-looking café with some Moroccan-looking old men sat outside. But then a dilapidated little establishment turned out to be a shop called The Pasty Shop, a shop selling pasties. This place was fucking with our heads. It was hot out there. Damned hot. Malarial even. And that's hot.

We ducked into a pub to eat, down by the Governor's residence (the Convent). The TV was on in the background as we munched our pie and chips. Pubs here obviously face a dilemma, given the climate. Do you serve the warm beer of Old England, or the cold refreshing fizz of your cool and refreshing Med beverage, the lager beer. Our pub had solved this conundrum by serving London Pride (a bitter) freezing, freezing cold, with bubbles in it. A great British compromise, if quite unpleasant to drink. Fizzy, extra-cold bitter: it is not the British way.

Gibraltar TV is quite something. The big TV event that night was a debate by party leaders in advance of the next day's election, but before that we caught the end of a sports programme.

THE NELSON TOUCH

Nelson had a quite distinctive plan at Trafalgar: no messing about – just sail into the middle of them and start shooting. In short, have it about them. In brief, have it up them.

Normally, opposing ships would sail into a line opposite each other and engage. Nelson's plan was to break the enemy's line, sail into the middle of them, and start shooting. Or as he put it: 'I shall go at them at once . . . It will bring about a pell mell battle, which is what I want.' He also said, in his formal orders: 'No captain can do wrong if he places his ship alongside that of an enemy' – and fires at it.

Basically: just go up to the enemy and fire cannons at them. It was a plan that relied on the British sailors' superior close-range gunnery. And being mental. We wouldn't claim to be military *experts*, but you can see how this sort of strategy might go wrong.

When Nelson explained it to his officers before the battle, apparently some of them started crying. With joy! Nothing pleased these guys like total war, and they couldn't contain themselves. They wept. They probably hugged.

It was intensely brutal, terrifying stuff. There were 'storm[s] of ball and grape', notes a military histor-

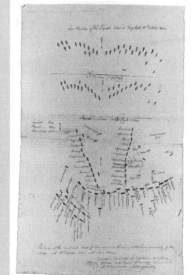

THE BATTLEPLAN FOR TRAFALGAR. WE DO NOT UNDERSTAND THIS DIAGRAM.
National Maritime Museum

ian. When British boarding parties poured on to the French flagship, they 'swathed paths of death and agony', the piles of dead so getting in the way that they had to throw the bodies overboard.

It worked, of course. It wasn't at Trafalgar that Napoleon met his Waterloo – that was somewhere else. But the French fleet was decimated. Although Napoleon still aspired to invade Britain, the age of great fleet battles was over, and Britannia ruled the waves (yes, they probably did sing the song).

When we came in they were keeping everyone updated on a recent dinghy racing event, listing every winner and every runner-up in every race; the next time we zoned in, it was time for full coverage of the women's five-a-side nine-pin bowling.

Then Joe Bossano of the GSLP ('looking after all our people'), and the sitting Chief Minister Peter Caruana of the GSD ('a government you know you can trust') appeared to debate the election issues. Casually speaking across the host, and familiar in the manner of men who have probably been rehearsing these arguments together for years, their main beef was sovereignty. They both wanted to keep it, essentially.

It was a bit like a small local council but on TV. (Some context was conveyed when Caruana trumpeted his alleged tripling of the health budget – 'increasing the number of nurses by nearly a hundred!'.) At a little over two and a half square miles, and with a population of just under 29,000, Gibraltar doesn't merely feel like a small town; it *is* a small town. It's like Truro going independent.

We left them to it, and went outside to see what else Gibraltar had to offer thrill-seekers from the old country. Answer: not much. In one sense this place did feel like provincial sixties Britain: come nightfall, it died on its fucking arse. Over in Spain, all of three miles away, they don't even think about going out until half past two in the morning. But here, at half past nine, the streets were already deserted, with nothing to do but dive into one of the shit drinking/smoking establishments. Now we knew why our friend the newsagent was so proud of his evidently revolutionary late opening hours. Nine thirty? The man's insane!

The cultural schizophrenia continued. At one point, we were playing pool with jumpy geezers with massive biceps and tattoos who kept disappearing to the toilets for more nosebag. Next, we were sitting in a bright little late-night bar with ornate tiles straight out of the back streets of Bilbao or Barcelona, our only company a group of elderly Spanish men playing cards, ordering *cerveza* in halting Spanish. It's all part of the magic of the place. Mostly we traipsed from one dire English-themed drinking hole to the next.

You know that couple that go out to eat at a pub and never say a word to each other all evening? They were over here too. Still saying nothing.

*

A Jules Verne short story, 'The Day of an American Journalist in 2889', imagines 200 years into the future when Gibraltar is the last territory of a British Empire that has lost the British Isles themselves. ('"Of all that once was England, what's left? . . . Nothing." "Nothing, sir?" retorted Francis Bennett. "Well, what about Gibraltar?" At that moment the clock struck twelve.')

It's a tale that conveys the tenacity of the bond between Britain and Gibraltar, a bond that holds strong even after Britain has lost interest and tried to move on. Immigration from Spain/intermarriage with Spaniards was a constant feature until General Franco closed the border in the 1960s. But the Gibraltarians – despite many of them both looking and speaking Spanish, and having names like Martinez – have no wish to be Spanish. Judging by their vehemence, they would rather die than be Spanish. Hand us over to Spain? You might as well hand us over to the Inquisition!

Jack Straw came in 2002 offering a form of joint sovereignty between Britain and Spain. After all, we're all Europeans now. 'No!' said the Gibraltarians. 'No! To Spain!' In a referendum on the proposal, in an 88 per cent turnout of the population, 98.97 per cent rejected Mr Straw's initiative. Jack Straw is used to being unpopular, but not that unpopular. But as far as Spain is concerned, for the people of Gibraltar there can only be one answer: No! To Spain!*

We settled down at a café/pub on the high street for breakfast. Our guidebook boasted of restaurants and bars catering for 'all sorts of tastes – Indian, Moroccan, Chinese, Spanish, Italian, English, etc.'. It was mainly the last one, though. Fish and chips, egg and chips, pie and chips, chips . . . all these cuisines were readily available.

So, inevitably, we ended up at an all-day pub for a full English. In our humble opinions, it was one of the worst full Englishes in the world. And, to be honest, when it comes to bad full Englishes, our opinions are far from humble (in this, if

* A Gibraltar 'national anthem' – composed in the 1990s by Peter Emberley – sums up the prevailing ethos: 'Gibraltar, Gibraltar, the rock on which I stand/ May you be forever free, Gibraltar, my own land.' The finale repeats these lines more emphatically: 'Gibraltar! Gibraltar! My own land!' The message is clear: the Gibraltarians will not now, nor will they ever, pay duty on cigarettes.

in nothing else). This breakfast was, we agreed, easily the worst either of us had eaten for at least a decade, cold burnt oil dripping readily from cold fried bread that had evidently been fried twice: once to cook it, and once to warm it up again before leaving it to cool down again and then serving it. Yum.

After the breakfast to end all breakfasts, we strolled past a polling booth, where we were handed leaflets for candidates called things like Gomez, and the Trafalgar Cemetery, on our way to the cable car up to the ridge. We were going up the Rock. This was quite exciting, as it involved going in a cable car. It's like *Where Eagles Dare*, with added monkeys.

The Rock is now largely given over to a nature reserve for the monkeys. There are around 230 Barbary macaques ('apes') here, the only wild monkeys left in Europe. A legend claims that if the monkeys ever leave, British rule in Gibraltar will fall – like the ravens at the Tower of London, but monkeys. This is silly, though: the ravens could always fly away (if they hadn't had their wings clipped), but what were the monkeys going to do? Apart from anything else, they looked like they couldn't be arsed.

At the top, looking down into the vast blues of the Atlantic and Mediterranean, the Rock's greatest asset became fully apparent. It stands at the narrow mouth of the Mediterranean, a big stony gatehouse. It was particularly and increasingly useful for Britain, as it controlled the sea routes to important colonies like India and Australia via the Suez Canal.

Now a stop-off point for British and American submarines, and reportedly a listening station earwigging North Africa, there are myriad underground tunnels used exclusively by the military – this in addition to the famous eighteenth-century siege tunnels open to the public. They're all just driving round down there underneath us, we thought, being militaristic. (They've got their own bakery in there, apparently: 'I love the smell of fresh rolls in the morning . . .') Gibraltar was attacked as late as the 1980s, by the Argies. During the Falklands War, an Argentine plan to target British shipping in the harbour using frogmen (Operation Algeciras) was foiled – a plan that appeared to have been copied from the 1950s Gibraltar-based war film *Silent Enemy*, starring Sid James. (Not sure if they all did the laugh or not.)

But who cares about war? You just want to know about the monkeys. And why not? There was something unfunky about these monkeys. One sat on the circular concrete stairwell leading from the cable car to a viewing platform sucking the flavour from a burger wrapper. He wasn't all that cute in and of himself, but who could resist a monkey eating a burger? Who?

Up on the viewing platform, another monkey grabbed the T-shirt of a German kiddie, harassing him until he finally dropped his milkshake and fled, the monkey hungrily licking up the unctuous pink spillage. Clearly a British monkey. Down a track to another gun placement, a tribe of monkeys draped themselves over the half-ruined steps and doorways, looking vaguely like the apes in the 'King of the Swingers' lost city scene in *The Jungle Book*, only without the singing or dancing or any display of enthusiasm for life whatsoever. These looked like seriously lazy fucking monkeys.

A MONKEY EATING A BURGER.

They only seemed to perk up when there was a chance of obtaining junk food with menaces. Anyone peeling off from a group munching crisps was fair game to these fisty primates. At one point, they started staring at us. We stared back. We met the simian psychos eyeball to eyeball, but we didn't like it much. Then, just when it looked like it might go off, some off-duty Navy ratings turned up in a white Land Rover and fed them a Mars Bar. They liked the Mars Bar, but one of them still pissed on the 4×4.

A large sign explained the problem: the monkeys were suffering from 'an excess of monkey/human interactions. This results in the macaques becoming stressed and

A MONKEY'S BUM.

they will bite.' Visitors are implored: 'Please do not feed the macaques . . . they will become obese.' The sign concludes: 'Too much contact with people is resulting in some packs losing their family structure and causes splits in the group.' Stressed, violent, atomised, obese: we were witnessing a broken monkey society. We blamed the absent monkey fathers. And the monkey nanny state.

We would have gone to the furthest summit, O'Hara's Battery, to gaze to the Atlas Mountains in Morocco, but suddenly a Levantine wind hit the east cliff and vapour started whipping over the ridge, blowing past the disconsolate monkeys like a crazy nutter with a giant dry-ice machine.

We couldn't really come to Gibraltar without checking out the Great Siege of 1779–83, when Spain took advantage of the American Revolution to try and get its ball back. Many good men died holding on to this rock. It was a pretty full-on siege. The sort of thing where they end up drinking their own piss.

Gibraltar has many, many bastions (and gun emplacements, and ARP shelters . . .), and we headed straight for the best.

Following the casements and barracks along the harbour front – passing a mosque stationed in an old Nissen hut; you know, just to fuck with your head a bit – we reached the King's Bastion, a chunky great affair of chunky grey stone rocks, designed by General Sir Robert Boyd, proud defender of the Rock in the Great Siege.

Near the bastion we come across some cannons. This was hardly a surprise occurrence by now, but a plaque revealed them to be cannons not from some Gibraltarian siege or other, but from the Crimea, presented to the people of Gibraltar by Queen Victoria. 'What shall we do with these spare cannons, Your Majesty, acquired keeping the Ruskies out of India?' 'Oh, give them to Gibraltar: they fucking *love* cannons.'

Boyd was proud of his bastion. So proud, in fact, that he demanded to be buried within the stone walls. After he died, that is. Boyd did not love his bastion so much that he wanted to be buried within the walls while still alive. On his death, his body was laid in a special chamber within the walls. We tracked down the plaque that marks the spot, iron railings protecting the stone, in a slightly obsessive statement of defensiveness. A siege plaque with a siege mentality: this we had not seen before.

MONKEY GUARDS ENTRANCE TO THE MEDITERRANEAN.
ALAMY

The King's Bastion was now being rebuilt as a leisure complex, replete with ice rink, cinema, bowling alley and 'discotheque'. This could prove problematic. They would be dancing next to Boyd's grave and not on it, of course, but God help them if they started playing, say, the 'Macarena'. He'd probably come bursting out of the walls shouting: 'Give me "Knees Up Mother Brown" or give me death!' Then he'd start drinking his own piss.

The Gibraltar government website calls the siege tunnels – dug out of the northern cliff-face during the Great Siege – 'perhaps the most ingenious defence system devised by man'. They're only tunnels with some cannons poking out of holes in the rock face, though. Their creation was certainly quite a feat, but surely man has devised more ingenious defence systems than that? Radar, say?

Still, we went down, looked through the holes in the cliff and saw below, on the other side of the airport runway, Spain, the land of the Spaniard, and the Spanish. We took photos of the cannons still pointing out at Spain, forever vigilant. To complete the effect, some cannons pointed directly at La Linea, just across the border (the name means 'the boundary line').

A properly thriving city, La Linea houses many of the workers who by day make the Rock what it is. By night they go home and have a good time in what is apparently a more buzzing place. We looked down with a certain longing.

Our taxi driver was not totally sure why we wished to go to Rosia Bay, a semi-derelict concrete-encrusted inlet about a mile away from the centre, surrounded by a commercial dockyard and a building site. Would we not prefer to go up the Rock? They have monkeys. But it was here, in Rosia Bay, that Nelson's corpse was brought ashore, pickled in a brandy barrel, after his stunning victory against the combined French and Spanish fleet at Trafalgar.

At the hallowed spot there was no monument, no memorial, no crowds of proud and grieving patriots, just a stone staircase down to the quay that reeked – reeked – of piss. Like, really stank – of piss.

With Spain declining after the Treaty of Utrecht in 1713 (where Britain formally secured the Rock, plus the right to sell slaves to Spanish colonies), France became the prime bullyboys to beat: both much wealthier than Britain (with an economy twice the size) and more populous (with three times the population). During the so-called 'long eighteenth century' from 1688 to 1815, Britain and France were at war for 60 years out of 127. They were like kids who when the teacher came along and pulled them apart still managed to get some good kicks in. Only with the winner gaining mastery of the world.

As our taxi driver had a fag, we walked about, climbed on the dilapidated concrete jetty, watched a man fishing, considering how important this site was for Britain becoming boss of the globe instead of the French.

After the battle, the *Victory* was fixed up, and the brandy in which Nelson's body had been pickled (mixed with camphor and myrrh) was exchanged for wine when his body was put into a lead casket. Some hair was cut off and sent ahead to his mistress, Lady Hamilton. The sailors reputedly drank the brandy, mingled with Nelson's blood and death fluids – to imbibe the spirit in the spirits, to absorb their leader's fighting strength, to taste the taste of the man Byron called Britannia's God of War, and to get really, really pissed up for free.

We could hear their voices now, echoing through the ages, shouting at each other and getting lairy. Probably some of them were sick, what with having just drunk a dead man's fluids. We imagined them being sick. We didn't need to imagine them pissing in the stairwells. There was absolutely no need at all to imagine that aspect of things.

Nelson was pretty British, of course. Mentally so. In 1776, while convalescing from malaria, he had a vision of a radiant orb hanging above him. This, he decided, was an orb of Britishness. 'A sudden glow of patriotism was kindled within me and presented my King and Country as my patron.' 'I will be a Hero,' he added, 'and, confiding in Providence, I will brave every danger.'

Just 12 when he joined the Navy as a midshipman (and only 15 the first time he sailed to the West Indies), Nelson had already had an arm shot off at Tenerife. At the Nile, a bullet cut his head open, leaving him a bit, well, troubled in the head.

LORD NELSON: LOOKS LIKE HE'S DREAMING. PROBABLY ABOUT KILLING FRENCH PEOPLE.
Corbis

He seemed to take all that kind of thing in his stride, though. He was pretty into war, and ships, and warships: on shore leave at home in Norfolk, he amused himself by digging a man-o'-war-shaped pond, and sailing miniature ships on it. Maybe he practised for Trafalgar by jumping on the ships, flailing wildly around the pond in full regalia throwing bits of rigging and water-lily around willy-nilly, constantly falling over in the water he was churning up in an infernal scramble with himself? We just don't know.

We gazed out across the azure blue. Thanks to Nelson's victory a few miles out into these waters, Britain was spared being ruled by a bunch of distant grotesque oligarchs who would not have given a hoot for the rights of the ordinary British citizen. (Instead, Britain continued to be ruled by its own grotesque oligarchs). If you're getting into the spirit of things.

Thanks to that extraordinary victory, Britain was free. Free to conquer other people. And amen to that.

*

In the evening, we took stock. There really was little else to do. We were world-weary. But not weary of the world as a whole. Just weary of this bit of the world. Imagine a visit to your most boring relative, if that relative was also a militaristic drunk (which they may be). (Actually, a relative who is also a militaristic drunk sounds sort of interesting, in a way that Gibraltar most definitely is not.)

It was a desperate evening. We felt like we had been walking up and down Main Street for about three years. And it wasn't exactly revealing hidden depths, like an onion of mystery peeling away its layers of allure. That didn't happen. But we set out again into the nightlife, clinging to the idea that there must be somewhere nice to go just around the corner, even though we knew there wasn't because we'd already been round that corner and all the other corners.

A nadir was reached in a pub run by an ex-member of the Royal Ulster Constabulary. We sat wordlessly nursing lagers beneath the landlord's framed truncheon.

Back in the courtyard of our hotel, though, we did meet quite a funny guy – a builder from Hull called (we think) Tony who regaled us with stories about his colourful past.

The bar of our hotel seemed to be a bit of an expat hangout. The first night, we stumbled into a heated debate between four middle-aged men about Europe, and how it keeps fucking everything up all the time – all the bananas and that. Britain was quite a wrong place, in quite a fundamental way. They felt this very strongly. It had something to do with the erosion of rights. But the rights they seemed most keen on were the right to be homophobic and smoke fags everywhere all the time. They were so pissed off about immigration into Britain that they'd emigrated from Britain and immigrated into . . . Spain.

Tony was altogether a different kettle of chips. He told us he'd been caught spraying YORKSHIRE on to the new road signs when Hull was designated part of Humberside. Escaping jail only when bailed out by a proud local businessman , his cause was all over the local media. He'd also played in Hull bands as a contemporary of the Housemartins ('Fatboy Slim? Best of luck to him . . . the jammy cunt.').

Tony had a decisive analysis of old Blighty's problems, and that was that it's 'fucked'. He gave short shrift to his new 17-year-old workmate who suggested on leaving that Tony might have a problem getting up for work in the morning what with having just consumed 25 lagers: 'Don't fucking worry about me,' he said. 'I've been doing this for longer than you've been born.' We had absolutely no doubt at all that Tony would be up for work the next day, and it sort of made us proud to be British. We would be not be oversleeping either, of course: there was no way on earth we were missing the plane out of here.

WAS THE BRITISH EMPIRE ACTUALLY OKAY?

Empire's coming home. Not like last time, with its tail between its legs – no, with its head held high. Because the new champions of British history are taking back the Empire. They're sick of hearing about how the British Empire was 'really bad'. They think we should 'stop apologising' for Empire. If anything, it's them who should be saying sorry to *us*. (Maybe you weren't apologising – what with it probably not being your fault. Well, anyway, don't start.)

LORD CURZON, A MOST SUPERIOR PERSON. PICTURED HERE WITH MOST SUPERIOR WIFE AND TIGER.
Photoshot

This big new idea is gaining ground among new-right historians, Labour prime ministers and Prince Charles. But it raises important questions. Firstly, which empire should we not apologise for? The 'First Empire', mainly involving the Americas and encompassing the sixteenth to eighteenth centuries? Or the 'Second Empire', largely involving the Raj and the late-Victorian Scramble for Africa? It's hard to say which needs praising most, what with the first being built on slavery and genocide and the second on white supremacy (yes, that old toss-up again).

These anti-anti-imperialists seem to be infected with the residual idea that Brits – or 'benign' Western imperialists in general – are somehow always best: even our colonialism has to better than everybody else's. Of course, for all the new imperialists' efforts at bigging British 'gifts' like the banking system, the English language and, er, cricket, when push comes to shove, they can't really deny the Empire's many minor flaws. So their best response is: if the British hadn't done it, someone else would, and they might have been worse. In his Empire-loving book *Empire*, historian Niall Ferguson (if Empire-loving historians had an emperor it would be Niall Ferguson) concludes: 'In the twentieth century too [the Empire] more than justified its own existence, for the alternatives to British rule represented by the German and Japanese empires were clearly far worse.'

Finally, then, a position on which we can all agree: 'The British Empire – not quite as bad as the Nazis!'

FIFTEEN

WALK A CURRY MILE IN MY SHOES

THE FAST
AND THE FURIOUS
FIFTH COLUMNS
A CURRY

FROM THE IMPERIAL finery of Gibraltar to the post-imperial pomp of Manchester, just round the corner from Moss Side.

Britain's most famous Curry Mile is the Wilmslow Road south of the Manchester city centre, in Rusholme. The whole idea of a Curry Mile is mythic for many in Britain – the merest mention gets people all excited (A mile of curry? That's *fantastic*!). And this is the largest concentration of curry houses in Europe. You're never short of a curry here. After nightfall, it's a brightly coloured locale: jewellery shop windows give off a golden glow, neon lights drag you into the many various palaces of curry. It's a highly glittering scene – like Las Vegas, but with far better food (curry, in the main) and much less gambling. Imagine a long, busy road with lots of neon-signed curry houses on either side of it. That is what it looks like.

The restaurants here have historically been mostly frequented by white students and locals, although apparently more Asian people are eating out here these days. It's a great testament to integration that British Asians have started increasingly doing such quintessentially British things as going for a curry.

But this night, 12 October, was definitely major Asian festival night: Eid al-Fitr, the festival celebrating the end of Ramadan. The Muslim community was showing out by driving around in fast cars, playing loud music – the dung-ga-dung-ga-dung-ga-dung of bhangra filled the cool night air – and otherwise hanging out in laddy gangs of lads.

Families promenaded up and down, little girls sporting flashing bunny ears, past stalls selling nuts and jewellery. Shops sold Eid cards, and proudly displayed gifts for children such as the board game Junior Quran Challenge.

And always, always, *always*, there were the cars: BMWs, Ferraris, Lamborghinis, S-Type Jags. High-performance motor vehicles, rented for the occasion. The fast is over, let's go fast: that was the message. Except that they were all stuck in traffic. What to do? Just rev it up, basically. Parked cars were being revved up. Cars stuck in traffic were being revved up. These were, frankly, fuel-inefficient cars being even more inefficient with fuel than normal.

It was also business as usual for a Friday night here, of course. Students milling about on their way out, or gathered round large tables, enjoying a curry. The very occasional

Wahabi-looking chap in a white skullcap floated past, giving them and their boozy ways a dirty look. But the main thing was the cars. Did we mention the cars?

Some kids were gathered around a parked-up silver Porsche. A red Ferrari then pulled up over the road, and 20 mobile phones rose almost in unison to take a photo. A group of coppers went to check it out. This attracted even more youths. There was some badinage. We walked over to take a picture. 'You go for it, mate,' said the driver.

Another car came past with young blokes waving out of the windows. On the pavements, gangs of lads swaggered along the street glancing about at further gangs of lads. This was more macho swagger than actual menace – but then again, probably not totally devoid of menace either. The police were not taking any chances and were, correspondingly, absolutely fucking everywhere. On horseback. On foot. In police cars. Everywhere. One passing white woman asked a policeman what was going on: 'I thought it was a riot or something . . .'

Previous years had seen some trouble, which had led to a clampdown on cars being driven in an 'anti-social manner' – that is, car-drivers swigging bottles of champagne and then waving the bottles out of the window. But young male Muslims causing trouble because they were imbibing alcohol was definitely preferable to young male Muslims wanting to impose the kind of state that bans alcohol. And actually, even a quick look at media reports for previous years' festivals will elicit plenty of predictions of violence, but not many reports of actual violence.

This year, certainly, the only riot was a riot of colour – on flags, the splendid multicoloured neon restaurant signs, shiny clothing: families showing out in strong prime colours decorated with gold and silver braiding and frills. We kept strolling. Some young lads sprawled over an empty parked Jag to have their picture taken. A gang of crew-cut teenagers wearing traditional robes stood in the middle of the road waving a massive Pakistani flag, shouting in jubilation. So how did they feel about the end of Ramadan? 'I feel *ruff* . . . I'm a bad bwoy, ya know what I mean?' He jutted his chin out sternly to back up his claim.

A young bearded guy in his early twenties, who had come down the M62 from Bradford for the occasion, interpreted the festival in a way that would presumably be more recognisable to Muslim clerics. 'It's not just about fasting. It's about not swearing too,' he said. 'Just generally thinking well of others.'

Ever since Britain has had immigrant communities, they have been painted as an 'alien wedge' sadly positioned on the other side of the clash of civilisations (100 years ago, it was all about Jews being bomb-carrying anarchists). In 1978, opposition leader Margaret Thatcher sent a message less dog-whistle than full-on klaxon by talking of fears about the 'British character' being 'swamped' by

EID IN MANCHESTER: YOU CAN GET THERE BY BUS.

visitors from Pakistan, the very people still most often painted as the most alien wedge of all. Tonight, though, all the revving up fast cars, hanging out with your mates looking hard, queuing up for an ice cream . . . it didn't look *too* alien.

Mind you, any passing prurient white Brits who did find this kind of activity overly 'other' would not be alone. They could be joined in their distaste by other Muslims. One Muslim message-board correspondence we saw suggested that the response to all this un-Islamic boozing and hiring of cars was best represented by a cute little emoticon of a yellow blob in shades firing off a machine gun. If people within this so-called alien wedge are alienated by their fellow aliens, this doesn't sound like *that* much of a wedge. Not like a sort of Roman phalanx of Muslims. Perhaps Muslim people are diverse – you know, like all the other sorts of people.

These days, though, you don't have to be a rabid right-winger to be worried about a Muslim invasion, or to conflate all Muslims with the (obviously grotesque) Jihadists. You can also be Martin Amis, the novelist moonlighting part-time just up this very road at Manchester University. In that day's

Independent, the novelist (spurred on by a 'literary spat' with Manchester University colleague Terry Eagleton) had written an open letter to columnist Yasmin Alibhai-Brown, who had criticised his absent-minded fantasy, expressed in an earlier print interview, about strip-searching Muslims at random. Amis had said: 'There's a definite urge – don't you have it? – to say, "The Muslim community will have to suffer until it gets its house in order." What sort of suffering? Not let them travel. Deportation, further down the road. Curtailing of freedoms . . . Discriminatory stuff.'

So, strip-searched ideally – or just harassed or roughed up a bit, you know? 'I don't want to strip-search you, Yasmin,' Amis reassured (yet again, providing an utterly unforgettable literary image).

But we must excuse Amis for his slip – it was just, he explained, a 'thought experiment'. So, you know, he possibly didn't mean it. He did mean it, of course. But he might not have. And that's the main thing. Certainly it's in keeping with all his other pronouncements on the apocalyptic dread-threat posed to Western rationalism by Muslims en bloc.*

'Thought experiments'? We've all enjoyed those things . . . you know, really scary racial ones that leave everyone else in the room looking at each other nervously wondering whether you've just flipped your fucking lid right off the top of your mental bonce. Don't you have them? Oh, right.

At about half past ten, as we were beginning to tire of wandering up and down the pavement watching cars revving their engines and were ready to sit down for a you-know-what, we saw a crowd gathering in a side street to watch a car being winched on to a tow-truck. No doubt this was the result of some of that 'anti-social' behaviour we'd been warned about.

---

* Like, for instance, his quite spectacular fears about Britain (indeed the whole of Europe) being swamped by mega-breeding Muslims. Yes, they're only 3 per cent of the population *now*, but boy, are they breeding. Next, we'll look round and they'll be over 50 per cent. Don't turn away – he's looked into it and everything (well, he's read a book by neocon nutter Mark Steyn). Amis warned in another newspaper interview: 'You mustn't start getting in a tizzy about white supremacism when you read these figures.' Maybe he should work up a PowerPoint presentation. The fucking freak.

Frankly, we were terrified. Just imagine what Britain would look like if such lawlessness was allowed to spread throughout the land. Imagine the 'British character' being swamped by testosterone-crazed geezers all out looking for a bit of excitement. Driving around with flags attached to their cars. Some even drinking alcohol. Possibly to excess! Every Saturday night. Even small towns. Then, indeed, we shall be lost . . .

They should get Martin Amis in, we decided. To strip-search someone.

MARTIN AMIS: POSSIBLY CONTEMPLATING THE MUSLIM POPULATION EXPLOSION.
Corbis

GOD TOLD THEM TO DO IT: BRITAIN'S TOP IMPERIALIST NUTTERS

RICHARD WELLESLEY, 1ST MARQUESS WELLESLEY: As Indian governor-general, threw money at bejewelled coaches, a Ganges yacht and put it about so much his brother the Duke of Wellington wanted him castrated. Boasted to a female friend: 'I will heap kingdoms upon kingdoms, victory upon victory, revenue upon revenue; I will accumulate glory and wealth and power, until the ambition and avarice even of my masters shall cry mercy.' Women like that sort of talk.

CHARLES JAMES NAPIER: This commander-in-chief in India shared his tent with his horse, Red Rover (who was there at his deathbed). Not that we should read too much into it.

JOHN NICHOLSON: A great military hero, the evangelical 'Hero of Delhi' inspired jingoistic songs, praise from Kipling and young Victorian boys to sign up to imperial duty. During the Uprising, was noted for slashing down with his sabre to split rebellious sepoys in half. 'Am I cruel? For I confess I did enjoy the opportunity to rid the world of these wretches.' Was he cruel? Well, yes, he was.

MAJOR-GENERAL CHARLES GEORGE GORDON, AKA GORDON OF KHARTOUM: Wished he'd become a eunuch at 14; he also had a fascination with boys (not that we should read too much into it). Called by London officials a 'Christian lunatic', Gordon defied orders to withdraw from Khartoum in 1884–5 (well, there were natives to kill), instead feasting on turkey and Bass's Pale Ale while waiting for the original Mahdi Army. When they arrived, his severed head was paraded around on a pole. You can't help thinking he had that one coming.

SIR GEORGE TAUBMAN GOLDIE: The swashbuckling freak who invented Nigeria and famously envisaged a British dominion from the Niger to the Nile compared his own personality to 'a gunpowder magazine' (that's not a magazine about gunpowder). Once rented a room off the Strand, where he set up a Gatling gun, aiming it across the Thames. So it's safe to say he preferred north London. Strangely, an atheist.

HERBERT KITCHENER, 1ST EARL KITCHENER: Obsessed with avenging his soulmate Gordon, Kitchener eventually clashed with the Mahdi at Omdurman. We say clash, but the enemy were simply mown down by machine guns in a slaughter Kitchener described as 'a good dusting'. A repressed homosexual, he never went anywhere without his trusted gang of unmarried officers, the so-called 'band of boys'. Ironically, one of his famous First World War recruiting posters read: 'YOU ARE THE MAN I WANT'.

CECIL RHODES: Rhodes, the man who invented Rhodesia (and South Africa), said: 'We are the first race in the world, and the more of the world we inhabit the better it is for the human race.' Neither married nor showed the slightest interest in sex (maybe he had sex with Britain in his dreams?). Instead, set about single-handedly dominating the southern African diamond trade via Maxim-gun-related slaughter and forced labour. See, just think what you might achieve without all those base desires cluttering up your life?

CECIL RHODES: POSSIBLY NOT TO SCALE.
World History Archive/Topfoto

ALFRED MILNER, 1ST VISCOUNT MILNER: A 'British race patriot' who believed the 'superior race' should wage total war to achieve world domination. Sounds a bit Nazi-ish, that. As does his 1901 decision to build the world's first concentration camps (in which over 40,000 people died) during the Second Boer War.

ROBERT BADEN-POWELL, 1ST BARON BADEN-POWELL: The Hero of Mafeking, who staved off the Boers for over 200 days; author of *Scouting for Boys*; lover of slaughtering black people (he once held an illegal execution of a 'fine old savage' in Matabeleland, just for kicks) . . . Enjoyed looking at pictures of young boys in the nude ('Stayed with Tod. Tod's photos of naked boys and trees. Excellent.'). Not that we should read too much into it (maybe he just liked trees). Wondered about linking the Scouts to the Hitler Youth. His 1939 diary noted: 'Read *Mein Kampf*. A wonderful book.' Not that we should, etc.

GEORGE CURZON: While at Oxford, wrote the lines: 'My name is George Nathaniel Curzon,/ I am a most superior person.' Stupendously posh and pompous, he found the British in India too common. Responded to millions dying of famine by outlawing charity. Once banned the singing of 'Onward Christian Solders' from an official event because it claimed that 'kingdoms rise and wane'. The British Empire? Wane? Never! Not with such fine men to lead it.

SIXTEEN

GOD'S FAVOURITE PEOPLE

GUNPOWDER
TREASON
PLOT

THE POPE IS being escorted along the crowded night-time Georgian high street, while fireworks and bangers go off above his head. Dressed in full vestments, his right arm is raised and he is holding a crozier. He is being held well above the crowd, kind of like on the Popemobile. Only it's not the real Pope, it's a papier-mâché Pope. And, actually, he's being carted off to burn on a towering pyre of flame. So it's a good job it's not the real one.

Members of the crowd – many of whom look like perfectly normal, everyday members of society – are hissing and booing at the Pope and shouting: 'Papist bastards!'

Others yell, with genuine malice: 'No popery!'

Meanwhile, above our heads, a huge banner hangs across the street declaring: 'NO POPERY!'

Then some members of the procession walk past carrying a blazing sign – a metal grille lit up in flame – that spells out the words: 'NO POPERY!' In fire.

A message was emerging here. And that message was: no popery. Putting your message across with fire really drives the point home, we felt.

Tonight, for one night only, Lewes, the East Sussex market town picturesquely perched amid the undulating South Downs five miles from the coast, is playing host to a partially sanctioned festival of bonfires, fireworks and irresponsible flinging of bangers. It is not playing host to any popery. (Honestly – the way these people go on about the Pope, you'd think he used to be in the Nazis or something.)

LEWES, BONFIRE NIGHT: THIS YEAR'S THEME WAS ANTI-POPERY.

The fifth of November is a full-blown Protestant red-letter day – in its own way the biggest Britain day of all. If Britain had a Fourth of July/Bastille Day type day, a day to celebrate the formation/evolution of the British nation, the natural choice would be 5 November. A special day. (A special day for burning papists.) It commemorates (obviously) the Catholic plotters who tried to blow up Parliament in 1606. That's definitely one factor to remember remember. And then, in 1688, as William of Orange stood poised to pile in and send Britain's last Catholic king, James II, packing, he deliberately chose this day to land his forces in Torbay, the soon-to-be-crowned William II winning over the populace with reassuring banners: 'The Liberties of England and the Protestant Religion I will maintain.' (And so began Torbay's central role in world history.) Britain's subsequent economic successes were taken as a sign of God's approval. How have the British celebrated the fact that they are God's chosen ones? By having a big riot, usually.

So this Lewes Bonfire Night procession is actually a quite authentic, non-bleached-out version of ages-old tradition. Here, more than anywhere else in Britain, the notorious Protestant Bonfire Boys kept the old hatreds aflame when most of Britain started letting go and moving on.

From the eighteenth century, the authorities were keen to tone things down. But the people still just loved to burn shit. Well into the nineteenth century, rowdy mobs eager to celebrate the Fifth 'in the traditional way' rampaged round on Bonfire Night in such well-known anarchic hotbeds as Horsham in Sussex and Guildford in Surrey. In Guildford, the people would send 'plunder' parties out to steal 'fences, gates, doors . . .' – you know, all the fun stuff. In 1859, they stormed the police station after the police refused to come out and have a fight with them. A notice posted on Horsham Town Hall in the 1770s by some of the townsfolk, when there was an attempt to ban the festivities, read: 'It is determined between us to have a fire of some sort, so if you will not agree to let us have it in peace and quietness, with wood and faggots, we must certainly make some fire of some of your houses.'

In Lewes, in 1857, a local vicar, John Neale – he wrote the carol 'Good King Wenceslas' – found himself being savagely beaten up for his supposed Catholic tendencies; describing in a subsequent letter to *The Times* being knocked to the ground and giving himself up for lost at the hands of the Lewes mob, 'only too notorious in the annals of lawlessness'. (You know how mobs are. Soon, even people who quite liked his carol started laying in, perhaps shouting: 'Feast of Stephen THIS, you fuck!')

These days, it's all a bit of fun, though. Pyromaniacal fun that families are officially advised to stay away from, but a bit of fun nonetheless. Well, except for the blowing up of the parking meters. The people of Lewes have singled out many targets with their 5 November bonfire effigies, burning likenesses of Margaret Thatcher, George Bush and, er, Geri Halliwell. But what the people of Lewes hate most of all, more than Thatcher, more even than Halliwell, is paying to park their vehicles in Lewes town centre (a recent imposition). They have combined this strong hatred of parking charges with their great love of fireworks – by blowing up the parking meters. With fireworks.*

This year, the local police chief, Superintendent Cliff Parrott, had decreed that the tolerance of recent years' parades was being abused and now wished to roll back the revellers' long-held freedom to be grossly irresponsible with explosives. It was a crackdown – on bangers! Rumours that miscreants would be taken by 'snatch squads' and detained in a hall somewhere in the centre of town further angered the townsfolk. John Winter of the Lewes Borough Bonfire Society declared: 'They can't throw us all in jail!'

The intense noise all around suggested the police were not getting their way. The mob didn't feel overly Protestant. No one was demonstrating much of a work ethic, or noticeably deferring pleasure. Instead, sparks were flying. The various fancy-dress processions (pirates, Napoleonic solders, Zulus) were literally walking through fire – stomping through the flaming squibs that had fallen from the torches to pepper the ground. Flaming tar barrels were run down the high street, the dark was lit up by the flashes of smoky red flares. Bangers and fireworks were fizzing everywhere. More bangers than before. More bangers than *ever*! In narrow little lanes, drunken teenagers let off Roman candles and, gurgling with pleasure, watched them splurt into the air. A rocket went flying off into a churchyard (not a Catholic church, just a church church), with youths rushing off gleefully in the opposite direction.

* They also ran an amazing and heroic, if slightly touched, boycott of a local pub that, taken over by a rival brewer, refused to stock the certainly very tasty local beer, Harvey's. This went on for a year or so before the brewery caved in (the sweet taste of victory! and beer!), and came to be followed in detail by the national press and its commentators (Nick Cohen called the boycotters 'magnificent'). Very determined, the people of Lewes. If someone could devise a way of somehow blowing up an NCP using beer, they'd be like pigs in shit.

A 12-foot-high effigy of Superintendent Parrott came past, processed around town in all his bespectacled, gap-toothed glory, clinging on to a massive red rocket flying over an effigy of Lewes Castle (now *that's* attention to detail. Oh, and he had another rocket stuck up his arse). Before him, there had been the flaming crosses; 17 of the buggers carried precariously down the narrow street. 'Hmm,' we thought. 'It's not often you see flaming crosses these days.' Each one commemorated one of the 17 Protestant martyrs burnt in Lewes High Street during the 1555–7 Marian Persecutions, when the country was still darkly split between the Catholic and Protestant religions. Henry VIII's Catholic daughter Mary 'Bloody Mary' Tudor would cheer herself up by murdering Prods, and her dirty foreign husband, Philip II of Spain, had great designs on incorporating England into the vast Habsburg Empire, like a big Catholic bastard.

The Marian Persecutions were not totally useless, though. The full gory details made for great Protestant propaganda – most famously in John Foxe's *Book of Martyrs*, first published in 1563. In Scotland, John Knox found that Foxe's book inspired his belief that every good Protestant had a right to

LEWES, BONFIRE NIGHT: THIS YEAR'S THEME WAS ANTI-POPERY.
Rex Features

slaughter every idolater, if they got the chance (Knox and Foxe: would have made a great anti-Papist comedy act). When republished in 1732, this book became strongly bound up with the survival of the plucky post-Union Britain, and was among the few titles one could expect to find in working-class households. So it was kind of an early misery memoir. You know, one of those really anti-Catholic ones.*

For hundreds of years, before and after Union, Catholicism represented the Evil Empire, the mysterious, tyrannical Other that would extinguish all our liberties. As the Armada approached in 1588, people talked of how it had amongst its ranks one ship carrying only whips – to lash them back into the Catholic faith. There was state-sponsored anti-Catholicism, and plenty of room for private freelance anti-Catholicism, too: sixteenth-century Lincolnshire gentleman Richard Topcliffe kept a rack for torturing Catholics in the comfort and privacy of his own home. The authorities didn't seem to have a problem with this. Plague? Papists did it. Great Fire of London? Come on, it can't have been an accident. For a few hundred years, anti-Catholicism went in waves, taking different forms at different times for various reasons, but what we're saying here is that at no point did Catholicism become 'popular'.

Near the river, the police were having difficulty. Something was kicking off somewhere else and a single-file line of 12 policemen and -women had to negotiate the higgledy back streets to get there. At the front, the leader had the Lewes A-Z open and shouted to his followers: 'Alley on left.'

They sped off down a seemingly empty alleyway, presumably to some scene of fire-based carnage, at a light run. We

---

* As a taster of Foxe's insatiable fascination with burning martyr flesh, the passage on the protracted death of Oxford martyr Nicholas Ridley tells how flames burned at his 'nether parts' but only scorched his skin, so more faggots had to be brought so that 'his nether parts did burn' properly, while only singeing his upper body, before a third load of fire did for him, and how he was still speaking to Jesus until his tongue was too swollen to speak, and 'he knocked his breast with his hands until one of his arms fell off, and then knocked still with the other, while the fat, water, and blood dropped out at his fingers' ends'. Foxe concludes: 'Seeing a man of so great dignity, honor, esteem, and so many godly virtues, with many years of study, of such excellent learning, to be put into the fire and consumed in one moment. Well!' Well, indeed.

SOME OTHER GUY

So 5 November is mostly about burning Catholics. Or, in the case of Guy Fawkes, hanging them, hacking off their nadgers and thrusting them in their face, tearing out their heart for inspection by the baying crowd and then dragging them round behind a cart. Ironically, the only thing they *didn't* do was set fire to him.

While the captured Fawkes was being furiously tortured, the others – including leader Robert Catesby, 'the prince of darkness at the centre of the Gunpowder Plot', in the words of historian James Sharpe – fled from London. They ended up in the Midlands, assistance from their fellow Catholics evaporating by the hour. They now wrestled with the classic dilemma that plagues religious-political fanatic conspirators to this day: if it's all going tits up, is that God's will?

THE EXECUTION OF THE PLOTTERS.
HEART HELD UP FOR INSPECTION.
GOD'S WORK.
MEPL

They had a cartload of arms and gunpowder with them. The powder got wet, so they decided to dry it out when they reached Holbeach House in Staffordshire. By putting it next to the fire.

When the gunpowder exploded – blinding John Grant and injuring Henry Morgan – was this rank stupidity, or divine intervention? The conspirators were shaken. There was a disagreement . . .

MORGAN: What work is this, oh Lord? I am injured! I am injured! And Grant is blinded.

CATESBY: It's a pisser all right.

THOMAS WINTER: Yes. And who left the gunpowder out in the rain again, Catesby, you twat?

CATESBY: God made me do it.

The conspirators made their final stand at Holbeach House. The mortally wounded Catesby exhibited a suitably dramatic, almost Hollywood, touch by dragging his bleeding body across the floor to die clutching the feet of a statue of the Virgin Mary. So he was definitely a Catholic.

followed a little way, to see them disappear around the corner straight past what looked very much like the midpoint of a drug deal. At the sight of 12 baton-carrying police officers trotting past, both dealer and customers stood stock still, wide-eyed, clearly believing that pretending to not be there was momentarily a mighty fine tactic. (At least the drug-dealer was showing some of that famed Protestant work ethic, getting down to some good business, albeit not business of a wholly Puritan bent.)

Pretty soon the processions had snaked through the town and disappeared off to their various bonfires. (There are five bonfires – one, or even two, not being nearly enough to satisfy the people of Lewes.) We climbed the dark street that snakes up the Cliffe. Fireworks were by now filling the night sky, and the Cliffe was supposedly the place to see it all going off.

This was, essentially, a big teenage party. Our progress was stopped whenever another drunken teen set off another Roman candle by someone's doorstep. Which would be: most doorsteps. Funnily enough, one of the houses on this steep lane apparently belongs to Arthur Brown, the sixties singer famous for singing the song 'Fire', which is about fire, while wearing a hat that was on fire. Were Mr Arthur Brown to appear tonight, standing on his doorstep, with his head of flames, surrounded by bangers and bonfires and fireworks, shouting about being the God of hellfire and bringing you fire, and gonna take you to burn, that would really have been something, we thought. He didn't, though. Maybe he was out. Maybe he's had enough of fire.

At the top, we could look down on an immense cavalcade of fireworks and bonfires; very pretty, in a Bosch-comes-to-Sussex sort of way. The Cliffe Bonfire – upon which the Pope would be doing his burning – looked like it might easily overtake the whole town. Bonfires were originally made of bones and intended to drive away evil, and there is obviously something quite purgative about settings things on fire. But we weren't sure whether we felt purged. ('Do you feel purged?' 'Not sure.') We instead considered how Catholic burned Protestant, then Protestant burned Catholic, then Protestant banned Catholic from public office and roughed Catholic up in the street. And so on.

We left town with the fireworks still in full flow, spying as we went another group of police officers, this lot all standing stock-still, huddled together in their bulky yellow bodices, in an otherwise empty street, in reverential silence. We followed their collective gaze along a side street to one of the spectacular fireworks displays going off on the edge of town. We wanted them all, as a giant red and green starburst lit up the night once again, to go: 'Ahhh!' But they didn't.

On the national news, the night's main story concerned a terrapin in Wrexham having a rocket firework tied to its back with masking tape and then being fired into the sky in what the RSPCA claimed was a copycat crime aping a Virgin Media Broadband ad featuring a cartoon tortoise being launched into space. And so the wheel of oppression turns: this day the Catholics, the next the terrapins. Where will it all end?

SEVENTEEN

ALL THE ART IN THE WORLD'S NOT WORTH A MEAT PIE IF YOU'RE HUNGRY

WORKSHOP OF THE WORLD
WORKERS OF THE WORLD
A CHAMPION OF THE WORLD

BLACKBURN: BIRTHPLACE OF the modern world. It was mid-December, and we were off to Lancashire, the 'first industrial society', to try to make sense of industry, and, er, society. While we were there, we also wanted to soak up a bit of Northern-ness. We might even rediscover our proud Northern roots . . . roots that have not, to the best of our knowledge, ever actually existed. But all modern people come from the North, in the same way they come from Africa. And who doesn't love the North? Our North. The North!

First up, we had a date in Blackburn – with a little lady called Spinning Jenny.

You know the spinning jenny. Or you remember hearing of the spinning jenny while trying to stave off sleep as the sun poured on to your back through the classroom window panes, lulling you towards unconsciousness . . . ah, the sleeping, the calmness . . . Yeah? Well, you were fucking wrong about that, so sort yourself out. She's a lady. An industrial lady.

The train pulled into winter-afternoon Blackburn, rows of redbrick terraces lining the hillsides. Blackburn was once Cotton Town – a boomtown expanding exponentially, mills springing up all along the snakey river. Cotton was Britain's biggest industry – yes, cotton spinning was Britain's biggest money-spinner – back when Britain was the Workshop of the World. (Imagine being a workshop for the whole world. Imagine how dusty everything would get.)

There are no cotton mills here now of course (the last ones stuttered to a close in the eighties leaving the working-class population feeling somewhat redundant, both metaphorically and indeed literally). But we needed to conjure cotton factories of the mind. Blackburn was quite helpful in this respect, having left some of the mill buildings standing. (One had a St George's flag draped from it.) They were big, made of bricks: Northern.

By the Town Hall (municipal, Northern), we stopped to look at the statue of an eminent Victorian. The stone plinth was covered by a temporary wooden board, so obscuring any name panel. We stood in the pedestrianised street wondering who it might be. There was a statue of Gladstone somewhere in town, but this didn't look like Gladstone. He was whiskery, but not Gladstone whiskery.

As we paused, a little middle-aged guy in tracksuit bottoms and a pinstripe cotton shirt came over and started smiling at us, noting our interest in the statue. We smiled back.

'There's another one over there!' he shouted, pointing off down another street.

'Right. Who is it?' we asked.

'Don't know!' he replied. 'There's another one over there!'

Then he trotted off. We never did find out who the statue was – or who our new friend was. But there *was* another one over there. He was right about that.

We wandered into the museum (proud, Northern) and through to the main room on the ground floor: the best room; the room containing all the machines; the room of pride. And there she was – right in front of our eyes: Jenny (Ms) (Spinning). This was the machine – a square rack with eight spindles and a turny, wheely thing – that, more than any other, invented the modern world. Single-handedly.

We stood and looked at the spinning jenny. It really brings things home, we agreed, looking at things up close (it's almost as good as actually bringing stuff home).

SPINNING JENNY. PLUS FEMALE WORKER.
DON'T KNOW HER NAME.
MEPL

Of course we knew before that a machine that could spin lots of yarn would be more productive than one person spinning away at a single wheel. But we didn't *know* it, not really, not like we did now. It didn't *look* that modern, but looks can be deceptive.

This was a copy of the one first made by local weaver James Hargreaves in 1764 (or thereabouts)* with his pocket knife; just one bloke and his little knife, whittling away at bits of wood, inventing industrialisation . . . His motive – perhaps hilariously – was to free 'the poor weavers from the bondage in which they had lain'. He ended up inadvertently inventing factories, of course, leading to compulsory bondage for all – including the kiddies.

* Hargreaves reportedly named the spinning jenny after his wife Jenny. Although some claim he named it after his daughter Jenny. The only problem being his wife wasn't called Jenny and neither were his daughters. So what Jenny he named it after remains a mystery. (Others claim the word is a derivation of 'engine' . . . BORING!)

So was Blackburn's son hailed for his invention? Was he heck. Sensing these new spinny things were bad news, in 1767 local weavers broke into his house and burned his supposedly liberating machines, going on to smash every spinning jenny for miles around.

Machine breakers are often portrayed as thickies standing in the way of progress (often as downright Luddites), but then again, they were trying to stave off unemployment and starvation, which actually sounds kind of intelligent.*

You can definitely see why the machines might piss people off. One 1832 description of a Lancashire cotton mill gives a flavour: 'Whilst the machine runs, the people must work – men, women and children are yoked together with iron and steam. The animal machine – breakable in the best case . . . is chained to the iron machine, which knows no suffering and no weariness.'

So it was quite hard work.

But what about the inventiveness, we wondered, looking at all the inventions? People like to talk about British inventiveness. Well, Jeremy Clarkson does.† But it seemed quite straight-forward, standing in front of Jenny. Given Britain's Empire (and thus access to markets and raw materials), and the tremendous demand for cotton that couldn't be met by handloom weaving,

---

* Earlier we'd strolled past the BBC Lancashire building, which bore a plaque commemorating the Plug Riots of 1842, when Blackburn workers went from factory to factory pulling the plugs out of the even more new-fangled steam-powered equipment. The Army fired on the unarmed demonstrators and the leaders were condemned to death. When they pointed out they were only trying to avoid being starved by a cartel of cotton barons, the judge compassionately commuted their sentence: to deportation to Tasmania.

† Clarkson claims that virtually everything that has ever mattered in human history has come from 'a man in a shed in Britain': 'Everything. The internet, penicillin, the mechanical computer, the electronic computer, steam power, the seed drill, the seismograph, the umbrella, Viagra, polyester, the lawn-mower, the fax machine, depth charges, scuba suits, the spinning jenny . . . I could go on, so I will. Radar, the television, the telephone, the hovercraft, the jet engine, the sewing machine, the periodic table . . .'

Polyester *and* lawnmowers? Tremendous. Oh, and the periodic table was made by Dmitri Mendeleev, who doesn't sound very British (he was, in fact, a Russian). Not that it matters – being a scientific explanation of the natural world and all. Presumably, by the way, when he says 'a man in a shed' it's not the same man (and shed) each time? Or is it?

AS IT SAYS ON THE PICTURE ITSELF, WHAT YOU ARE ESSENTIALLY LOOKING
AT HERE IS COTTON WEAVING IN LANCS.
MEPL

someone was likely to come up with a solution. It's hardly surprising that the spinning jenny was invented by a Lancashire
weaver rather than, say, some guy in Borneo. Demand for
invention begets invention. Rather than some weird genetic
inventiveness voodoo.

In the end, poor old Hargreaves was ripped off countless
times after failing to patent his invention and was hounded out
of Lancashire by the weavers, who hated his guts. Perhaps he
ended his years going: 'But . . . but, I thought it would be
good!'

We looked around the other machines, wondering what they
all did. Stuff, probably, we agreed – you know, with the thing
there.

Luckily, a retired machine manufacturer under the museum's
employ came in, only too ready to talk to anyone about the
machines he had worked on. Being told all about the workings
of large metal machines – about all the bits that go round and
the bits that go back and forth, and all the other bits – by an
elderly gentleman in a thick Lancastrian burr? Fred Dibnah
would be proud.

When Blackburn was Cotton Town, Manchester was Cottonopolis. They were cotton fucking mad up here. Cottonopolis

sounds almost cool – you know, if it wasn't for all the child labour and stuff.

As we pulled into Manchester's Victoria Station in the evening, one thing was apparent. Women were absolutely everywhere. Women. Everywhere. Coming down the station steps. Women. Out and about. Women. Walking along the platforms. Gangs of women. Pouring off trains. More women. Swarming through the streets. Women women women. We half expected to hear Ernie K-Doe's 'Here Come the Girls' blasting from the skies. What was going on? Where were all the men? We knew Northern women were 'feisty', but had this feistiness spilled over into outright overthrow while we were on the train from Blackburn?

Then, just outside the station, we heard a voice. A male voice. A lone, hectoring male voice that made everything clear. 'Anyone need any tickets for Take That?' yelled a tout.

So that explained all the women. Tonight, Manchester's MEN Arena would be playing host to four men. Four brave, noble men of the North. No Robbie of course, but this lot didn't seem to mind – tonight the MEN Arena was the WoMEN Arena. (Or the WoMEN and some GayMEN Arena. And best of luck to it.)

It was a raw night. After dumping our bags, we hit town. By now, there were some men about, many of them hopping around in the cold drinking lager from plastic cups and eating bratwurst hotdogs at the enormous German Christmas market that covered the whole of Albert Square in front of the monumental Gothic Town Hall (because these days nothing says 'British Christmas' like a vast German Christmas market). A truly gigantic illuminated inflatable Santa looked down on the happy, sausage-munching scene.

Never ones to turn up an opportunity for fun, we figured: hey, it's Thursday night. We're in Manchester. Let's track down a mural of a massacre of vote-demanding workers by the pissed-up Manchester Yeomanry. So it was off to the Free Trade Hall.

On the way, we tried to look at Manchester afresh and absorb its very Cottonopolis-ness – the cotton exchanges, the Gothic libraries, all that stone . . . It looked like Manchester. We cut up Brazenose Street and noticed something neither of us had paid any attention to before: a statue of Abraham Lincoln. Lincoln had never been to Manchester (not even just clubbing). But the statue commemorated his thanks to the people of Lancashire for their support in the American Civil War, as opposed to the whole of the British establishment – both Tory and Liberal – who demonstrated their undying opposition to slavery by, er, supporting the Southern slave owners.

This was, it must be said, pretty internationalist of the cotton-workers (particularly considering the starvation caused by the resultant cotton famine). The statue was next to a stall called Muncher Futterkrippe (Schnitzel Bratwurst Fleisch-pflanzer) – Original German Kitchen!

That was quite internationalist too. (No one had even sprayed the phrase BOCHE SHOP on it . . .)

Finally, we reached our quarry: a Radisson hotel. But not just any Radisson hotel. A Radisson hotel with associations of slaughter. Can you say that for many Radisson hotels? Don't know.

This was now the centre of town, but it was once all fields – St Peter's Fields. On 16 August 1819, a peaceful demonstration of 100,000 men, women and children had gathered here to call for parliamentary reform. The country was literally run by a closed shop of the super-wealthy who thought the people were all scum (This is no exaggeration: Wellington considered vote reform 'evil').

This was the great and fabled struggle for British democracy. But it was democracy in a real and direct sense. Since the French Revolution, the British ruling class had lived in fear of revolt. The middle class didn't have the vote: the new industrial cities like Birmingham and Manchester didn't have MPs even. And the working class was kept at near starvation level. The radical leaders were often middle-class professionals; but the mass of support was in the working class – which was organised, quasi-militarily trained in many cases, and putting the fear of God up authority. Their demands were for universal suffrage, annual parliaments and an end to import controls that kept up food prices. With no massive state apparatus, these demands meant curtains for the old order. Revolution was on the cards, which were on the table, and also in the air: it was that serious.

In St Peter's Fields that day, the Yeomanry (a volunteer police–army made up of butchers, publicans, tradesmen, etc.) had orders to intervene if radical orator Henry Hunt tried to elect an unofficial MP-style representative for the city, as had happened in Birmingham. (There were even cannons in reserve around a corner down by the G-MEX, which hadn't been built yet, but still . . .)

Pissed, the yeomen steamed in anyway – and when the crowd knocked them off their horses, were followed by the Hussars – cutting through the crowds with sabres, killing 15 and injuring hundreds, probably more than 400. The events were satirically dubbed Peterloo, to mirror Wellington's military victory four years earlier, by Bradford writer James Wroe (the government chucked him in prison as revenge). Actual Waterloo troops were used on the day.

Manchester's newly enfranchised middle class built the Free Trade Hall on the site of the fields in the 1850s. After hosting the Sex Pistols gig everyone claimed they went to (we actually *were* there – in the pictures, we're the two four-year-olds down the front), it's now part of a five-star hotel, with added health spa.

PETERLOO, 1819: BECAUSE BEING A BRITISH SOLDIER WASN'T *ALL* ABOUT MASSACRING FOREIGNERS.
The Bridgeman Art Library

We went inside, looking for the Peterloo mural kept from the old Free Trade Hall. A jolly young concierge in a smart black and white uniform was happy to help, pointing the way with a smile: 'Oh yes, the massacre . . . the mural's just up the stairs.'

We don't think he should necessarily have shook his head in memory of the innumerable crimes of the ruling class, dipped in blood, feasting on the fruit of the workers – but he acted like the very idea made him downright chirpy. Do the bastards *make* him do that?

The mural was hung right next to the staff room. You could see this as a warning to hotel staff not to get too uppity, if it didn't seem more likely that it was just the least public spot to put it without it actually not being in the hotel. Sadly, the mural itself was a pale, washed-out affair: we hadn't expected Goya, but fucking hell.

Respects paid, we went off for a Chinese at one of Manchester's many fine Chinese restaurants. This Chinese restaurant, we noted, was full of Chinese people. Always a good sign.

In the morning, we stopped off for a cup of tea with Nick Mansfield, director of the People's History Museum – formerly the National Museum of Labour History, formed as a repository for labour-movement and working-class history (the museum itself was closed for redevelopment). We asked Nick about the name-change, which had been controversial: 'National Museum of Labour History: doesn't really sound like an exciting day out, does it?'

Nick, we knew, was an expert on the struggle for the vote. Obviously a big part of the Britishness debate is the idea that Britain somehow *is* democracy, that our Britishness is bound up with our democratic principles thanks to some kind of innate British reasonableness, possibly handed down from the heavens – but at the very least handed down by British politicians: the best, and most liberal, politicians in the world.

'People are incredibly ignorant about the mechanics about when people got the vote. They assume, "Oh, sort of Magna Carta . . . something like that,"' said Nick. 'But it's incredibly recent. Absolutely incredibly recent. Really, in terms of one person one vote, not until after the First World War was there a major shift. Not just women voting but working class voting.

BANANAS IN PYJAMAS

To stifle public anger following the massacre at Peterloo, the Tory government issued the repressive Six Acts banning 'seditious' writings, large meetings and unofficial weapons training ('What are you doing with that pike?' 'Nothing . . . just practicing STABBING YOUR FUCKING HEAD IN!').

But after a decade, full-on radicalism finally resurfaced in the Reform Bill crisis of 1830–2 in which, while Parliament ummed and aahed about how far (or not, mostly not) to spread the franchise, the country was busily turning itself upside down. Well-informed, well-armed crowds would form from nowhere and then, fairly frequently, riot furiously. In Birmingham, according to one report, 'the workmen walk about talking of nothing but the Bill'. That's not meaning the previous night's episode of *The Bill* (*The Bill* hadn't even started then).

The Merthyr Rising of 1831, an insurrection against the state pawnbroker seizing furniture from the poor (a bit like the IKEA riot, then, but not), saw workers holding the town for four days against the forces of the state, which feared revolution would spread throughout Wales and the Midlands (this was the first time a red flag was raised in Britain).

In Bristol, radicals besieged a hotel where their corrupt local Tory MP was holed up until he fled over the rooftops in his underwear in the dead of night (cool).

Finally, Wellington's Tories folded and the new Liberal government passed the 1832 'Great' Reform Act which ended some rotten boroughs and slightly extended the franchise through the middle classes – not quite the ticket, really. This event is eulogised as part of Britain's fine upstanding 'golden thread' of liberty and democracy, *exactly* the sort of thing we should be celebrating in our great British heritage. Despite, at the time, the Great Reform Act feeling more like a Total Kick In The Teeth For Most Of The British People Reform Act.

If there is something to celebrate here, it's not the generosity of the British state. It's people chasing Tories over rooftops in their jimjams.

'People really did have to fight and die. Not just the Chartists [*huge working class movement for universal suffrage and annual parliaments*], but also the First World War. The labour movement and most of the Labour Party did a deal, threw in their lot with the wartime government to help recruit and get the factories to fight through the war. This was a deliberate policy. It got the Labour Party off the ground and made potential working-class voters less deferential, and that led to the welfare state. But it was literally a blood sacrifice.'

Crikey.

All of this of course makes something of nonsense of the idea of a single 'national story' – a narrative of the past that we all share. It all seems to depend on whose point of view you're looking from. You have to think that many of our foremost patriots, great lovers of great British democracy like Peter Hitchens, only got the vote thanks to the kind of bolshie bastards who would make them choke on their powdered egg. We'd joked with Nick about a banner we'd seen in a book that said 'Down with the Bishops! No Peers!' It was from 1831, but it was a slogan you could still raise today. While there would clearly be less chance of getting a sabre up you for your pains, the vote and democracy have obviously proved themselves not to be synonymous with each other.

The story is sold as pioneering British capitalism leading inevitably to pioneering British democracy, sort of like conceptual lovers, British ones. But to us it seemed less about the gradual unfolding of the democratic blanket, more the development of capitalism on the one hand, and democracy on the other: fighting like a couple of pissed rats in a sack. So it's quite hard to see what's actually shared here given that the people who hold all the power and wealth in Britain *still* apparently have a problem with sharing.

The lesson appeared to be: when people fight for things, they can make progress. When they don't, it gets taken away: it's a story without an ending. So perhaps most people's experience of living in Britain owes more to Peterloo than Waterloo. And these things that seem to pushed into the background in the official 'national story' – radicalism, class, the right not to be completely fucked over . . . well, they all seem to be quite international things. It's almost enough to make you think you might have something in common with foreigners!

There are no cotton factories in Lancashire now of course.

But cotton goods don't generally fall from the sky. These days, child labour has been outlawed . . . sorry, we mean outsourced. Workers, often quite young ones, in China and other parts of Asia are going through the same struggles as their Lancashire forebears: the right to form trade unions, the right not to be maimed by large-scale industrial machinery . . . All that old stuff.

Not that this has any direct relevance for us here in Britain. Except for all the stuff they make.

It should probably be admitted at this point that the North of England has made a major contribution to British popular culture. The cities around these parts have counted in a way you can't really say for Reading, or Berkshire generally (it's probably something to do with all the cities). What we don't get, though, is why the North is so reticent about bigging itself up. Cities like Liverpool and Manchester have much to be proud of, and should find some way – any way – of expressing pride in their achievements. People like Phil Redmond or Paul Morley should be using their positions in the media to tell people about the fabulous things the North-west has offered us over the years.

Before leaving the North, we decided to sample some of this culture: culinary culture. On our journey north, we had been determined to fight cliché every step of the way, sort of like knights or Chartists or something, but without the actual threat of violence. But then we became aware of an event happening in Wigan at the exact time we were going to the North-west that we felt we had a duty not to ignore – yes, that's a *duty*: it's only the World Pie-Eating Contest!

Wigan is a mill town *and* a pit town (there were once 1,000 pit shafts within five miles of the town centre – now *that's* mining). It's also a pie town. The annual World Pie-Eating Championships took place at Harrys Bar, once a rather grand Victorian bar in the Clarence Hotel, the competition arena crammed up one end of this narrow tiles-and-mirrors boozery. We arrived just in time to overhear reigning champion Brendan Brockbank telling a radio reporter that he doesn't even like pies much: 'It's all the pastry,' he explained.

You could cut the tension with a pie slice. The audience consisted almost solely of the pub's regulars, hard-drinking men who have settled into a middle age that often involves having liquid for lunch. One man was asking his contestant mate about the nature of the competition pie. His friend reasoned: 'A pie's a pie, innit, Terry . . .'

The whistle blew. The contestants, lined up behind a table, were out of the traps and into their pies. We looked one way, then the other; here a contestant has a swig of beer; there it's a dog with its face in a pie (sorry – we should have explained about the dog: one of the contestants was a dog). They munch, taking swallows of beer as they go . . . Shouts of 'Come on, Fred' and 'Come on, lad.'

At one point, a steward in a white coat with a piemaster's hat noted a contravention of the rules: 'Do not drink the gravy! Do *not* drink the gravy!' Manhood. Adrenalin. Virility. Pies . . .

As we neared a minute, there was noise; a kerfuffle. A flurry of contestants raised their arms to show their pieless hands. Pub owner Tony Callaghan declared a dead heat between last year's champion and newcomer Adrian Frost at 55.48 seconds.

LIKE HOT POT? LIKE PIES? . . .

This meant one thing: it's a pie-off! 'Clear the arena.' ('That were never a dead heat,' countered one spectator. 'Were it fuck,' concluded his companion.)

This time there's something different. Frost is sipping water. Small bite, little sip of water. Brockbank is barely into his pie, but Frost is on his last mouthfuls. It can't be, but it is: 34 seconds. It is textbook munching. (Barely has Frost got his triumphant hand in the air before the crowd turns on Brockbank: 'You're an 'as-been!' shouts one man. 'He's still chewing,' says another, incredulously. 'Yeah, you're shit!' shouts another again. We're all *thinking* it, maybe, but bloody hell: give the man a chance to finish his pie.)

In a short ceremony, Callaghan handed the glittering trophy to Frost, World Pie-Eating Champion for 2007. 'Adrian, make sure it don't change yer life,' warned Callaghan.

'Oh, I won't change, mate . . . I'll still turn up for work tomorrow . . .'

Before heading for the station, we enjoyed a small detour.

Because it's not all pie-eating contests in Wigan. There's also a new shopping centre. We took our quick whiz through the Grand Arcade – a spanking new mall that's straight out of Walter Benjamin, via Fritz Lang's *Metropolis* – because it had promised us a statue of local laddie George Formby. (And you try keeping Steve out of T K Maxx.)

We found the Emperor of Lancashire at the rear entrance, on the way out to the car park (you'd be unlikely to see the statue on the way in from the car park, it being shielded from that direction by a wall). Poor George. Maybe he'd have a song for the occasion: 'What a bunch of bloody *bas*-tards/ They've stuck me by the stairs . . .' (And it doesn't even look like him! Fucking hell: it's not difficult: half of him's teeth, the other half's ukulele; how hard can it be?)

Leaving George and heading back through Malltropolis we were then, weirdly, thrown out of the shopping centre for trying to take a picture of its enormous Christmas tree. It really was a very big tree. And two really big blokes did invite us quite emphatically to leave the premises. (Shopping centres, eh? The new high street.)

We walked back towards the station, grabbing a pie each, deciding – after some consideration – on meat and potato.

The meat and potato turned out to be burning hot shiny gloop that only vaguely tasted of either meat or potato. These were the world's hottest pies. Standing on the station platform juggling hot gloop around our mouths to avoid burning them, we felt we hadn't done very well on the pie front.

The ones at the pie-eating competition looked great. Maybe a pie isn't just a pie, after all.

JOURNEY TO THE CENTRE OF THE EARTH

While we were in the North-west, we couldn't resist a small detour. Well, a detour of sorts. It was also a voyage to the Centre of Everything . . . and how can that be a mere detour? It's more of a tour.

We headed into the hills. Up in the hills of northern Lancashire, we had discovered, was the geographical centre of Britain. It's not often you find yourself near the geographical centre of Britain. This was not the middle in any 'furthest from the coast' way – it's only about 20 miles from Morecambe Bay. This was Britain's centre of gravity – meaning that, if Britain's Strongest Man were to spin Britain on his fingertip, this would be the ideal place for him to pick up Britain. (How many Britains could balance on the head of a pin? Not that many.)

It was about half past five and pitch-black by the time we pulled in to Clitheroe, which was coincidentally the birthplace of Jimmy Clitheroe, the sixties comedian who dressed as a schoolboy and had his own ITV series co-starring the inimitable Molly Sugden. (Jimmy Clitheroe was from Clitheroe and he called himself Clitheroe. But that was not a stage name. His real name was Jimmy Clitheroe. He lived with his mum.)

Anyway, we were only passing through Clitheroe. We were on our way to a phone box ten miles up the Ribble Valley. Of course we were.

We hopped into the nearest taxi and asked: 'Can you take us to the middle of Britain, please?' Or words to that effect. The Asian taxi-driver did not think we were exactly mad; he did know the phone box and had taken people there before. But, and he was fairly insistent on this point, 'never at night'. People did come to look at the phone box in the middle of Britain. They combined this with marvelling at the stunning valley views. But they did not do so in the dark.

As we wound around the country lanes, looking at the outlines of the majestic hills against the dark-blue skyline, our new friend kept telling us how beautiful this area was and implored us to come back when there was some daylight. (It probably was a bit stupid, looking back. But hey: if you can't drive round night-time rural Lancashire in a taxi when you're young(ish), when can you?)

After a 15-minute journey, we came to the outskirts of the little village of Dunsop Bridge, and a phone box by a stream. The sign inside explained: 'You are calling from the BT payphone that marks the centre of Great Britain'; and that this was BT's 100,000th phone box, unveiled by Ranulph Fiennes in 1992. It didn't say how he got here. Maybe he trekked over from the North Pole.

We're a bit like Ranulph Fiennes, we decided. You know, on a quest against insurmountable odds and all that. And, okay, we hadn't diced with polar bears, snow-blindness, diarrhoea and frostbite, but we had been to Gibraltar and been the subject of the mild if friendly approbation of a taxi-driver.

A PHONEBOX. BRITISH.

We stood by the phone box, waiting for the phone to ring.

BRITAIN'S TOP MYTHICAL CREATURES

BLACK DOGS: Whether Cu Sith of Scotland, Gytrash of northern England, or Black Shuck of East Anglia, Britain is overrun with devil dogs. Big black buggers that emerge (sometimes from the sea) at night, portending doom. If it comes from the sea, watch out for it shaking water all over you. Just before ripping your throat out.

HOBBY HORSE: Horses, but predatory people-horses who appear in Padstow as part of the May Day celebrations, symbolic of frolicking mischief, grabbing at a particular lucky lady and dragging her beneath his skirts in an an unholy parody of bestiality. Don't worry: kids love it!

THE GREEN KNIGHT: The supernatural monster-knight who, when beheaded by brave Arthurian knight Sir Gawain, picked up his own head, which started asking for a rematch. The anonymous writer of the poem *Sir Gawain and the Green Knight* really, really hated the Wirral: 'Few lived there/ Who loved with a good heart.' So, sort of a medieval Boris Johnson.

BLUE MEN OF THE MINCH: Blue-skinned mermen who lured sailors from their ships into the Minch, the sound between the Hebrides and the Scottish mainland. Thought to be a folk memory of Moorish galley-slaves abandoned by Viking pirates. Fascinated with rhyming games, they challenged their victims to verbal duels. So, African rappers challenging sailors to throwdowns on the Western Isles . . . isn't that unusual enough? Without giving them fish-tails? Just how short were these people's attention spans?

BONELESS: A disgusting mass of gooey white flesh, like a giant jellyfish, that would wait in ambush and engulf travellers in remote lanes in Oxfordshire. Kind of ancient folklore meets Hollywood B-movie. You'd think the collective unconscious would have moved on a bit, but no.

BONELESS.
The Kobal Collection

QUEEN MAB: The faerie queen who drives her chariot across men's noses, providing dreams of wish fulfilment (yes, that probably does mean sex dreams). According to one theory, Britain's fairies are folk memories of Bronze Age beaker people driven into the forests by incoming Celts, occasionally foraging near the iron-wielding newcomers. Folklorist Marc Alexander explains: 'One has only to glimpse a Lapp briefly in the brooding Scandinavian forest to guess how trolls came about.' Ah yes, glimpsing a Lapp briefly in the brooding Scandinavian forest – what a day that was . . .

WILL O' THE WISP: A mysterious glistening light that lured travellers from paths into deadly bogs. Thought to be caused by methane produced by decaying organic material. Not actually mythical, though, as it had its own telly series in the early eighties.

BOLSTER: This Cornish giant, who regularly stole villagers' cattle, became smitten with a pious local lady called Agnes. His lovelorn swooning got in the way of her praying, so she asked him to prove his love by filling up a hole in the Chapel Porth cliff with his own blood, but the hole ran down to the sea! So it never filled up! And he bled to death! The bleeding to death of a lovestruck giant is commemorated in Bolster Day. A 'great day out for all the family', apparently. A great day out watching a giant bleed to death.

BEAN NIGHE: Scottish fairy washerwoman whose appearance portended violent death for those whose shirts she was seen washing. Her long breasts would be thrown over her shoulders. How to approach her: a man should steal up behind her, seize a nipple and start sucking, calling her mother. The Bean Nighe is not commemorated in any great days out for the family. And thank fuck for that.

GLATISAUNT/GLATISANT, THE QUESTING BEAST: This evil Arthurian beast had the head of a serpent, body of a leopard, hind of a lion and legs of a deer. This sounds silly, and it is. But it's also a properly fearsome creature that symbolises chaos and incest. Jesus. Imagine symbolising incest! Symbolising chaos sounds okay. But not incest. Some of these myths are a bit much, really.

WINTER

EIGHTEEN

THE TIME OF OUR LIVES

A CHRISTMAS CAROL

DICKENSWORLD THEME PARK
(WHICH EXISTS)

DELIVERANCE

IN THE MIDDLE of the Christmas season, a highly seasonal season, came our fourth seasonal marker, the winter solstice – a time when people on these isles have traditionally tried to keep warm. We were going to drive away the midwinter blues with metaphorical fire only, banding together with our fellow man at the Charles Dickens theme park in Chatham, Kent: Dickens-World (which exists).

DickensWorld (which exists) has been highly appropriately sited in the Medway town where the literary titan lived for a few years as a child while his father worked in the Naval Dockyard – so there's a proper historical link right there. It's on a factory outlet park next to the river, sandwiched between an M&S and a Nando's. But really, what's so very un-Dickensian about that? Dickens would have worn clothes. Wearing clothes was what his age – the Victorian age – was all about. Put it on, and keep it on. That was the general message.

We were determined to enjoy ourselves. This was little short of our office Christmas party. And what could possibly go wrong? Dickens was very Christmassy; he virtually invented the sodding thing. Theme parks are full of families, and families – well, *they're* as Christmassy as hell. So imagine a Dickens theme park that promised us carols, a Christmas tree and a production of *A Christmas Carol* too, full of families, at Christmas. It might snow. Hey, maybe Slade would turn up?

Crossing the enormous car park that stretched off into infinity (well, at least as far as the bowling alley), we couldn't help but notice the huge picture on the exterior wall, above the entrance: a giant pair of hands cupping a working clock above the phrase: 'THE TIME OF THEIR LIVES'.

Was this supposed to mean something? We looked at it for a bit. Weirdly – in fact, coincidentally – it started moving. It transpired that, every hour on the hour, the clock moved back to reveal the prow of a boat, which moved partly forward through the aperture. The boat contained a large model of Dickens with his arms around

DICKENSWORLD, CHATHAM: A WORLD OF DICKENS.

a boy, a girl – Dodger? Little Nell? – and a dog . . . Fucking hell, that must have been some ideas meeting.

We paid our money, took our tickets and went up the narrow stairway towards Victorian London, 'up the stairwell representing the transition from the modern world to the 1800s'. Rounding a corner, the warehouse opened out to reveal the dimly lit nocturnal cityscape; we crossed a ramshackle wooden bridge over a waterway and past some tottering slum dwellings. The fake Dickensian scene was vaguely effective in a West End scenery kind of way. Some other visitors floated past underneath us on one of the slowest boat rides ever.

We were brought out into the central courtyard – an open performance space surrounded by fake Victorian shops and eateries that were in fact shops and eateries. Here we joined about 40 families watching some am-dram youths who were just coming to the end of a mini-play of *A Christmas Carol*. 'A merry Christmas to everybody! A happy New Year to all the world!!' roared a young actor playing Scrooge just having seen the error of his ways. Ersatz, dim Victorian street lamps barely illuminated the scene.

After the play finished and Scrooge (really, among the very youngest-looking Scrooges ever) left the central area, some fake snow – not even very much – fell from the roof. As the paltry fall of snow came down, spectators milled around the space trying to eke out at least a touch of bonhomie. What really stood out was the young Muslim woman in a light pink headscarf standing in the middle of the throng with her hands thrown up into the air, welcoming the fake snow. That was definitely the most Christmassy thing that had happened so far.

We tried to keep our mood Yuletide. Before we went, we'd read visitors' complaints that the young people playing the Dickens characters didn't seem to know what they were doing, that nothing was working, that the whole thing was an unmitigated disaster. But we thought that was just the internet telling lies again, like with 9/11.

But it was true, there was just nothing much here. There was the Great Expectations Boat Ride, with a sign saying you would get wet, which might be all the fun in the world on another occasion but didn't seem an ideal thing to happen on the shortest day of the year. (Even though this ride looked rubbish, they had those signs that say: 'QUEUING TIME FROM HERE: ONE HOUR'. These signs gave us the fear.) Then there was Fagin's Den, which turned out to be a tiny soft-play area – no picking of pockets, although you could maybe nick some very small shoes, if you were that way inclined.

After a failed, slightly traumatic attempt to go into the Haunted House (a man in the top half of a Victorian undertaker's outfit and the orange bottoms of a velour tracksuit – we couldn't work that out either – shouted at us for going through an open door and told us to stand behind a rope, but we didn't even know where the rope was), we climbed the stairs to the upper level, and sat down with about a hundred other punters inside the Britannia Theatre.

Here, the Ratcatcher host joshed with the audience about selling their children, and where the fire exits were located.

The main show consisted of animatronic characters in the galleries to the side of the stage – Bob Cratchett, Mr Pickwick and the like – telling us in fantastically terrible cockney accents what a great writer 'Mr Dickens' was. We wouldn't claim to be *experts* on animatronics, but isn't the point that they're supposed to actually move? These just kind of lurched forward when it was their turn to 'speak'. They also kept saying things like 'Interesting, don't you think?', 'This is entertaining and fun', and 'This has truly been a momentous occasion' – as if in some sort of freaky suggestion mind-control experiment. (£62 million this place cost. It's amazing what £62 million doesn't get you these days.)

Emerging back on to the upper level, we surveyed the Victorian street scene below. At the edge of the performance arena there was a large Christmas tree, which we now noticed had only one string of (white) lights on it. Next to it stood a young man done up like the Artful Dodger in the film. He started playing the banjo. This was inevitably reminiscent of *Deliverance*, known for its famous banjo scenes (obviously) but also other, much darker overtones. There is a reason the BBC have never seen fit to make *Deliverance* a Boxing Day afternoon staple.

Dickens loved Christmas. The festival had been close to dying out in the early 1800s but, with his 1843 novella *A Christmas Carol*, Dickens gave it a shot in the arm, and also gave shape to the modern British family Christmas (games, gifts, a general feeling of goodwill to all). Dickens loved family values as much as the next Victorian. He didn't always love his own actual family, though. He and his wife Catherine used to really get on each other's tits (not just at Christmas, but all the time); he referred to her in letters as 'the donkey', she suffered from post-natal depression – which can be a hindrance if you're giving birth to ten children. The Dickens family Christmases must have been a hoot.

Here's Dad with the games and the presents, and the stories – oh, the stories! Then, at some point in the afternoon, after one too many, he starts shouting abuse at Mum before jumping in a carriage down to Peckham to give his mistress one.

Still, isn't that always the way?

MRS DICKENS, LOOKING FORWARD TO CHRISTMAS.
Corbis

Along from the theatre was the pub, essentially a high-street chain pub, called the Six Jolly Fellowship Porters after the lowlife riverside local in *Our Mutual Friend*, Dickens's immense 1864–5 novel about 'money, money, money', all human life endlessly commodified, all human relations poisoned by the relentless churn of the cash nexus, life expectancy in the cities (at the supposed height of Britain's greatness) falling to 26, with everything boiling down to a big pile of crap – cleverly symbolised in the novel by a big pile of crap (the 'dustheap' of refuse and human waste around which the plot revolves). Actually, DickensWorld (which exists) did convey this general idea quite well, so that was a plus.

We decided to head to our homes, to continue our quest even during the holidays by having a traditional British Christmas with a Christmas tree (German idea imported by the Windsors/Saxe-Coburgs) decorated with traditional Christmas lights (America, 1880), eating turkey (native to the Americas) and watching a panto (French). Because that's what the Great British Christmas is all about. Not forgetting Santa, of course (the Turkish saint as reimagined by the Germans and the Coca-Cola Corporation). (The Coca-Cola Corporation *and* the Germans. Jesus.)

Our Christmas party had not been the best Christmas party we had ever been to. In truth, we didn't expect DickensWorld (which exists) to feel like all our Christmases had come at once. But this was like none of our Christmases had come at once.

Back outside in the expansive car park, we went across to the M&S, which had abundant cheap boxes of quality mixed nuts. So all was not lost. Quite a lot was lost, though.

NINETEEN

PICK YOUR ENEMY
AND SHOOT HIM

NAZIS
BLITZ
WAR
THATCHER

THE SECOND WORLD War is one war at least where it's crystal clear who the baddies were. It was the Nazis. Nobody likes Nazis. Well, except Nazis. They're very much on their own on that score. Well, there's crypto-Nazis – but look, anyway: the British people united behind their betters, naturally concerned not to be invaded by Nazis (who, as we have already established, were bad), but kept a watchful eye on their betters, and hoofed them out of office as soon as the war was over. Not all the British people of course. Some of them were busy selling contraband nylons or burgling other people's houses during the Blitz. But most of the Brits.

But how to fully experience what the British people went through, how sorely they were tested and not found wanting? If only we could somehow be transported through time to an air-raid shelter, with the sound of the Luftwaffe at full throttle overhead, raining down hell on to Blighty's broad shoulders. Luckily, we were in luck: they had just the thing at Winston Churchill's Britain at War Experience (which exists). We would go to Winston Churchill's Britain at War Experience (which exists) for an hour, we decided. Our finest hour? Who knows?

It was right underneath the London Bridge station arches ('*Underneath the aaar-ches . . .*'), on Tooley Street. We weren't sure to what degree Winston Churchill was providing us with Winston Churchill's Britain at War Experience (which exists), given that he had been dead since 1965. Maybe he came to them in a vision and inspired the enterprise ('The tourist . . . must have . . . somewhere else . . . to go . . . in the Borough/ London Bridge area . . . that isn't . . . the London Dungeon . . . or the market . . .').

Paying for our tickets at a 1940s-style cinema booth, we went through into the exhibition and were immediately presented with mannequins sheltering in rough woollen blankets on wooden bunks.

The exhibition was very tatty, with an authentic smell of damp. In wartime, everything gets a bit tatty, of course, so that's kind of authentic. War is also terrifying. And this was at least kind of spooky. There were the life-size dummies in soldiers' mess tents and a gory, actually just bloody weird, massive blazing building recreation with firemen beating back the flames and a pile of naked mannequin parts – limbs everywhere – piled up on the ground; here, a dead and discarded mannequin baby. (Maybe Winston Churchill got the young

Chapman Brothers in on work experience to help out. Winston Churchill meets the Chapman Brothers on work experience: you know, that whole genre.)

The Experience was packed full of propaganda posters and other evidence of how the war effort was packaged for the masses. We thought about how this is sort of how the war is seen now: like a 1940s information film. Everyone pulling together. Great days. You even get thought pieces in liberal newspapers about how great all the allotments were and how, in these days of global warming and recession, maybe we should be a bit more like people in the war; turning the war into just another lifestyle fad, largely gutting it of its whole war/politics aspect.

It's as if we're being encouraged to see the war straight out of those propaganda films called things like *BRITAIN CAN TAKE IT*. Or the ones they did for US servicemen coming to Britain: 'John Briton doesn't want war, but once he's riled, there's no stopping him . . .' That kind of thing.

Propagandists had reason to idealise Britain and the war effort: they were making propaganda. There probably weren't actually all that many bluebirds over Dover. Not even in the 1940s. We had been particularly struck by the 'It's Your Britain Fight For It' campaign, a series of beautifully designed post-cards and posters by Frank Newbould, an official war artist. They are lovely, colourful images of life in rural Sussex: a fair visits the village of Alfriston, a shepherd tends to his flock on the South Downs – everything picked out in big blocks of colour. Very effective images of the kind of idealised England we had looked for back in the heady days of summer – back before the war came, the golden days . . .

It's all bollocks, of course. The people going off to fight, or enduring the Blitz, did not – nor would they ever – live in rural Sussex. But no one was going to produce 'It's Your Britain Fight For It' cards featuring slums full of kids with rickets and TB living in one-room flats in tenements crowded against rail-way lines, were they?

We sat down and watched a film showing footage of the home front, the Blitz, the devastated streets, with extracts from letters and diaries. It was narrated by John Thaw. Occa-sionally, when the moment required, it would cut to an audio of Winston Churchill intoning one of his key speeches. Obviously, Churchill's wartime speeches are the surest way to send tingles down the spine of any full-blooded British person. Here it comes again, that hypnotic lulling burble . . . 'NE-ver was so much owed by so many . . . we shall NE-ver surrender . . .' There was probably a lot more to being a great orator than saying 'NE-ver', but when the strings kicked in, he could have just said 'NE-ver NE-ver NE-ver NE-ver NE-ver NE-ver NE-ver NE-ver NE-ver NE-ver NE-ver NE-ver' for hours on end and the British heart would always be stirred. Resistance is useless! No one, but *no one* can deny the full-on emotional clout of a sentimental drunk during times of war.

We took in the film's survey of damage, and damaged people: 'Everything is becoming unclean,' wrote one ARP warden after clearing out bodies from a bombing raid. 'Tomorrow is never.' We also picked up tips on what to do during an invasion: 'Pick your enemy – and shoot him . . . The average Britisher's brain works quicker than the average German's.'

WINSTON CHURCHILL: IF ANYTHING, SHOT BETTER AFTER A FEW DRINKS.
Corbis

The weird thing is that the longer the British people stood bravely behind Churchill against Hitler, the more they pulled away from their own betters. We were pulling together! By, er, pulling apart. Even in 1941, in his propaganda essay *England Your England*, George Orwell noted a massive shift in the army and the home front for a more equal society free of the grotesque class divides and privilege exemplified by people like, well, Winston Churchill. 'This war, unless we are defeated, will wipe out most of the existing class privileges,' Orwell predicted (as it turned out, not quite correctly).

Soldiers were reading (not just pin-up mags) and realising that Britain's old rulers were often a bit Nazi themselves. We've all seen Anthony Hopkins in *The Remains of the Day*. We know the score. Churchill had been an admirer of Mussolini, and sympathetic to Franco: he was clearly full square behind the whole not being invaded by Nazis thing, but still: bloody hell.

Most soldiers and civilians were determined there would be no repeat of the aftermath of the First World War. Lloyd George had promised a 'country fit for heroes', with the house-building programme dubbed Homes Fit for Heroes. In reality, many were given the opportunity to stand in the unemployment line, for heroes.

We turned a corner to be faced with the Anderson shelter. We opened the doors and crouched down to enter, shutting ourselves into the dim light. It was a bit like sitting in a sauna, only not as hot – backs against the corrugated-iron walls. The noise of aerial warfare was blasting in our ears – a single speaker pumping out a nonstop loop: sirens wailing, plane engines thrumming, bombs whistling, explosions . . . It sounded like a spot of avant-garde noise-rock, possibly Japanese. It sounded like war.

A mustachioed tourist opened the doors, saw us sitting there listening to the noises of war, testing ourselves, and politely closed the doors again.

Britain was under attack. We were hiding out in our shelter. Just like our grans (who were tested and not found wanting). We finally got up to leave. Just at the precise moment we reached the door, hand on the handle, a young female Euro-tourist opened the door suddenly and came face-to-face with our pale, war-torn faces – and screamed. War is hell.

DECORUM WAS MAINTAINED.
Imperial War Museum

After the war, Labour was swept to power – the first majority Labour government; a landslide. Britain was ruined, on the point of starvation even, but people refused to be short-changed this time. The new Labour government offered a New Jerusalem. This wasn't the Middle East Jerusalem, but Blake's Jerusalem: a land of equality and fairness where the fruits are shared by all. The new dawn! The new Jerusalem!

In practice, there were limits to this new utopia – as anyone who has been to Croydon can attest. But wars against poverty and disease? They're the best sort of wars.

Maybe Winston Churchill's Britain at War Experience should have shown the footage of Churchill touring his victorious nation and being booed by crowds in football stadiums yelling 'WE WANT LABOUR!' That was more strictly speaking Winston Churchill's Britain Post-War Experience, but it would have still provided a fitting climax.

In the shop, we admired the 25-quid ceramic Winnie with lapdog, bomb wreckage tea-towels and the freaky Blitz colouring book. (More golliwogs. We were over being surprised to see golliwogs by now. It had become a normal thing to happen in the run of events for us.)

A wall of letters from a class of eight-year-olds from Watford expressed gratitude for their day out. One said: 'My best part was the shop as it had so many good things in it.' Another: 'The Blitz Room was really fun because I like dark things that are dark.'

That's the youth of today for you.

So Britons were tested and not found wanting. Imagine being found wanting . . . a whole nation, being found wanting. 'Sorry, you were tested and you failed that test. You have been found wanting.' What a pisser that would be. ('Can we have another go?' 'No. You're run by the Nazis now.' 'Pisser.')

The Empire was holed under the waterline, though, and Churchill had failed in one of his key war aims: 'I have not become the King's First Minister,' he declared in 1942, 'to preside over the liquidation of the British Empire.' But the game was up. Australia and New Zealand realised Britain could no longer protect them in the East, and started to look to America; India was independent by 1947; African countries were emboldened by their own role in the war (as India was post-WWI), and started to break free . . . America was in the ascendancy. Churchill even told Roosevelt he wished he *was* American. (Bloody hell: neo-fascist, British, American – make your fucking mind up.) Suez finally proved that the old colonial powers could not act without at least the tacit support of the US.

But Old Blighty had one last throw of the old-school dice left in her . . . the Falklands. We didn't think we could leave war Britain, imperial Britain without considering the Falklands.

GOAL!

On 1 July 1916, Captain W. P. Nevill kicked off the Battle of the Somme – quite literally, with a football. The company commander had brought over four balls, one for each platoon, and offered a prize to the first platoon to score a 'goal' in enemy trenches – 'subject to the proviso that proper formation and distance was not lost thereby', naturally. History does not record what the prize was, as it was never awarded: sadly, but perhaps not unsurprisingly, Captain W. P. Nevill was killed stone-dead by machine-gun fire as soon as he followed his ball over the top.

Clearly, nothing inspires the common soldiery to near-certain death like a posh bloke kicking a football – but, you know, what a twat. The First World War represented the dizzying highpoint of British patriotism. In a speech to potential recruits virtually celebrating the outbreak of war, future PM Lloyd George was moved to declare: 'The stern hand of fate has scourged us to an elevation where we can see the great everlasting things which matter for a nation – the great peaks we had forgotten, of Honour, Duty, Patriotism, and, clad in glittering white, the great pinnacle of Sacrifice pointing like a rugged finger to Heaven.'

Obviously, most people who joined up were not thinking they would be literally sacrificed and many rushed to enlist for what has been called 'the most popular war in history'. It wasn't just the promise of football. There was also the enticing prospect of helping out 'plucky little Belgium'. People must have thought quite highly of Belgium in those days. 'Father! Mother! I'm to war! Belgium's in distress!'

It wasn't *just* about Belgium, though. There was also the assassination of a single Austrian Duke for the whole world to go to war over. Oh, and the inevitable clash of colony-hungry European powers now the globe had been mostly carved up: so worried were Britain's rulers by Germany's aspirations that they officially redesignated relations with France as 'cordial'. If that isn't a sign they saw war as inevitable, what is?

In all, over 700,000 British lives were lost in this power-struggle. Amazingly, almost as many soldiers volunteered as were conscripted. Pals regiments saw mates from towns and workplaces sign up and serve together (this plan was soon ditched because all the sons in the street getting killed at once brought home the reality of the war to people in too undiluted a way); women were encouraged to brand non-volunteers cowards; some companies like Nestlé made it clear they expected young male employees to volunteer (and you thought Nestlé had always been a force for good) . . .

One of the most celebrated aspect of the British recruiting drive of course remains – quite jaw-droppingly – the freaky posters of freaky General Kitchener pointing out, freakily, and saying 'Your Country Needs You.' Imagine the feckless youth of today being inspired by a poster campaign like that. They'd probably just draw a silly moustache on it or something. Anyway . . .

The war's general popularity declined after the initial 'non-dying' phase came to a blood-spattered close, and by the end, Lloyd George thought that workers full 'not of depression, but of passion and revolt' might stick a big rugged finger up *him*.

Still – footie, though, eh?

THE WIVES ALSO FAVOURED HUN-RELATED CARNAGE.
Swim Ink 2, LLC/Corbis

(America, by the way, thought Britain would lose the Falklands war.)

Luckily for us, just around the corner on HMS *Belfast*, the huge grey cruiser moored up in the Thames between London Bridge and Tower Bridge, there was an exhibition celebrating the Falklands. It was winter, too, so we thought it would give us an idea of what it was like in the Falklands: cold, essentially.

HMS *Belfast* is 'a vital and enduring reminder of the reality of naval warfare in the twentieth century'. Or a rotting symbol of British sea power marooned next to much more popular tourist attractions like the London Dungeon and Tate Modern. It had seen lots of action: supporting advancing troops in the D-Day landings; guarding vital supplies convoys; sinking the *Scharnhorst*; launching the career of Spandau Ballet . . .

The north London New Romantics famously got themselves a record deal by holding a party on HMS *Belfast*. 'Philip Salon [notorious transvestite club promoter] turned up in a wedding dress covered in lightbulbs and saying, "Where can I plug myself in?"' We thought about this, briefly: a man covered in lightbulbs.

On the way up the gangplank, we overheard a mother on her mobile, talking about how she'd just taken her three-year-old son, beside her with another younger child in a buggy, aboard the *Belfast*: 'We thought it would be fun,' she was saying. 'You know – like a pirate ship. But it's all serious stuff about war, and it's so *grey* . . .'

Grey? War? What exactly was this woman expecting from a fucking great big battleship? (Which has, by the way, a wooden deck, which is sort of surprising.)

The Eyewitness Falklands exhibition was a modest one-room affair deep in the bowels of the ship – past the lovingly re-created ship's bakery and dentist's surgery, beyond the mocked-up mess featuring old-school tins of bitter – deep down in a room near the torpedo launching technology and the tobacco stores, only a bit further down than that, was the exhibition.

The Falklands was old school. They even managed to have a ship-to-ship surface battle. How quaint! In the age of smart bombs decimating areas systematically expunged of any media presence, it seems like another world.

The exhibition was short on giving reasons why the war needed to happen and big on *Boy's Own* derring-do, like the civilian catering worker shooting down an Argentine jet with a machine gun. Apparently he had a *Combat* comic-style speech bubble above his head, which read: 'Eat steel, Argi pig-dog! Atención! Atención! Aaaaaarrgggghhhhhhhhh!'

The war will have had some impact on us at the time, of course, being barely of *Commando*-reading age: we were but boys; all of ten, babbling shit about the Black Hole and Condorman all the time . . . We would have been agog at news of dramatic firefights at places with new-found war-comic names like Tumbledown Hill. Corned beef was, of course, off the menu (which was a great sacrifice, but then, that's war).

But the 1980s seems quite late in the game for a so-called post-imperial power to be chalking up major war crimes. Thatcher used to show visitors to Chequers the chair she was sat in when she ordered the sinking of the *Belgrano*, the ship sunk sailing away from the Falklands. 'I was in the bath when I decided to privatise British Gas . . .'

In the exhibition, Field Marshal the Lord Bramall quotes Churchill on 'willpower' prevailing. We will NE-ver surrender. So it's just like the Second World War, really. To these guys, there is no question of the importance of this war – even if it is largely an invention of their own minds. Something very unfortunate that came across in this exhibition is how much the top brass appear to have really enjoyed themselves. It's nice to get out – and, well, they had done all that practice – but some of these guys come across as fucking desperate to have a war.

Retrospectively, many of the contributors claim toppling the Argentine junta as a war aim: Britain, the home of democracy, claiming credit for one of the few occasions when it wasn't actively supporting a South American dictatorship. (In fact, having a war shored up the desperately unpopular Galtieri, a bit like – well, a bit like Maggie.)

The whole thing was actually a massive cock-up. Thatcher had wanted to hand sovereignty of the islands over to Argentina, and then lease them back – thus guaranteeing the islanders' communities. But the deal went tits up. Argentina took it that Britain wasn't bothered about the islands – even making diplomatic noises in that direction. But when they invaded (six months prematurely, as it turned out: they also had their overeager officers desperate for war), Thatcher decided that in fact these rocks were crucial for Britain, that it was vitally important that young men died so those rocks remained British. No deals, no negotiations: we will NE-ver surrender.

'Great Britain is great again,' said the Tory election posters. Where 'great' means 'back chinning dagos like we've never been away – come on! Hey, India, the French . . . want some?'

MARGARET THATCHER, TANK COMMANDER.
Corbis

Victory turned a lame-duck prime minister limping from day-to-day survival into the all-conquering titan everyone remembers: 'We have ceased to be a nation in retreat,' she said. 'We have instead a new-found confidence – born in the economic battles at home and tested and found true 8,000 miles away.'

She could now turn her attention to attacking the unions and the welfare state, romping the 1983 election ironically by the largest margin since Labour won in 1945. ('I wish I had had a war,' lamented her Labour predecessor, Jim Callaghan. The twat.)

So was Britain great again? Not really. Anyone who believes Britain is 'great' – i.e., without substantial room for improvement – has quite possibly not been to Britain. Even the people who were saying Britain was great seemed to despise most of the people in it, banging on about enemies within and workshy scroungers.

We ambled back down the gangplank wondering whether, in a funny sort of way, Britain was still at war. We agreed that it was.

TRADITIONAL BRITISH SPORTS TO REVIVE FOR 2012

In 2012, the eyes of the world will be on Britain – a perfect opportunity to reinvigorate our sporting traditions. Could be demonstrated by Lord Coe.

BEAR-BAITING: On his marathon nine-day morris dance from London to Norwich (no, really), the famous Shakespearean clown Will Kempe was mobbed by crowds. In Stratford, knowing of his love for the sport (the very same Stratford that is hosting the Olympics: bear-baiting's coming home), the locals prepared some bear-baiting. Kempe recalled being annoyed because he couldn't see for all the crowds. How disappointing to only hear the bears roaring but not actually see them being baited, *at your own party*. See also duck-baiting (which sounds like it wouldn't work, but they *made* it work).

NO ANIMALS WERE HARMED, ETC. (WELL, APART FROM THE BEARS.) *MEPL*

CNAPAN: Medieval football matches in which whole towns of men would chase a small wooden ball made slippery by being soaked overnight in animal fat. Legs and backs were broken, clumps of hair pulled from heads and clothes ripped off. Some death. In his 1603 *Description of Pembrokeshire*, Welsh antiquarian George Owen noted: 'It is a strange sight to see a thousand or fifteen hundred naked men to concur together in a cluster . . .' We'll have to wait until 2012 to see if he was right about that.

CUDGELLING: Smacking your opponent around the head with a big club. Old school!

SHIN-KICKING: Step One: two men, probably drunk, lock arms in a grapple. Step Two: kicking. Popular in England's north-west; an 1843 report of a contest near Manchester spoke of two men 'both in a state of nudity with the exception of each having on a pair of strong boots'. A stirring image that somehow never made it into the works of L. S. Lowry.

RATTING: Trained terriers kill as many rats as possible in a special ratting pit. Foreshadowing Olympics scandals to come, rats were sometimes doped for a higher kill rate. Bit of a dark one, ratting.

SMOCK RACES: A race for women. The smocks would have to be wet, of course.

NAID BERC: The name of this Welsh rural sport can be roughly translated as 'jumping over a stick'. Which gives a fair indication as to what's involved here.

THRASHING THE HEN: A hen is placed in a sack and carried on the back of the 'hoodman', who stands in a circle with bells on his coat. The contestants are blindfolded and given sticks. Then they beat the hen to death. Possibly more of a pastime than a proper sport.

SMOKING MATCHES: A country fayre favourite. Who can smoke a pipe full of tobacco the fastest? Or who can keep the tobacco alight for the longest? The PC brigade would probably complain that smoking matches 'promote smoking' or somesuch nonsense.

TWISTING THE LEGS OFF A COW: In the 1820s, a Highland Games at Inverarry apparently included twisting the legs off a cow. Only one man managed to twist all four legs off and it took him over an hour. So do leave adequate time for this one.

TWENTY

YOU CAN'T DUMP ME BECAUSE I'M DUMPING YOU

ENGLAND
SCOTLAND
WALES
THE BIG-NOSED BARD OF DORSET

IN TERM OF Britishness, the question of the year was this: was Britain breaking up with itself? You know, properly this time, not just talking about it like before.

Alex Salmond had been pretty popular, with around 60 per cent of Scots thinking he had done a good job (roughly the same percentage as thought Gordon Brown 'should start smacking himself around his own fat face'). Okay, the SNP, without a working majority, got through its first budget by Salmond threatening to resign, and by ditching most of its election commitments. But don't worry, said the First Minister, I have a plan (rubbing his hands): oil. Salmond – who kept managing to rub his hands even though his hands were tied – was promising jam tomorrow. Well, oil tomorrow. ('Scotland in 2017 – independent and flush with oil, says Salmond.')

Come independence, Salmond had promised a clean break. Okay, sure. There won't be massive arguments and tortured small-hours shouting. That sort of thing never happens. Except that, as we all know, break-ups rarely go *that* well. You don't often hear: 'It was fine, actually, everyone's friends, you know?' It's more about still having murderous rages even years down the line. And what effect would the custody battle have on the North Sea oil? Will no one think of the North Sea oil?

So confident were the SNP that they'd already started building the Scottish Empire. In February, the Scottish First Minister announced plans to reorder the borders – and annex Berwick. Berwick-upon-Tweed had changed hands 13 times before but had

ALEX SALMOND: IN RARE 'NOT LOOKING PLEASED WITH HIMSELF' POSE.
Corbis

been English since 1482. A poll had shown that 60 per cent of the town's residents preferred to be ruled from Edinburgh (they were after things like free personal care for the old folks, etc. rather than an abiding sense of belonging to the clan of Scot);

and Salmond, not usually an opportunist by nature, seized this opportunity. 'Borders are fluid,' he said, probably rubbing his hands a bit. Again.

The fallout between Scotland and the Labour Party was definitely proving trying for the Scottish Labour Party. At the Scottish Politician of the Year awards, the Scottish leader Wendy Alexander's press adviser Matthew Marr was heard shouting at Alex Salmond, calling him, and we quote verbatim here, 'a cunt'. Well, we've all been there, when all the turmoil of a separation gets too much, hitting the bottle and calling the Scottish First Minister 'a cunt'.

There was also the intriguing sniff of adultery: Salmond was sick of a Scotland dominated by Whitehall. But was there someone else? The nature of any independent Scotland was thrown into stark relief when loony-eyebrowed billionaire Donald Trump announced he wanted to celebrate one of Scotland's most beautiful and wild stretches of coastline by building a massive golf-course on top of it. Billionaire Trump's plans for a 'golfing paradise' on Menie Links north of Aberdeen was stuck thanks to one stubborn proud Scot, Michael Forbes, who refused to sell up. The American sneered: 'Take a look and see how badly maintained the property is. It's disgusting. There are rusty tractors, rusty oil cans . . .' This makes you wonder . . . has Donald Trump ever *seen* a farm?

'I OWN YOU.' *Andrew Milligan/PA*

Surely this is an easy one for the Scots Nationalist cause: a madpants American billionaire businessman loudly insulting a stubborn proud Scot. And so it turned out that for the SNP there was indeed no choice. Well, Trump does have gingery hair.

'They say that money talks; not with me it doesn't,' Mr Forbes said.

No. Nor with the SNP neither.

So the Scottish Parliament may have few powers, but Salmond was doggedly exploiting them in the interests of big business – sorry, in the interests of Scotland.

To see the devolved, possibly even disintegrating new Britain in action, we hopped on a train to Cardiff on the Tuesday after St David's Day – to check out the Welsh Assembly.

These were high times for Welsh confidence. Wales had recently been crowned Kings of Britain, having beaten both Scotland and England in the Six Nations rugby. The victory over England had been particularly sweet and crushing: Wales winning by 26 points to 19. The day before, the media had been full of England's alleged invincibility: ('I'm ready to run through brick walls for my country,' said James Haskell.) But on the day, England had been a shambles. After one Mike Phillips try, BBC pundit Brian Moore reported of his Welsh colleague Jonathan Davies: 'He is whooping, jumping up and down. He's squeaking.' Squeaking? Jesus.

We knew Cardiff from days of old. We had drunk of its barrels, we had supped at its table, we had looked round its castle. We had, not to put too fine a point on it, been students there. But we hadn't been to the New Cardiff where Everything had Changed. When we were there, Cardiff Bay was just a bay. Next to Cardiff. But now . . . now it was like Barcelona, only better.

The sun was out. And where there was once a vast expanse of waste ground, now there were some coffee shops. And who doesn't like those? It used to just have a lightship and a Norwegian church (they were still there), so this definitely represented a step on.

It also had the Assembly buildings and the £106 million Wales Millennium Centre, the vast handsome copper-roofed monster that some locals have called 'the second biggest white elephant in the Bay'. This was billed as the new opera house for a resurgent nation. When we passed, it was showing Gary Wilmot in *Half a Sixpence*.

By the water's edge, next to the shops, was an intriguing public artwork acknowledging the area's Tiger Bay past – saucy melting pot and red-light district. It's a statue of what looks like a brassy black woman (complete with authentic-looking nipples poking through her blouse), a dog and a man (docker?) reading a paper. What was the message here? Let's all think back to Tiger Bay's saucy past by checking out this large pair of bronze knockers? Dockers read newspapers too? Dog is man's best friend? Metal is good? The sea is good? . . . To be fair, it kept us amused while we munched our packet sandwiches.

NEW SCULPTURE, CARDIFF BAY. A BIT RUDE.

Outside the Tesco Express, a bin caught fire, seemingly spontaneously, and we watched a very vexed security man put it out. So there's definitely more stuff going on down the Bay than there used to be.

We entered the Senedd (the Assembly), which resembles nothing so much as a huge mushroom, perhaps in acknowledgement of the magic ones that grow so abundantly in the moist fields of Wales.* Taking our seats in the circular gallery above the debating chamber – a sheet of curved glass between us and the Members below – we sat back and waited for Questions to the First Minister, Labour's Rhodri Morgan, leader of Labour and Plaid Cymru's Orwellian-sounding One

---

* This huge 'shroom of Welsh oak is encased in glass, with a pointy-sided metal nun's hat (think poster for *The Sound of Music*) on top. Quite good, actually. The sides of the building are transparent: symbolising the transparency of the democratic process. You can literally look in and see what they're doing. You can only see the foyer, but even that gives you a real sense of what's going on, in the foyer. (If they ever draw the curtains, we'll know we're all fucked.)

Wales coalition. Except the First Minister wasn't here. Nor was the Deputy First Minister. They'd sent some other bloke along. He was all right.

To be honest, though, we wanted more. It's as if the Welsh local councils have devolved upwards all the most tedious bits of their business. Maybe all the councillors at Rhonda-Cynon-Taff are laughing behind their sleeves, debating global warming and the Middle East then knocking off early for a pint, safe in the knowledge that they've offloaded all the crap about school dinners to the Senedd. 'What do you think they'll be debating now?' ask the councillors of Caerphilly Borough Council as their tray of drinks arrives in a sunny pub garden. 'Bargoed relief road, I expect. For half an hour!' Then they all laugh like drains.

What we're saying here is: the Welsh Assembly is tedious. At one point, a party of 50 or so schoolchildren trooped into the gallery and sat down. About three and a half minutes later, they all trooped out of their national debating chamber, none the wiser. None the wiser, but bored out of their fucking minds.

Even the Assembly members don't pay much attention to the Assembly. They all have computer screens in front of them, and many were typing emails. One Tory member (a bald man with a trim white beard) had seemingly perfected the art of being asleep with his eyes open. He kept stock-still for around 20 minutes. Just long enough for a truly refreshing power-nap. (A Member was once apparently reprimanded for, during a crucial debate, buying himself a suit on the internet.)

Maybe the chamber's on fire when Rhodri's in town. Maybe it was more combative before Labour and Plaid Cymru got pally. Maybe the Assembly is just very boring. Probably the latter, and probably because it has powers roughly equal to no powers at all. If the Scottish Parliament, in the (reasonably accurate) words of Simon Jenkins, 'has all the powers of a pre-Thatcherite town council', the Welsh Assembly has powers more along the lines of a parish council. (Maybe even a pre-Thatcherite parish council? Did Thatcher come even for the parish councils? What a *bastard*.)

So this is the bright new devolved democracy, is it? Because to our eyes it looked – sorry about this – just bollocks.

Later, we stood at the end of Queen Street, the main shopping street, and considered the statue of Nye Bevan, chief icon of the iconic postwar Labour government and midwife of the NHS. Cardiff has quite a wild selection of statues; but Bevan has by far the best spot. We thought about how the NHS – Britain's favourite institution – had been birthed by a ruddy great Welshman.

How much of Britain's possible break-up was down to the extinguishing of all-Britain Labourism? we wondered. The collapse of the Labour vote in Glasgow – aka Red Clydeside – made all the difference in the SNP's one-seat victory in Scotland. In South Wales, so the old saying goes, they used to weigh the Labour votes, not count them. Not any more (they do have to count them now).

Hoping to make sense of it all, we met up with Neil McEvoy – an ex-Labour activist and a former Labour city councillor who was now active in Plaid Cymru. It's safe to say that no one represents the decline of Labour and the rise of Other Stuff like Neil's shift. Plaid was nowhere near SNP levels of support, but oddly it was now making inroads in places far removed from its rural/West Wales heartlands . . . including solid Labour areas of Cardiff: a Welsh city hitherto largely immune to the lure of Welsh nationalism.

Settling down for a curry on Cowbridge Road, we chatted with Neil about this changing scene. The social democratic agenda of the modern Plaid is the stuff that people like Neil – and some Labour voters – have responded to. But Plaid isn't a social democratic party with a nationalist face; it's a nationalist party with a social democratic face. And Neil had definitely, well, become a nationalist.

'Wales is a colony. It's still got a colonial mentality,' he said.

According to this thinking, the Welsh and Scots must be freed from the inferiority complex born of English expansionism. Is that right? we wondered. Self-determination, Neil was arguing, would free the essential progressive drives of Welsh society: 'You don't have to sell red-green politics in Wales. People in Wales already want to buy it.'

It was obvious from all the young Cardiffians nodding and saying hello in a bar we went on to afterwards that this was one local politician who was going places. Possibly, in fact, by being in touch with his locale.* 'In Plaid,' said our new friend

---

* As it turned out, more so than we could have imagined. Neil was elected as a Plaid councillor two months later, as the party took *all three* seats in the

(in fact, an old friend of Alan's), 'I'm considered middle-aged.' (He's in his mid-thirties.) 'For seventeen- to eighteen-year-olds – they don't want a party tainted with corruption, they haven't got any truck with royalty, or endless compromise.' Labour was 'finished', he said – both as a force for social change, and as an electoral outfit.

'But what about us?' we wondered. We're not colonialists; we're English, by accident of birth, and aren't we just going to get left behind? What about English people who deserve free tuition too, and would instead be left staring down the shot-gun-barrels of perpetual Tory government?

'Catch up!' said Neil. To this we responded . . . well, actually, we didn't really have a ready response to this one. For Neil, it was Plaid that was taking up the housing cases and the cam-paigns for school playing fields and if England fancied the look of all this, then all well and good.

Stepping back, though, we just couldn't get past all the nationalism. Plaid preach an independent Wales within Europe as the democratic alternative to Britain, that old prison-house of nations stitched up by the English. And, yes, Britain is an undemocratic institution that often does feel like it's been stitched up by the elite that is, yes, often based in London. But, bloody hell, have they not seen the EU?

Being stitched up is definitely a problem for people globally. It really does need addressing. But it's hard to see how a good way of starting is by building more frigging borders.

And what about England? For its part, the cause of 'English self-determination' is largely media jibber-jabber pushed by same old same old right-wing motormouths like Garry Bushell and Simon Heffer.

The headline-grabbing polls saying that 60 per cent are for an English Parliament ask: 'The Scots have got something you haven't and everything would be okay if it just wasn't for those bastards from West Lothian stealing all your democracy, do you want the same? . . . Or, er, not?' As soon as other options are introduced (like special sessions of English MPs to discuss

solidly Labour Fairwater ward. Two months after our class–nation/ Wales–Britain chinwag, Neil took the Plaid group into coalition with the Liberals, and became Deputy Leader of Cardiff County Council. He summed this experience up with a text message of perfect eloquence: 'Nuts here m8.'

England-only matters), support plummets (to around 20 per cent). There has been some sort of rise in 'English consciousness' (it's okay to giggle at that phrase), but it's almost entirely in response to devolution for Scotland and Wales.

We had a go at searching out the most vocal pro-English Parliament group, the English Democrats – part of a cross-pollinated, shape-shifting mutant fringe taking in UKIP, Veritas and other weird campaigns that only seem to exist on old-fashioned-looking internet sites featuring lots of pictures of flags. They had a candidate in the London mayoral elections – a bloke from Fathers 4 Justice – but we could find no public meetings at all: that's none; none at all.*

But there is one – at least one (if not, in fact, only one) – progressive English patriot: Billy Bragg. Was Billy the answer? Could Billy save us?

We obtained a copy of his 2006 book, *The Progressive Patriot*, and read some of it – attacking books you haven't read, or even opened the cover of, being a profoundly shoddy way of behaving. We felt afeared. For chaps of our age and general inclinations, slagging off Billy Bragg feels somehow very wrong – like swearing at your grandad. Sadly, though, his book was crap.

We felt cheated before we even started. Here was Billy Bragg, the man who had once sung, emphatically, that he was not in favour of a New England: 'I'm not,' he sang on numerous occasions in the song 'New England', 'looking for a New England.' And here he was now, looking for a New England. What next? He never even owned a Vauxhall Velux? He was not and never had been a multitasking mine-dock-railway worker in the 1930s?

Bragg firmly believes in reclaiming Englishness for the radicals, once writing: 'It's time we on the left stopped denying that the English identity exists, reconnected with our radical tradition of Levellers, Abolitionists, Chartists and Suffragettes and began to engage positively in the debate about what it means to be English.'

* The candidate, Matt O'Connor, withdrew from the race shortly afterwards – saying, basically, that they didn't have any activists. He was particularly affronted at the lack of turnout to support him on St George's Day. And if the English Democrats can't get their English shit together on St George's Day, when can they?

'The politics of identity' is a phrase that reoccurs throughout Bragg's book. They are indeed the first four words of the Introduction. And a sense of identity is okay; but how does all the soul-searching lead to better things happening in the world? Might it, in fact, be something of a distraction? Or did the Levellers/Chartists/Suffragettes – only one of whom, the Levellers, was purely English, and that was only because there wasn't a Britain yet – bear banners declaring: 'Fight for the Right to Engage Positively in the Debate About Who We Are!'?

We'd wrestled with the question 'Who are the English?' ourselves, of course, and decided it was a rubbish question. How does Billy define the English? Well, it's complex: there were all these invasions and waves of immigration and that, and . . . it's complex. Anyone, really. 'Being English is a state of mind.'

Yeah yeah yeah, and everyone loves the Clash, but: Aaarrrrrrgggggggghhhhhhhhh!

One thing was still bothering us. The 15 per cent of Britain's population in Scotland and Wales have the perfect right to independence if that's the bag they're into. Equally, a federal Britain is another feasible possibility. To a certain extent: whatever. Britain is, without doubt, a dog's breakfast: a 300-year-old artifice drawn up for business reasons, taking three somewhat dysfunctional demi-nations to create – oh look! – one almighty mother of a dysfunctional nation. Nations, eh? But why are separatists gaining in popularity now? Why are ideas that we find – frankly – wildly old-fashioned, and a bit whiffy, making a comeback?

Academics suggest the EU makes the case for small independent nations more credible; or there's the end of Empire; even the end of the Cold War . . . But the main story in Britain for the last 30 years has been Thatcherism (and its offspring) breaking up the welfare state, hitching government to big business while also centralising power in Whitehall (which is in England). Nationalists don't have to do much to look vaguely caring compared to the competition. Free prescriptions? Ooh, that sounds nice. All this has to be a consideration.

But then again, there's only so many hours in the day and are there not, to put it bluntly, more important things to worry about? You know, what's that fucking ticking sound? Because just when what is needed is someone to stand up to big business over global warming, what is all this Scottish nationalism powered by? Oil! Christ, even Scotland would probably suffer from global warming somehow or other . . .

And look: old school ethnic and blood nationalism is a pretty discredited beast in these parts, and the SNP and Plaid are at pains to say they're new school civic nationalists who want to represent everyone within their borders. They are inclusive and anti-racist – of course they are. But, come on, it's not entirely *not* about all that heather and mountains bollocks, is it, really? Not out there. There's surely some sort of Celtic dog-whistle thing going on here. All of which makes you question Billy Bragg's description of these parties as straightforwardly 'progressive' (and indeed answer that question).

GARRY BUSHELL. OI!
Rex Features

Finally, more importantly, what about us? Will *no one* think about us? Stuck, through no fault of our own, with English über-patriot Garry Bushell banging on about what defines the English: 'It's defiance. Whether it be King Alfred standing up to the Vikings, Colonel H at Goose Green, or the Metric Martyrs giving the finger to Brussels. No one likes us! We don't care!'

Billy's all right. We can just put him in the corner with a pale ale and he can tell the children all about the punk wars. But not Garry. Please not Garry and his big beardy chops.

Oh my *God*! Don't leave us with him! Even on the rebound, we're not going out with that.

TWENTY-ONE

WHICH WAY DOES HE TURN ON THE PLANE?

THE 'COM-MUN-I-TY'
A COMMUNITY
CARE IN THE COMMUNITY

BRITAIN IS BROKEN. Not in a Scots/Welsh way. In a racial way. Well, that's the view even the liberal media were prepared to flirt with on the fortieth anniversary of Enoch Powell's 'Rivers of Blood' speech.

Anniversary clips shows considered post-9/11, post-7/7 Britain and asked: 'Was Enoch right?' Was this 1968 statement of the alleged essential incompatibility of races as perceived by a right-wing, patrician Tory really not a failed prediction of race war in the 1960s after all; but a Nostradamus-like prediction of the Islamist terrorism in the twenty-first century? Throw in some clips of the Brixton and Toxteth riots, which the Tory government's own patrician analysis said were caused by social deprivation, and the picture of a fundamentally racially divided Britain just got stronger, said these clips shows. Okay, everyone knows Britain is much less racist than it used to be, and this is ahistorical: but is it any the less true for all of that? Is it?

Well: was it? We needed to find out. To hear about all this, we went to Birmingham in February for 'An Audience with Jon Gaunt – Live and Undaunted'. First we had a drink under the Burlington Hotel, where Enoch Powell had given his 'Rivers of Blood' speech: in the Bacchus Bar, a slightly tatty and surreal homage to classical bingeing. There was no great significance to this, and no great insight was forthcoming; but we did do that. Then we walked up to the Town Hall, idly discussing the proposition that this part of Birmingham looks 'just like Paris', readying ourselves for a bit of Gaunty.

To his fans, talkSPORT shock-jock and *Sun* columnist Jon 'Gaunty' Gaunt is one of the few people in the media with the guts to tell The Truth. He's a 'true Brit' patriot, who loves Britain, who takes no prisoners, accepts no quarter, is not afraid of being 'post-PC'. He is the self-styled 'voice of the common man' – because the 'common man' is, like Gaunty, sort of a cross between Richard Littlejohn and Chris Moyles, only louder. One paper called Gaunty 'The Mouth of Britain'. We wanted to see what would come out of Britain's Mouth.

Gaunty often gets labelled a bigot – many of his callers are foam-flecked racists – but he is loudly and proudly in favour of our multiracial Britain. You can't get him on being a racist: 'Ask my Sikh mate . . .' Gaunty calls Ian Wright 'the greatest living Englishman'. So he's as not-racist as you like. (The Coventry native was *there*, supporting Two Tone, during

Two Tone: he's *met* the Specials . . .)

Then again, he does write *Sun* columns demanding we lock up more than 200,000 Muslim radicals headlined 'Time to round up the enemy within'. Lumping together a diverse group of people from various countries (if not continents) as 'them' and proposing draconian action against all of them using terms like 'shipping out' and 'cleaning off the streets'. That doesn't sound massively not-racist.

As we had a beer in the bar beforehand, we eyed up the rest of the crowd – it was a real mixture of people, a real mixture of white people; mostly middle-aged, predominantly male. The merchandise stall was selling some 'Gaunty for Prime Minister' T-shirts (the bespectacled chubber standing in front of Parliament). To be fair to the audience, there weren't many takers. (We overheard one guy explaining who Gaunty was to his mother-in-law. 'We'll take your mother, it'll be a treat for her.')

As he strode out on to the massive stage, it was immediately clear Gaunty was going to struggle to fill the space. For an opening gambit, he produced a teddy bear and declared a competition to name it. Mild confusion from the audience until Gaunty boomed: 'You bunch of Brummie *morons*. The punchline is meant to be "Mohammed"!'

This satiric reference to British teacher Gillian Gibbons, arrested in the Sudan for allowing her pupils to call their teddy bear after the Muslim prophet, set the faltering tone for the evening. Was it more weird than painful? Hard to say.

Oddly, it appeared that Gaunty might actually be *important*: this very day, housing minister Caroline Flint had floated plans to throw the workshy out of their council properties – an amazing idea, one rumoured to stem from New Labour's panic about failing support among the 'talkSPORT demographic' (having not yet fully appreciated its failing support among *all* demographics). Well, Gaunty's on talkSPORT and he wasn't impressed: 'Yeah, like they're going to throw people out in the street!' he said.

Gaunty was into his stride now. Britain has been broken by feckless criminal youth and liberals being soft on Muslims. Of course according to his autobiography, *Undaunted*, Gaunty has at various times been a feckless criminal youth and a liberal thespian trying to establish a Coventry Bauhaus, on drugs – but now, now he's the voice of the people, and he has never – *never* – been soft on Muslims.

Sometimes, it was downright emotional. He took comments from the audience about a recent incident on the train to Brighton, involving three youths who invaded Gaunty's empty carriage and defecated in the guard's van. As they were poring through their shoplifted DVDs, he got up and left: 'I was a coward, I'm always going on about these feckless kids, how you've got to stand up to them . . . Don't get me wrong, I wanted to kill 'em, I wanted to take those kids into that guard's van with a baseball bat and beat them to a pulp. But I wasn't brave enough, I wasn't fit enough . . .'

He trailed off, movingly.

Gaunty has one of the strangest catchphrases there has ever been: 'Which way do I turn on the plane?' He turns left. You're supposed to shout 'Left!' Into first class. Not like the rest of us, the herd, the common man, turning right. No: left. Jon Gaunt, who has more money than us, turns left when he gets on a plane.

'Was that you, Baggies fan? "You torn roight"! No, I don't turn right. Baggies fans turn right.'

To be fair, Jon Gaunt is no Enoch Powell – and not just in the lack of classical references. He barely skimmed past straight immigration – saying it should be 'managed'.* And he ignored any head-on race issues, except to go on about how not-racist he was (he's met the Specials, apparently). Mostly he talked about how much money he earned. The crowd were

---

* He didn't say anything about it this evening, that is. Not that he doesn't spend most of the rest of his time going on and on about it. He thinks all immigration should be halted because the country is 'full up' and being 'swamped'. You know, that sort 'managing'. One where everything is 'Tom, Dick and Abdul's' fault.

WHITE KNIGHTS

These days, even the white supremacists aren't racist. They're just really into white stuff. In recent years, Nick Griffin has re-aligned the British National Party – to worrying degrees of electoral success – as a 'patriotic' party that's literally light years away from all the old jackbooted neo-Nazis (well, inches, anyway).

A NAZI.
Corbis

They're just really into British history, myths, legends, wars (not just race ones, either). Their elite funding group is called the Trafalgar Club (and it's a tight ship: unlike the main parties, mired in donations controversy, the BNP like to keep their funding whiter than white). Their internet shop is called Excalibur (yes, their internet shop is called Excalibur) and sells a greetings card called 'Winter Stonehenge Scene' (send one to your gran). They're even getting into English folk, with Nick Griffin raving about Kate Rusby on his frankly incredible blog. Maybe you can catch him down the front at the next Green Man Festival.

In their inclusive view of history, the BNP can embrace everyone: Arthur *and* the Saxons. All British history, in fact, up to when it started to involve non-white people. Interviewed on *Newsnight*, Griffin responded to survey results that half the white working class said that immigration had benefited Britain, explaining: 'Absolutely, the Huguenots, the Jews and the Irish, that's entirely true.' Yes, the white ones.

But it's not all white-might history fun. There's also the very real danger of the BNP taking either control of the council, or a Westminster seat, or both, in Barking. This is Labour territory of course, and the hot issues are traditional Labour issues: services, jobs, and housing – topped up by rapid population change. You'd think Labour would be making electoral hay out of this if – er, oh no, hang on.

A great addition to the New Labour legacy, then: giving the fascists a free go.

about to collectively nod off when he pulled out his ace: 'the Muslims'.

'We've now got a situation where they're treading on eggshells because they're worried about upsetting [he spits out the words in a contorted whine] the com-mun-i-ty . . .'

'Ugh!' The woman sitting to our right flinched at the merest thought of lots of Muslims.

'We don't need pint-sized Hazel Blears giving 17 million pounds of my money and your money to make Muslim women more assertive when they're dressed like FUCKING Daleks.'

The crowd went wild at this point. They'd been sat glumly in their seats for most of the show, but they were *loving* a bit of hating the Muslims – it was like he'd suddenly scored a goal from nowhere. They were really shouting in support now.

'What we need to do is tell people that this is Great Britain, this is the greatest country in the world. This is the most tolerant country in the world. This is a country where you can be what you want to be. And that is why every Tom, Dick and bloody Abdul wants to come here! . . . If we've got an enemy within, let's bring back internment, let's get these people locked up . . . Are you with me or are you agin me?'

There's proper cheering now. He's really getting worked up. This must be a climax of sorts.

'In Leeds, they're trying to say Gaunty's a racist and a bigot [there were some moves to get his show banned there]. I'm none of those things. I'm a patriot. I'm a Brit. I love my country. And it's my country as much as it's my Sikh mate in the audience's country. As much as it is my Muslim friends' and black friends'. This is *Great* Britain! Don't let the bastards grind you down!'

At the interval, people were standing in groups in the bar wondering about the shitting-on-a-train incident and what they would have done. With four people, it would be okay. We drank gin – stiff ones – in the corner, and thought about internment.

And we had to ask ourselves: what's Gaunty up to? Yes, he strongly distanced himself from the BNP 'knuckle-draggers', but if Gaunty somehow believed he wasn't giving his audience some dark kicks by skirting thrillingly close to race-hate, then he might actually need mental help. I'm not racist, but . . . I can continually shout kinkily hostile anti-Muslim pseudo-comedy, really shout it into a mike, to a whooping crowd of whites.

Who *don't whoop at anything else I say*. It's not the sort of thing you find yourself doing by accident, really, is it?

We returned for the second half. 'I just want to say one thing before we go on, We've got two lads in the audience, I'm not going to tell you where they're sitting, but we've got two brave boys in the audience just back from Afghanistan.'

Massed audience clapping. Really loud. Then the punchline: 'Yeah, they're from Tipton, they were fighting for the fucking Taliban!'

Only moderate laughter. 'You liked that one, didn't you,' he beams at a woman in the audience. 'You'll be telling everyone that one, won't you, eh?' Fucking hell, we thought.

Strange one, Gaunty. He's right about one thing, though. The middle class has stitched up the media in a way unimaginable 20 years ago. The media is populated almost exclusively by people who don't have a clue about, in Gaunty's phrase, 'ordinary guys and women who are struggling to turn a pound'.

But everything in Gaunty-world was depressingly reductive. The middle class were spineless liberals who only stopped drinking their 'skinny lattes' to be soft on paedos and radical Muslims. And his working class was an almost psychotically embittered rump – besieged by the rising tide of paedos and radical Muslims.

Low pay, unemployment, the 'flexible' labour market, lack of political representation . . . change and insecurity is all around for the working class. Even those who aren't white. Maybe someone should start talking about this in ways that aren't fearful and self-defeating. Someone who isn't a gobshite.

Which way does he turn on the plane, again?

The train pulled into Leeds. The city centre is a glittering New Britain boomtown of hotels, luxury apartments and bars and, er, Royal Armouries. They've even got a Harvey Nicks! You might have heard about that. (People will still be talking about the Harvey Nicks in Leeds in the next century.)

A mile away, the south Leeds suburb of Beeston – the media's 'Home of the 7/7 Bombers' – stretches over the brow of a hill, with swooping views down to the city centre on one side. Its crumbling wine-red terraces are now slightly less crumbling thanks to some recent investment. But the repointing hasn't quite covered up the fact that this place is fairly obviously out of the New Britain loop. There probably aren't too many Harvey Nicks bags making their way back here.

This is where Gaunty's jackboot would fall. Would Gaunty do the interring himself? we wondered. How many blokes would you need to inter some jihadists? What do you think? Call us now, or email . . . We're talking about internment today . . .

After the 2005 atrocity – the worst ever terrorist attack on British soil – the media was naturally obsessed with working out how Britain could produce something so alien as violent jihad. Many descended on this suburb, where three of the four bombers came from. What they found, generally speaking, was a south Leeds suburb. Rather than, say, some kind of Jabba the Hutt's bazaar in *Star Wars*, only with more terrorism and Yorkshire accents.

We weren't under any illusions that we'd find The Answer either, but we did hope to get a little flavour of life here. Arriving in the evening, we shared a delicious meal with a local resident, Asghar Khan, and some of his neighbours, in Asghar's front room. At first, he says, the authorities thought Beeston must be hiding more jihadists.

'But then they came and saw the sort of place it was . . . we condemned the atrocities immediately. They were shocking to everyone. I was really surprised they were from Beeston, actually. We've never had any problem with extremist preachers or anything like that.'

Beeston is home to one of one of Leeds's largest Muslim populations, but it's still very mixed, with no great history of strife. A week after the 7 July bombings, around 100 right-wing extremists gathered at a pub just outside the community. And that was that. The BNP were up for a race war: but then we knew that already. In contrast, a peace march into town attracted thousands.

The area was full of media and armed police for a fortnight. 'The really big question was always: how do we get home, there's a man presenting the evening news in the middle of the road,' recalled Neil Rhodes.

A few days after the bombings, there were some controlled explosions in two properties with people being told to stay indoors. Another neighbour of Asghar's recounted: 'There's quite a few drinkers live around here. And they didn't like not being able to go out to the corner shop for more supplies. They'd go out the front door and had the police shouting at them, get inside. Then they'd try sneaking out of their cellar doors and suchlike.'

The next morning as we arrived at the Hamara Healthy Living Centre, a bright new building on Tempest Road, people were busily readying the community café. The 7/7 ringleader Mohammed Sidique Khan once set up a youth drop-in centre further down the road loosely linked to the centre, a connection that led to this place being turned upside down on an almost continual basis for weeks.

Health development worker Rifat Razaq showed us around. Her children had attended the primary school where Sidique Khan worked as a mentor, and she had actually alerted the staff that he was being blamed for the London bombings. 'They were totally shocked,' she said. 'We all were.'

Everyone we met had been taken by surprise by 7/7. Gaunty says that 'the community' must root out the problem. Well, the people of Beeston didn't know there was a problem. Terror cells tend to be quite secretive. Not telling people what you're up to is very much in the nature of these groups.

Upstairs was a Vera Media office. These are the people who make *Black Books* and *Bremner, Bird and Fortune*. Those dangerous subversives.

Much of Rifat's work in the centre is focused on getting older Asian women to keep fit, do a spot of running around the park and cook with less ghee. It's a message for us all: eat less ghee.

Leaving the Centre, we considered how much hysterical hoohah about British national identity had been kicked up by the war on terror and then the 7/7 bombings. The bonds of Britain had been allowed to weaken. In the face of this new threat, what we needed to be, now more than ever, was very British.

But, surely, some kind of lack of British fibre in the diet really isn't the main issue here. Jihadists are a pretty internationalist bunch, all told (they don't mind who they kill). And it seems unlikely their mind warp would be penetrated by learning more about Nelson.

And as for everyone else, they are, in essence, doing what they do – probably quite capable of defining their own identity, but not fannying on about it too much either. We'd met lots of people here who'd like to 'integrate' a bit more please probably – which would mean readier access to good schools, or better-paid work, the sort of things people take pride in without being prompted.

We took a walk around Beeston, and couldn't help but notice all the ice-cream vans. There were really a lot. The red terraces –

BEESTON, LEEDS: JIHADISTS NOT PICTURED.

some of them back-to-backs – were punctuated by off-duty ice-cream vans. Evidence of people trying to 'turn a pound'.

Either that, or maybe the Beeston populace were trying to destroy the West from within by, er, making them eat lots of ice cream. Or maybe Mr Whippy is an Islamist these days.

But Britain is broken not just in a racial way. It's broken in a federal super-state way. For there is a spectre haunting Europe: Europe.

For the final stop on our 'Britain-in-peril' tour, we were going to Surrey. Many people in Surrey love feeling imperilled, sometimes imagining Surrey itself as an island in a rising sea of excreta. Sent over from Brussels, probably. Regulation excreta.

We were off to Claygate, an untouched quarter of Surrey suburbia, just round the back of Chessington World of Adventures. We were here for a public meeting of the Democracy Movement. The Democracy Movement sounds like something you might get in Burma. It's not, though. It's an extremely Eurosceptic pressure group that grew out of the late tycoon James Goldsmith's Referendum Party.

In the mid-seventies, Goldsmith believed Britain had so gone to the socialist dogs that he discussed with friends Lord Lucan and 'eccentric' zookeeper John Aspinall* (those cool guys) the possibility of funding a military coup – 'a Franco-ite counter-revolution' – against Harold Wilson's democratically elected Labour government. So it's that sort of Democracy Movement.

There were Greek and Indian restaurants around the village green, proving they were not out-and-out xenophobes here: it wasn't all Austerity Britain powdered egg and overcooked veg. In the large village hall nearby, the British faithful had gathered for a packed public meeting, a last grasp at saving Britain from the leaden stranglehold of Europe.

There were about 300 people in the room, elderly people mostly. Up on the velvet-curtained stage, behind a desk sporting an 'EU Treaty – Give Us a Referendum' banner, sat the chair and the main speaker: Daniel Hannan, Tory MEP for South-East England and possibly the most anti-EU member of the European Parliament. The issue of the day was the Lisbon Treaty, the redrawn version of the rejected Reform Treaty, that was busy being rammed through all over Europe and would, amongst other things, create a post of EU president. It was about to be voted on in Parliament.

Hannan, a regular *Telegraph* contributor, believed that if Britain ratified the Lisbon Treaty, this country would essentially have ceased to be. You might as well just draw a line through it on the maps. Throw the bloody maps away, for all the good they'd do you! The previous week, he had caused a stink by writing on his blog likening new powers for the European Parliament's German President Hans-Gert Poettering to Germany's 1933 Enabling Act that gave Adolf Hitler unlimited power. He apologised for hurting Mr Poettering's feelings. He hadn't meant to imply he was a Nazi. But it was too late: in the media furore, he was forever branded as that bloke who called a German MEP a Nazi. Yet another European injustice.

The atmosphere in the hall was quite lively. Things kicked off even before that bloke who called a German MEP a Nazi spoke. The Chair's quite lengthy opening remarks didn't seem to be going too well as he kept mentioning 'good work' done by the Liberal Democrats on the issue – there were murmurs in the audience, but he was mostly being suffered in silence. Then

* This is the John Aspinall who believed the British population should be reduced by 'beneficial genocide'. That John Aspinall.

BE BRITISH

Emerging from the citizenship ceremony in Hackney Town Hall (see Introduction), and wandering down Mare Street past the Hackney Empire, we'd wondered to our great amusement what would happen if 'native' Brits were made to swear a similar Britishness oath, in the sight of Almighty God, to 'Queen Elizabeth II, and her heirs, according to law'. Til death do us part. Well, beyond that even: God's on board. Which could come in handy.

Then, just a few days later – literally a few days – Lord Goldsmith delivered his report on Britishness. Called something like *Some Cobblers about Citizenship: A Report (Invoice is in the Post: For Immediate Payment)*, it explained how Britain had become such a 'divided country' that we now needed to restore a sense of 'belonging' . . . by all swearing an Oath to Britain on leaving school at 18.

Firstly, someone should tell them that, on finishing school, British youngsters often get a load of weed in, so the whole thing would take ages. Also, 'divided society'? 'Divided society'? Who did all the dividing then? Fucking Noddy?

'YOU WILL OBEY ME.'

This fabled Britishness is supposed to be what binds us all together, rich and poor, little and large. It's like a party, only it's an identity – and everyone's invited. But what does any of it mean? They can't say. Not because it's cobblers; they just, er, can't say. National security, probably. It's one of those ideas that's most useful the more vague it is: it's not about celebrating sticking it up Bony, but if we don't say that and some people think it is, what's the harm? As long as we find a way of everyone doing what they're told. It's inclusive and new and now, but it's also historical. It's a weird nonsense.

Okay, they do talk vaguely about 'British values'. Not just drinking and shopping, but also rights, liberties, civic respect. (Values mostly associated with the Enlightenment, which is not a country, but anyway . . .) So they're talking about a modern civic state, not some old-school ethnic nation going on a conquerathon – but one where they can play with nationalistic ideas a bit, handily disowning all the bad stuff. Just as long as everyone does what they're told.

Incidentally, when the citizenship class teachers sat a mock test in 2004 when the process started, they all failed. They were deported immediately, of course. Well, apart from the two who were shot.

a man, probably in his seventies but quite spry, got to his feet and interjected.

This man – one Len Avery, it transpired – wanted to know why the Chair hadn't actually read the latest version of the Treaty. 'Why are you an expert if you haven't even got a copy?'

Hannan had it covered. Balding but fresh-faced, he rose to his feet. His shirt, we noticed, was impeccably ironed. If we wanted to live in a Britain of deference to one's elders and betters, we'd defer to Daniel Hannan: he's clever. He's tall. He's not afraid to stand up to the Hun.

Hannan's quite a charmer – albeit overenunciating every syllable like he was putting on a comedy public schoolboy voice. He looks and sounds like a man in his mid-to-late forties who's a bit old for his age. Amazingly, he's actually in his mid-thirties. He might be the only person ever to have surgery to make themself look older. He might – might – have prematurely pulled his own hair out.

Hannan explained that very few people – including the MPs wishing to push it through – will have read the document.

'Can I respond to that?' asked the ageing Europhile.

DANIEL HANNAN, MEP: A VERY TIDY MAN.
Rex Features

At this, the whole hallful of middle-aged conservatives started baying.

'Sit down!' one snapped.

'RUBBISH!' shouted one particularly fierce woman at the back, sort of a Central Casting mix of Margaret Thatcher, Hyacinth Bucket and a vicious cat. Even her red cardigan was fierce. Big gold buttons. Old school.

'I thought this was a public meeting,' exhorted Len.

'Not when you're talking *nonsense*!' shouted someone else.

The Democracy Movement supporters soon saw off this threat to their freedoms and the old man sat down. (They were particularly affronted when he said he was still a Tory. This marks you out as a bit of a sellout in these parts. '*Shame on you*,' sneered Mrs Central Casting.)

Hannan began his speech, plaintively bemoaning in posh sing-song (he's actually British Peruvian) the loss of Britain. 'I can't be alone in sometimes feeling depressed at the little interest people have shown in the issue of our independence as a country . . . so it's heartwarming to come to this little patriotic corner of Surrey and find that here at least people treat the issue with the respect it deserves.'

Labour had promised a referendum on the EU constitution and the Treaty *was* the constitution. Britain was forgoing more power to Europe, and was being denied a say over whether that power should go to Europe.

We briefly pondered how awful the referendum would be. On the one side, there'd be this lot, using some shadowy gazillionaire's money to spray Little Englander nonsense all over the shop. Arrayed on the other side, of course, are the political class – arrogant, removed, wanting to increase state powers by the back door, and viewing voting generally as some sort of unfortunate disease people need curing of. It's hard to see how any democracy would be forthcoming.*

Really getting into his stride, Hannan started listing all the ways that EU meddling was infecting British lives and destroying our ancient ways. And it was just sort of, you know, car seats, and something to do with stamps. Is it weird that Europe tells us to put our children in child seats till the age of 12? Well, kind of. But it's also weird to think that this means that Britain has ceased to be. Nevertheless, Hannan continued in almost Churchillian terms:

'We are approaching the end of the game, our cards are almost spent, we can see the chips of the winnings on our opponent's side of the table. These are rather bleak times, I won't try and sugar-coat it for you . . .'

This was, we felt, powerful stuff. Feelings in the room were

---

* Gaunty had been to Europe, by the way; he'd done a live show from the foyer of the Commission. 'And the waste I saw . . .' he told us. What, in the foyer? What have they got: a platinum floor? A room full of free whores? What? Gaunty actually got into some trouble after his EU broadcast: off-air, a Dutch MEP said he thought Gaunty was a racist. Gaunty dug deep and went back at him for Britain: 'Fuck off!' he said.

running high. During the questions from the floor, there was a lot of shouting – either in loud agreement ('The country's LIFEBOAT!' someone shouted at the mention of UKIP) or in vocal disdain of anyone showing pro-EU tendencies (yep, that'd be Len again. Just Len). One elderly chap shot to his feet to bellow: 'It's a SOCIALIST SUPERSTATE! A SOCIALIST SUPERSTATE!'

A question – really, frankly, quite a weird question – about the effect the ramifications of the Treaty would have on the freedom to deal with traitors brought quite a long heckle from Mrs Central Casting about how, in these days of PC gone mad, you couldn't even put traitors up against the wall and have them shot. Fucking Brussels!

Oddly enough, Hannan ended by quoting Enoch Powell, the fervent anti-European rather than the fervent racist. A statement he had made almost 20 years before to the day in 1988 on Britain's passing of the Single European Act: 'We cannot pretend any longer that we have been hoodwinked or deceived, with every day that passes now the British people, by their passive acquiescence, pronounce the verdict upon themselves, that we were a nation once, we are not now.'

We almost felt like crying. These words, Hannan said, were more relevant now than ever. Britain was no more back in 1988. Now, in 2008, it was even more no more. Really, really, *really* no more. It was getting to the point where Britain was actually a minus country – a country that actually owed a deficit of country to the EU, because there was no more country left to give. And yet Europe incessantly demanded more country, and we gave it. Shame on us all!

This was the weirdest movement for democracy ever. Still, it was good to know that these dispossessed Home Counties Britishers were out there, biding their time, always ready and hopeful for some kind of fightback. In a little corner of Surrey, there was a hidden army of true patriots, cut out by the liberal elites from a country they belonged to more than anyone else had ever belonged to a country ever. This Secret Dads' Army was the twenty-first-century incarnation of G. K. Chesterton's Secret People of England, the people of quiet power: 'Smile at us, pay us, pass us; but do not quite forget;/ For we are the people of England, that never have spoken yet.'

We heard them speaking. They were all mad.

BRITAIN'S TOP TEN RACISTS

Happily, recent British history has not been flush with race-hate demagogues. In France, there's Le Pen. In Germany, there's . . . well, there was Hitler. But sadly, by some estimates, Britain did 'invent' modern racism: pseudo-scientific differences to legitimise slavery. And then there's all the racism. So, it's swings and roundabouts as far as Britain and racism goes.

THE TUDORS: One foreign emissary at the court of Henry VIII said: 'The English have an antipathy to foreigners, and imagine that they never come into their island but to make themselves master of it and to usurp their goods.' That's right: coming over here, usurping our goods!

LLOYD GEORGE: The Liberal Prime Minister, in his later years in opposition, argued for the need to attack the civilian populations of British colonies, saying: 'We have to reserve the right to bomb niggers.' Which wasn't very liberal of him.

QUEEN ELIZABETH I: In 1597, Elizabeth took against Britain's 'blackamoors', decreeing that there were 'here too manie' and demanding they all be deported. Then she did it again in 1601.

Maybe they could make another film: *Elizabeth – The 'Blacks Out' Years*.

ELIZABETH I: RACIST.
The Bridgeman Art Library

ENOCH POWELL: Powell's 'Rivers of Blood' speech to Tory businessmen in Birmingham in 1968 was inspired by Labour's new Race Relations Act banning housing/jobs discrimination. His apocryphal little old lady being harassed by black children – 'wide-grinning piccaninnies' chanting 'Racialist!' – was a landlady who would no longer be free to place 'No Blacks, No Irish, No Dogs' signs in her window. The poor little old racialist.

VIRGINIA WOOLF: The legendary novelist was an anti-Semite who married a Jew (no wonder she looked so down all the time) and made continual anti-Semitic remarks about her mother-in-law. This maybe makes her sound more like an old-school comedian than she really was. Virginia Woolf was – and we're sure we can all agree on this – not very funny.

TORY PARTY: In 1955, Eden's Tories discussed using a poster in the General Election saying 'Keep Britain White'. A slogan presumably intended to send out a surreptitious dog-whistle message to racists. (In 1964, the Tories won Smethwick from Labour in a by-election, on the slogan 'If you want a nigger for a neighbour – vote Labour'. It was during this by-election that the phrase 'playing the race card' was born. The Tories have celebrated this ingenuity by playing it ever since.)

PRINCESS MICHAEL OF KENT: Celebrated royal racist (imagine that!). Accused of racism after telling some African-American diners in New York to 'go back to the colonies'. But surely New York *was* one of the colonies . . . She then skilfully deflected the charges of racism by saying: 'I even pretended years ago to be an African, a half-caste African . . .' And she doesn't even live in Kent!

OSWALD MOSLEY: Fascism never quite took off in Britain, but in 1934, Mosley's British Union of Fascists did manage to fill Olympia – the place they do the home and holiday exhibitions (apparently Mosley's event was billed as the Ideal Race Exhibition. Something like that, anyway). So there must have been *some* fascists, maybe even all over Britain.

WINSTON CHURCHILL: The Greatest British Person ever. Sadly, really hated Indians and made frequent outbursts against this 'beastly people with a beastly religion' throughout the war effort until colleague Leo Amery wrote: 'I am by no means sure whether on this subject of India he is really quite sane.' Goodness gracious!

BORIS JOHNSON: Here comes the mayor of the most culturally diverse city in the world, reviving Powell's 'piccaninnies' – he said sorry, though. And publishing a Taki column claiming that 'blacks have lower IQs' – he said sorry for that also. And claiming Papua New Guineans were 'cannibals' – he apologised for that too. So, you know, he's at least sorry he got caught.

BORIS JOHNSON: APOLOGIST.
Rex Features

TWENTY-TWO

ALL THINGS BEGIN AND END IN ALBION'S ANCIENT DRUID ROCKY SHORE

POLISH PEOPLE
THE FLATLANDS
THE END OF THE WORLD

WE WERE NOW coming to the end. We had almost seen the year round, and the spring equinox, 21 March, was fast approaching – marking exactly a year since we had started. It had been a long, hard winter. But nature was, once again, renewing itself afresh. It was an end, but also a beginning: you know, shit like that.

For the final send-off to Britishness, we were thinking about the sea, the sea that laps the island of Britain, the sea that rises up around Britain, the endless cruel sea that surrounds us and lulls us and taunts us, the sea on which for time immemorial British people have floated themselves in boats. That sea.

We were going to Seahenge, the wettest of all the Henges, the Bronze Age timber circle only discovered on the north Norfolk coast by two amateur fishermen in 1998. We'd be attending another made-up druidic rite of spring. But this would be a made-up druidic rite that we ourselves had made up. We'd appreciated the druids' input, and we had learnt much from them, mostly about making up rites. But we'd also kind of had enough of hanging out with druids, and wanted to branch out on our own.

We would go to Seahenge, we decided, and offer up stuff to the sea. Foodstuff.

Strictly speaking, we were going to the *site* of Seahenge. Most of the wooden monument – exposed by a tidal/mud shift – had been controversially moved to King's Lynn (the druids didn't like that). Some of a second, related structure – Holme II – was still there, but whatever. The sea had offered up Seahenge, and to the sea we were bound. And there definitely, definitely wouldn't be any druids there.

On the train to Peterborough, we had a conversation about what to lug into the deep. Alan had quite a strong opinion about one aspect of our endeavour, which boiled down to: 'I want to throw a chicken in the sea.'

Steve thought this was wrong, that a whole raw chicken, even plucked, would send out an overly gross message.

Alan absorbed this idea for a moment, and then further explained his position: 'I want to throw a chicken in the sea.'

Steve suggested a sausage.

And on it went.

Much to the relief of the woman opposite, the train pulled into Peterborough and we got off.

Ah, Peterborough: shopping mecca of the Peterborough area.

Designated as a New Town in the 1960s, we read somewhere that Peterborough was one of the first places to be designed with the aid of a computer. Considering this would have been even pre-ZX81 days, some of the medieval buildings in particular really are very convincing, we agreed.

It's not often that Peterborough is on the cutting-edge of anything, but with 10,000 Polish workers arriving in the past three years, it had been at the forefront of globalised labour markets. These were clearly radical changes and we wanted to see how it had affected the local area. Any scare-stories about Poles bringing down the neighbourhood stumbled on the fact that, in large part, they weren't.

One Polish group complained about the attitude of the *Daily Mail*, saying that they used emotively negative headlines like 'Poles flood into England', then, when they started leaving again, the headlines were all 'Poles desert England' (coming over here, stealing our jobs, then sodding off and leaving us with all these jobs to do . . .). But hey, this is Britain! What do you want – logic? Consistency? A basically unpoisoned view of human relations? Not on your nelly!

We walked down Lincoln Road, the road that has come to represent the newly Polish-ised Britannia. It did have two Polish delis, neither of which had any customers except us. There were, it has to be said, some Poles around. Coming over here and diluting our culture. Otherwise, we would have seen a pure, undiluted culture of kebabis and Portuguese caffs. They were not being madly diluted; an entire street of caffs and kebabis was being diluted by two Polish delis.

Oh, and a Polish beauty salon. Will these Poles stop at nothing? With their haircuts and their nail treatments.

Okay, local services were probably stretched a tad by the sudden influx of people. But this bit of Peterborough looked more interesting to us than the other bit: the bit represented wholly and entirely by an enormous shopping centre.

We grab some sausage, bread and *serek* (Polish yogurt) to eat in the world's smallest rental car, and head out of Peterborough – and into the Fens. We are now entering the Flatlands. Home of Nelson. Home of Paine. The Flatlands. The world of chickens. Bernard Matthews. The place they filmed *Dad's Army*. The Flatlands. Mysterious. Bleak and yet not bleak. Very flat.

It starts to drizzle for a while. We idly discuss whether the road we're on, raised slightly above the plain, is on top of the original Roman road into Norfolk. It's safe to say that isn't the sort of thing we generally used to talk about a year ago.

The chicken question rumbles on. It is the fifth anniversary of the start of the war in Iraq. Outside the window, it's still flat.

On the radio, the Dean of Peterborough Cathedral was saying how he and other members of the city clergy would be marking Maundy Thursday by shining people's shoes just as Jesus washed his disciples' feet at the Last Supper and as Mary Magdalene washed Jesus' feet with her tears before drying them with her hair. Surely, though, he shouldn't just be shining people's shoes, he should be washing their feet with his tears. Having your feet washed by the Dean of Peterborough Cathedral's tears, and then dried by the Dean of Peterborough Cathedral's hair? That would really be something. Possibly slightly traumatic in a strangely unidentifiable way, but definitely fairly memorable. We passed the royal estate at Sandringham.

Finally, we found Hunstanton, the Victorian holiday resort where we were staying the night. Just a few miles away were the Burnhams – the quaint villages now known as Chelsea-on-Sea. If scientists' predictions about rising sea levels are even halfway correct, Chelsea-on-Sea will at some point in the relatively near future become Chelsea-Right-in-the-Sea. But we didn't want to go to Chelsea-on-Sea.

Hunstanton was not part of any putative 'British holiday revolution' – hotels with CD collections or mythical al fresco fish shacks. None of that bollocks. This was the real British seaside. Concrete. Tarmac. Sea.

At the centre of the town, a large green sloping down to the concrete seawall and beach. A massive amusement arcade stood in pride of place. Further along was a pub perched alone on top of the seawall. It all had the effect of making Hunstanton look remarkably empty. This was, it turned out, no mere effect.

The cliffs were good, though. They were falling into the sea. Massive notices warned: 'CAUTION! BEWARE OF CLIFF FALLS'. We felt them to be a powerful metaphor. Because nothing symbolises a Britain that is falling into the sea like bits of Britain falling into the sea. We didn't see any of it falling into the sea: it was a metaphor. But it was a metaphor that was actually happening. And they're the best sort of metaphors.

Because they're real. So they're not even metaphors. They were nice cliffs, mind. A layered cake of white chalk, red chalk and a brown sandstone called carrstone. Extraordinary, even. They're falling into the sea, though.

HUNSTANTON CLIFFS. PICTURED HERE FALLING INTO THE SEA.

We gather our items for the morning's ritual – foraging in what turns out to be the only food shop open in Hunstanton: a Spar. We stalk the aisles, hunting our items: a packet of bacon (pork was sacred to the Celts – and we like bacon); oats (you need a seedy thing for this sort of behaviour; they only have a box of ten Oat So Simple sachets, so we get that); some milk (reduced – bonus!); eggs (to symbolise renewal – and eggs); a cabbage (no real significance to that one; but it was marked down and just seemed like a good idea at the time) . . . We earnestly discuss the suitability of some other items, like a can of beans. Opening a tin of beans and throwing the contents into the sea? That would be stupid, we decide.

And then, a miracle: Steve finds a great British compromise in the chiller cabinet. Half a cooked chicken!

What could be more exactly a compromise between a chicken and no chicken than half a chicken? It's *exactly* halfway between the two. Not logically, obviously, but actually. It is in a sealed brown plastic tray. Steve holds it up, evidently quite pleased with himself. The chicken is go.

We go back to our room above a pub to stash our items. As we cross the bar, the barmaid looks our way – and, okay, we're basically coming into a hotel at night with some food shopping, and we'd already laid the whole going-out-at-dawn thing on her, but so what? She gives us a look that suggests she's seen our type before. We briefly wonder what type that might be.

Looking for somewhere to eat, we walk into the dark town again. It is windy. In the street, two ducks cross our path – just two ducks, one big, one small, having a nocturnal waddle down the middle of the road. Is it a sign? We struggle to work out the significance of ducks. Ducks in town, though? That's definitely apocalyptic, we conclude, in a small-scale sort of a way. (It would have been handy at this point, we feel, to have had a medieval bestiary on hand, the handy pictorial reference works detailing the alleged spiritual significance of each animal. Maybe we should have kept one in the car?)

In a curry house – well, *the* curry house – we sit beneath the sign of the stag. That is, a shiny seventies-ish framed gold and silver stag scene, all shiny and swirly. We ponder the significance of that while, er, eating a curry. Mainly, we eat the curry.

We have a drink at the lone pub perched on the concrete sea defences and look out to sea, stepping out into the wind on the darkened deck out front. Hunstanton is almost silent. There aren't even any cars around. It's a good place to consider the end of the world. We look in the direction of the cliffs to see if they are noticeably any smaller, but it is very, very dark now and we can't see them. We debate whether this reinstates them to the status of a metaphor again. The wind is up.

We look across to the lights on the other side of the Wash. Out to the lights of Skegness. Then over to where, in 1216, King John's entourage – avoiding places held by baronial rebels – was caught out by the tide and he had his crown jewels sucked down into the treacherous quicksand. That's 'crown jewels' in the literal sense of the term.

We had been to the coast all around the island of Britain, from Kirkcaldy to Cardiff, and one thing had become abundantly clear to us: this was – as far as we could tell – an island. An island, a loam-lashed lump, endlessly battered by the elements. The air. The water. Mainly those two. Not really fire. Certainly not earth. Britain has never been battered by lumps of earth lobbed over from Holland. But the first two, definitely.

The wind was really strong now. It had rained on and off through the evening, and the rain came again and seemed as if it was settling in. Yes: it was a dark and stormy night.

This east coast had always been in the front line as far as the elements go. But now other storms were coming too, all over Britain: money storms. Recent weeks had seen even global climate meltdown knocked off the front pages by the global financial meltdown. George Soros was predicting a meltdown on the scale of the 1930s. We'd had the credit, we'd enjoyed the credit, but now the credit had gone all crunchy. Luckily, Gordon Brown had promised that Britain was 'well placed' to weather the storm. Which was a strange thing for him to say, because he's not generally known for telling jokes.

We continue staring into the darkness. There, in the North Sea, is a lost civilisation. Well, not a civilisation, but definitely a few lost mud huts. In the last year, scientists have mapped out a prehistoric landscape of lakes, hills, marshes and rivers stretching over to Denmark – all once rich hunting ground for early human settlers, lost to rising sea levels 6,000 years ago. The region's Dogger Hills now live on as the Dogger Bank sandbank – famous from the shipping forecast – and it is these that inspired scientists to call this lost landscape, perhaps unwisely, Doggerland. Scientists, eh?

Some even fancifully believe this fertile stretch of land was home to the lost city of Atlantis. That's right, the magnificent seafaring utopia of fable doomed by megafloods and earthquakes – right out there under the briny (with survivors even bringing druidic lore to Britain). For Norfolk, think Atlantis. Not chickens. Atlantis.

We step back inside to get out of the rain. The pub is largely empty. But there is a dog who can open a bag of Mini Cheddars and scoff the lot in seconds. 'He does love his Mini Cheddars,' the barwoman says.

Back at the hotel, we fall asleep fearing the storm that is raging outside. Not in an apocalyptic way; more in a we're going to get very wet and cold sort of a way. But also a bit in an apocalyptic way: there's no point doing this kind of thing if you're not going to get into the spirit of it all.

Dawn. Well, before dawn. Very, very early.

We struggle out of bed and into our tiny car. There is – we can't help but notice – no storm. It is ludicrously calm. Even the sea has settled down; the waves coming in just aftershocks from the storm's work way out to sea the night before.

We drive east out of Hunstanton and on a few miles through darkened villages. Then down a track to the Titchwell Marsh bird reserve.

Leaving the very small car, we pass the closed RSPB centre with its sign telling us to look out for bearded tits (we think it means the birds, rather than twitchers), and set out across the reserve – a series of huge lake-like ponds. The birds are all up with the lark, making quite a noise. We follow the wood-enforced path across the bird park towards the beach a mile